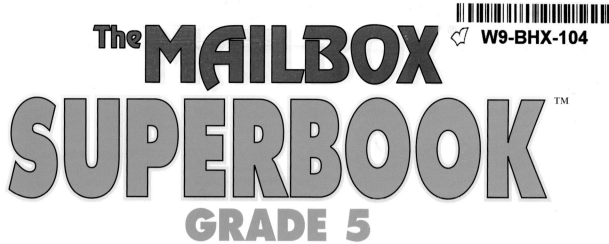

GRADE 5

Your complete resource for an entire year of fifth-grade success!

Editors:
Peggy W. Hambright and Thad H. McLaurin

Contributing Editors:
Elizabeth H. Lindsay, Debra Liverman, Stephanie Willett-Smith

Contributors:
Julia Alarie, Marcia Barton, Beverly Cartledge, Caroline Chapman, Colleen Dabney,
Therese Durhman, Carol Felts, Ann Fisher, Beth Gress, Terry Healy, Simone Lepine,
Cindy Mondello, Gail Peckumn, Bonnie Pettifor, Lori Sammartino,
Barbara Samuels, Marsha Schmus, Patricia Twohey, Cynthia Wurmnest

Art Coordinator:
Cathy Spangler Bruce

Artists:
Jennifer Bennett, Cathy Spangler Bruce, Pam Crane, Kimberly Richard,
Rebecca Saunders, Barry Slate, Donna K. Teal

Cover Artist:
Jim Counts

The Education Center, Inc.
Greensboro, North Carolina

ABOUT THIS BOOK

Look through the pages of *The Mailbox® GRADE 5 SUPERBOOK™*, and discover a wealth of ideas and activities specifically designed for the fifth-grade teacher. We've included tips for starting the year, managing your classroom, maintaining parent communication, and motivating your students. In addition, you'll find activities for reinforcing the basic skills in all areas of the fifth-grade curriculum. We've also provided reference materials for every subject, literature lists, arts-and-crafts ideas, holiday and seasonal reproducibles, bulletin-board ideas and patterns, and month-by-month activities. *The Mailbox® GRADE 5 SUPERBOOK™* is your complete resource for an entire year of fifth-grade success!

Library of Congress Cataloging-in-Publication Data

The mailbox superbook, grade 5 : your complete resource for an entire
   year of fifth-grade success! / editors, Peggy W. Hambright and Thad
   H. McLaurin ; contributing editors, Peggy W. Hambright ... [et al.]
   ; contributors, Julia Alarie ... [et al.] ; art coordinator, Cathy
   Spangler Bruce ; artists, Jennifer Tipton Bennett ... [et al.].
      p.   cm.
   ISBN 1-56234-201-0 (pbk.)
   1. Fifth grade (Education)—Curricula. 2. Education, Elementary—
Activity programs. 3. Teaching—Aids and devices. 4. Elementary
school teaching.   I. Hambright, Peggy W.   II. McLaurin, Thad H.
LB1571 5th.M35 1998
372.24'1—dc21   97-52035
                                                              CIP

Manufactured in the United States
10 9 8 7 6 5 4 3 2

TABLE OF CONTENTS

BACK TO SCHOOL

BACK TO SCHOOL

Not Just A Nametag!

Assist your students in learning about new classroom procedures with a little help from their nametags! Make one copy of the nametag pattern on page 13. On the boxed side of the nametag, list several procedures that you want your students to learn quickly. Next duplicate a class set of the programmed nametag onto heavy paper. Write each student's name on a different nametag; then fold and place the nametag on a desktop so that the name faces the front of the room and the procedures face the student's chair. These nametags will not only help you learn your students' names quickly, but can help to remind your students about some very important classroom routines!

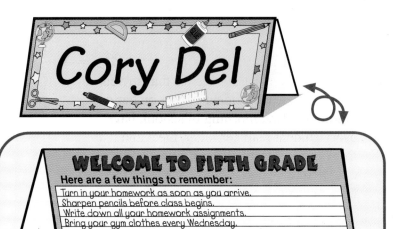

Cory Del

WELCOME TO FIFTH GRADE

Here are a few things to remember:
Turn in your homework as soon as you arrive.
Sharpen pencils before class begins.
Write down all your homework assignments.
Bring your gym clothes every Wednesday.

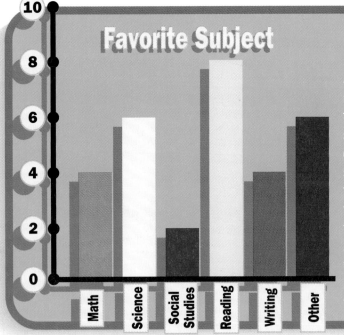

Favorite Subject

Math Science Social Studies Reading Writing Other

The Survey Says!

Send your students a welcoming letter that can double as a first-week graphing activity! Before school begins, mail each student a short, personal greeting. At the bottom of the greeting, include a tear-off section with a mini survey that the student should return to you on the first day of school. The survey questions could have the student list five things he did over the summer, name his favorite movie, and identify his favorite subject. On the first day of school, share the results of each survey question with your students; then have each student create a set of graphs that display the different data. Your students will be reviewing an important math skill and learning about one another at the same time!

Been There, Done That!

Allow last year's class to help you prepare your new students for fifth grade. At the end of the school year, have each student write a friendly letter to a student in your upcoming class telling him what to expect in fifth grade. On the first day of school with your new class, place one letter on each student's desk for him to read. Your new fifth graders will love getting advice from someone who was recently a student in your class.

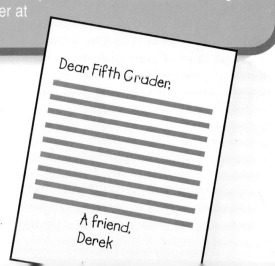

Dear Fifth Grader,

A friend,
Derek

The First Assignment

Arrival time on the first morning of school can get hectic! This activity will give your students something to do while you're busy meeting and greeting your new charges. Make one copy of the reproducible on page 14. On the copy, write a short letter to your students explaining how to complete the sheet and giving directions for other morning tasks. Duplicate a class set of the programmed sheet. Next personally address each sheet's letter to a different student. Then write the names of three classmates for that student to meet. Place each student's sheet on her desk. During the first morning of school, have every student read her letter, meet and list three things about each classmate whose name is listed on her paper, and complete the bottom portion of the sheet. By the time class actually begins, friendships will already be forming!

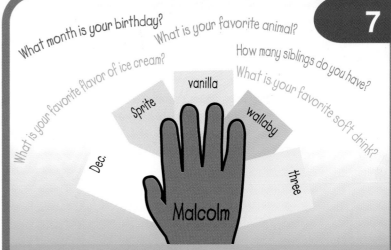

What month is your birthday? What is your favorite animal? How many siblings do you have? What is your favorite flavor of ice cream? What is your favorite soft drink?

vanilla — Sprite — wallaby — Dec. — three — Malcolm

What A Hand!

Deal your students a hand of cards that is sure to be a winner! Give each student five 3" x 5" index cards; then direct him to respond to each question above at the top of a different index card. Next have him write his name on the back of each card. Collect all the cards; then redistribute five cards to each student, making sure that no student receives his own cards. Instruct each student to walk around showing these cards to as many classmates as possible. As he does, have him sign the cards that match his own. After about 20 minutes, collect the cards. Then give each student a 9" x 12" sheet of construction paper and have him follow the steps below.

1. Trace and cut out an outline of your hand.
2. Use a black marker to write your name in the center of the cutout. (Meanwhile return the index cards to their original owners.)
3. Glue your cards to the hand cutout (see the illustration).

Display the cutouts with their accompanying cards on a bulletin board titled "What A Hand!"

Mystery Baby

Here's a fun get-to-know-you activity that can double as an attractive Open House display! Duplicate and distribute one copy of page 15 to each student. Instruct her to take the paper home and write three clues about herself on the lines provided. Caution her not to mention any physical characteristics in her clues or write her name anywhere on the paper. Have her attach a baby picture of herself at the top of the sheet and give it directly to you—without showing the picture to anyone—upon arrival the next morning. As each paper is handed to you, assign it a different number, then write that number next to that student's name on a class list as a key. Post the papers on a bulletin board titled "Name That Baby!" Then give each student a class list, inviting her to visit the board to name each baby. Reward the student who correctly identifies the most pictures with a small prize. Leave the bulletin board up so that parents can view it during Open House.

Name-O

Your students will be mixing and mingling in no time after playing this variation of bingo! Give each student one copy of the Name-O gameboard on page 16 and a handful of elbow macaroni or other small objects to use as markers. Instruct each student to walk around the classroom and have 24 classmates sign their names on his gameboard—each name written once in a different box. Meanwhile, write the name of each student in your class on a different slip of paper; then place the slips in a paper bag.

To play, draw one slip of paper from the bag at a time and read the name on it aloud. Have that student stand so that everyone can connect his name with his face; then direct the students who have his signature on their papers to place a marker on that box. Instruct the first student who covers five boxes in a row—vertically, horizontally, or diagonally—to call out "Name-O!" Award him a small prize; then have each student clear his board, and prepare to play another round. Continue play until each student has had his name drawn at least once. Soon all of your class members will be familiar with one another!

Name _____

NAME-O

Steve	Scott	Matt	Peggy	Tere
Jim	Jus	Allison	Jon	Joni
Erin	Diane	FR	Ken	Christy
Debbie	Sam	Stephanie	Nicole	Tim
A.	Dawn	Catherine	Ron	Amber

Hot Potato

This "spud-tacular" game will help your students learn their classmates' names in a snap. Have your class sit in a circle on the floor. Give two students who are sitting across from each other either a washed potato or a small ball. On your signal, have both students pass the potato to the person on his right. When you say "Hot Potato," instruct the two students holding the potatoes to say the other's name. Continue play until every student has been identified by name correctly. By the end of the game, your students should have their classmates' names burned in their memories!

"You're Jamie!"

What's In A Name?

Help each student learn more about her own name as she learns the names of her classmates. Check out from your local library a book of baby names. Assign each student the task of finding out the origin and meaning of her name as well as the possible reasons why her parents chose that name for her. Next have each student use her findings to write a name poem that tells the story behind her name (see the example). Display the completed poems on a bulletin board titled "What's In A Name?"

Deborah is a Hebrew name.
The **E**nglish changed it to Debra.
It means the **B**ee.
My par**R**ents liked the name and now it's mine,
But **A**ll my friends call me Debi.

GET-TO-KNOW-YOU ROUNDUP

This icebreaker can help your students get acquainted in no time at all! Program one index card with a different question for every two students in your class. Divide your class into two groups and instruct them to sit in two concentric circles on the floor so that each student in the inner circle faces a student in the outer circle. Next give each child in the inner circle a programmed index card; then allow him one minute to discuss the question on his card with the child across from him. Explain that *both* students need to share their thoughts during this time. After one minute, give a signal for each student with an index card to pass it to the child on his right and for each student on the outer circle to move one space to the right so that he faces a different partner. Continue in this manner until each student has answered all the different questions.

If you could visit anywhere in the world, where would you go? Why?

What is your favorite food? Why?

Of all the places you've been on vacation, which place was your favorite? Why?

Who is your favorite actor? Why?

What is the best book you've ever read? Why?

What is your favorite subject in school? Why?

What's the most unusual thing that's ever happened to you at school?

What is your favorite TV show or computer game? Why?

Where were you born?

No More Worries!

Ease the first-day jitters with this simple idea. During the morning of the first day of school, explain to your students that it's okay to be nervous and that teachers are sometimes nervous, too! Then instruct each student to write on a sheet of paper—without signing his name—any question or concern that he might have about fifth grade. Explain that you will address each question or concern during the next couple of days. Collect the papers and use a permanent marker to write each question on a different inflated balloon. As you discuss each question, slowly let the air out of that balloon. Students will enjoy seeing their worries vanish into thin air!

Will we have many tests?

Tony Capland

Bethany Kiser

Owen Troy

Trading Cards

Your students can feel like stars with this getting-acquainted project! Instruct each student to bring in a recent picture of herself. Then give each student one unlined 3" x 5" index card. Direct the student to paste her picture onto one side of her index card and write her name underneath the picture. Then have her use a black ink pen to write information about herself—such as her birthdate, height, place of birth, favorite food, hobbies, and so on—on the back of the card.

Collect the cards; then duplicate a class set of both sides of the cards so that each student can have a card of each classmate. Or simply paper-clip each card to a length of string stretched across a wall as shown so that students can remove one card at a time and read the back. What a fun way for students to learn about their classmates!

Partner Collage

Help your students get to know one another with this partner project. Pair your students; then give each pair two or three old magazines, one 11" x 17" sheet of construction paper, scissors, and glue. Instruct each student to scour the magazines and cut out pictures that represent himself—such as favorite foods, activities, colors, and so on. Next direct the pair to arrange its clippings on the construction paper in a way that shows the similarities and differences of the two students. Allow each pair to share its collage. Afterward post the collages on a classroom wall.

Student Cubes

Looking for a creative back-to-school activity to help your students get acquainted? These student-made cubes should do the trick! Duplicate and distribute one copy of the cube pattern on page 17, scissors, glue, and colored pencils or crayons to each student. Instruct each student to use the colored pencils to illustrate each side of the cube pattern as shown. Then direct the student to follow the directions for assembling the cube. Use the completed cubes as desktags, story starters, or simply as an attractive display.

See You In The Funnies!

Give each student an opportunity to share his summer experiences with this comical idea! Cut out several comic strips from a local newspaper. Pass out the strips to your students, giving them about ten minutes to read the strips. Next have each student choose one summer experience on which to base an original comic-strip story that he can create on a sheet of scrap paper. Explain that each comic strip should explain a summer experience in pictures. Next give each student a sheet of drawing paper and colored pencils for making the final copy of his comic strip. Remind each student to sign his strip. Display the completed comic strips on a bulletin board titled "See You In The Funnies!"

Creating A Model Student

Create a classroom full of model students with this novel idea! Draw a stick figure on a sheet of chart paper or poster board and label it "The Model Student." Have your students suggest the characteristics they think constitute a model student. Then draw a disproportionate feature on the stick figure that represents each suggested characteristic. For example, a student could say that a model student is a good listener. Then you could draw very large ears protruding from the stick figure's head. Students will love the ridiculous cartoon that results, and you'll be relaying important information about helping your students succeed.

Be considerate of everyone.

Return materials to their proper places.

Walk in an orderly fashion.

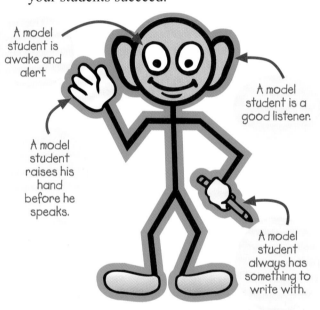

A model student is awake and alert.

A model student is a good listener.

A model student raises his hand before he speaks.

A model student always has something to write with.

Reasons For Rules

Allow your students to take an active role in creating the classroom rules. On the chalkboard, write three rules you feel must be enforced in your classroom. Then, as a class, brainstorm other rules that should be added to the list. Next divide your class into groups equal to the number of rules; then assign each group a different rule. Instruct each group to discuss why its assigned rule is necessary and what the classroom might be like if that rule were not enforced. Require each group to summarize its thoughts in writing. After the groups share their writings, allow the class to vote on which rules to implement. Collect the papers and create a master list that includes each rule and its accompanying explanation. Throughout the year when a rule is broken, refer students to this list. Your students can better appreciate the importance of each rule when it's written in their own words!

Rising Above The Negative

Show your students the effects of positive and negative words with this unforgettable demonstration! Obtain several Ping-Pong® balls, several small rocks, a permanent marker, and a clear fish bowl half-filled with water. Divide your class into groups. Instruct each group to generate two lists of words—one containing positive words that could encourage others and one with negative words that could discourage. Remind students that the listed words should be those that are allowed in a classroom. Allow each group to share their responses as you make two lists on the board. Circle any words that are repeated. Using the permanent marker, write each positive word that's circled on a different Ping-Pong® ball and each circled negative word on a different rock. Place all the labeled Ping-Pong® balls and rocks into the fish bowl; then have your students observe what happens. *(The positive words float, and the negative words sink.)* Ask your students to explain how this demonstration symbolizes the effect of positive and negative words on people. Guide students to realize that negative words can weigh a person down and make them feel low, but positive words can uplift. Your students won't likely forget the visual image provided by this lesson!

CREATIVE COMPLIMENTS

EXCEPTIONAL

Students will enjoy giving one another compliments after this word-search activity! Explain that saying or writing "good job" is a nice compliment, but that it can be overused. Pair your students; then give each pair a thesaurus and a dictionary. Instruct each pair to search the thesaurus to generate a list of words or phrases to use in place of "good job." Require that each pair use a dictionary to define each word on its list, and then use each word correctly in a written sentence. Allow each pair to share its two favorite variations with the class. Afterward collect the lists and choose 20 words to serve as the first spelling list for the year. After the test, display the new words of encouragement around the room as reminders for students to practice using them. What a *magnificent* idea!

MAGNIFICENT

SCINTILLATING

Sandra

Graffiti Board

Create a one-of-a-kind display with this quick and easy bulletin-board idea. Cover your board with black bulletin-board paper, rough side facing out. Place a box of colored chalk next to the board, and invite each student to visit the board during free time. Have him use the chalk to sign his name—graffiti style—and add a colorful picture. When every student has signed his name, recognize the person who penned each signature; then share something that you have learned about that student during the first few days of school. What a great way to make each student feel special!

Alex

Devin

Weaving A Web Of Compliments

Here's an activity that can bring a happy ending to that first week in fifth grade! Have your class sit in a circle on the floor. Hand one student a large ball of yarn. Instruct him to hold the end of the yarn and toss the ball of yarn to another student in the circle. Have the student who threw the yarn compliment in some way the student who caught the yarn. The compliment can be as simple as, "It was nice of you to lend me a pencil yesterday." Then direct the student holding the ball of yarn to hold onto a length of the yarn and throw the ball of yarn to another person. Continue in this manner until each student has received at least one compliment. Then call attention to the fact that each student holds a piece of a large web that interconnects the entire group. Place an inflated balloon on top of the web. Then challenge the group to work together to keep the balloon on top of the web—symbolizing that encouragement can help to keep everyone on this fifth-grade team feeling like they're on top of the world!

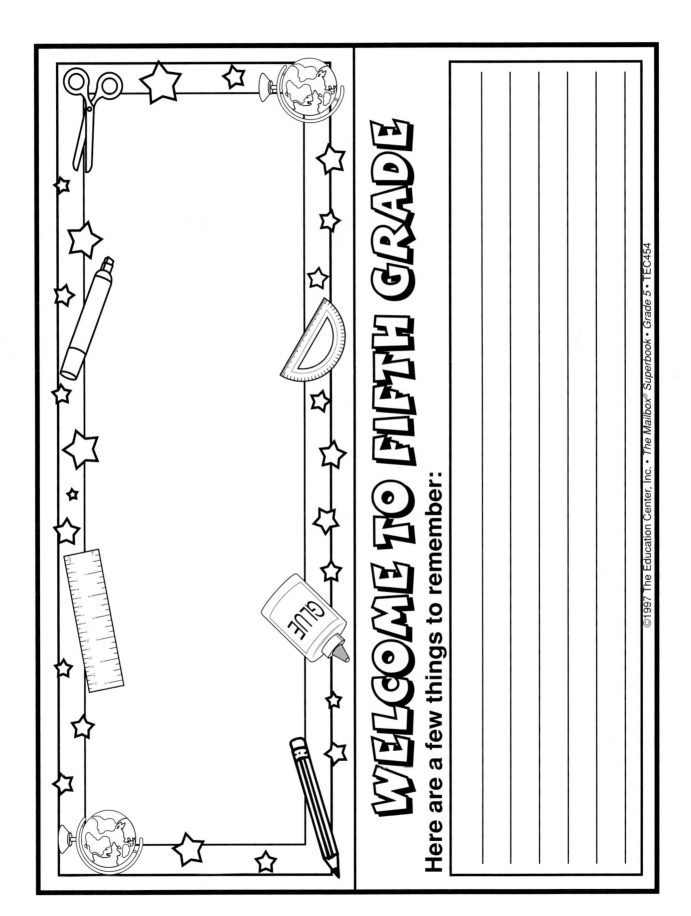

WELCOME TO FIFTH GRADE

Here are a few things to remember:

Dear _____,

———— Meet Some Classmates ————

_____   _____   _____
(name)   (name)   (name)

1. _____   1. _____   1. _____

_____   _____   _____

2. _____   2. _____   2. _____

_____   _____   _____

3. _____   3. _____   3. _____

_____   _____   _____

Polishing Up The Pledge

Refresh your memory of The Pledge Of Allegiance by using the words in the word bank to fill in the blanks below.

Word Bank

States   nation
flag   indivisible
all   Republic
   allegiance

I pledge

_____

to the _____

of the United

_____ of

of America and to the _____

for which it stands, one _____,

under God, _____ , with liberty

and justice for _____ .

Basic Facts Tune-Up

Sharpen your math skills by solving the problems below.

3 x 5 = _____   27 ÷ 3 = _____

2 x 9 = _____   40 ÷ 8 = _____

6 x 8 = _____   12 ÷ 1 = _____

9 x 5 = _____   49 ÷ 7 = _____

7 x 6 = _____   54 ÷ 6 = _____

4 x 9 = _____   35 ÷ 7 = _____

Note To The Teacher: Use with "The First Assignment" on page 7.

MYSTERY BABY # _____

MYSTERY BABY CLUES

Read each clue carefully and look at my picture. Can you identify me?

1. _____

_____

2. _____

_____

3. _____

_____

Note To The Teacher: Use with "Mystery Baby" on page 7.

Name _____

NAME-O

		FREE		

Name _____

NAME-O

		FREE		

Note To The Teacher: Use with "Name-O" on page 8.

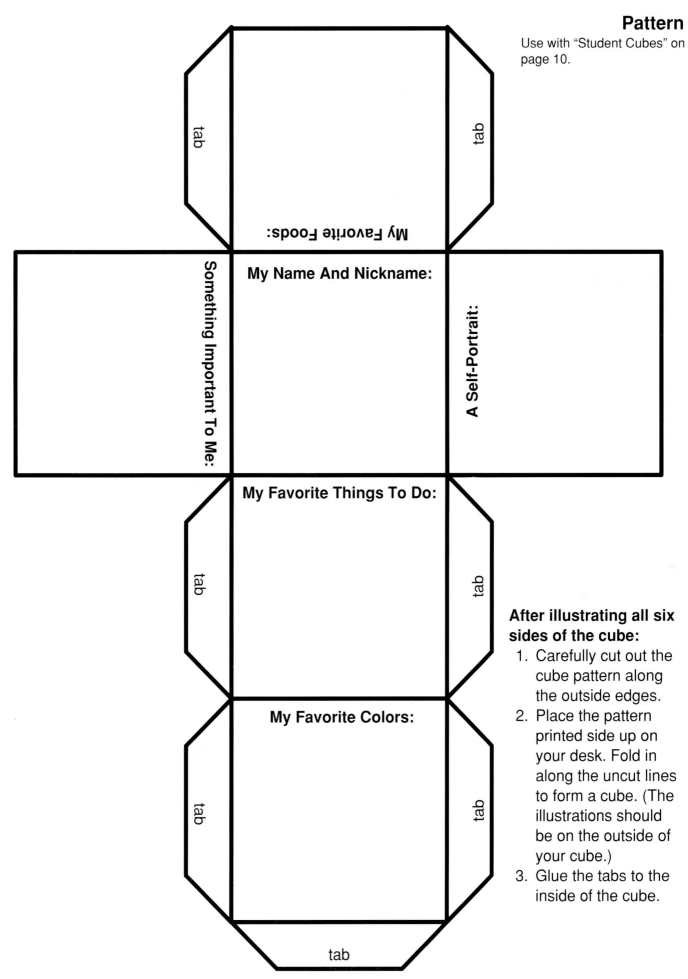

tab

tab

My Favorite Foods:

Something Important To Me:

My Name And Nickname:

A Self-Portrait:

My Favorite Things To Do:

tab

tab

My Favorite Colors:

tab

tab

tab

After illustrating all six sides of the cube:

1. Carefully cut out the cube pattern along the outside edges.
2. Place the pattern printed side up on your desk. Fold in along the uncut lines to form a cube. (The illustrations should be on the outside of your cube.)
3. Glue the tabs to the inside of the cube.

The First Day!

Can you believe your first day in fifth grade is almost over? Read the heading for each illustration below. Then use the lines provided on each shape for your responses.

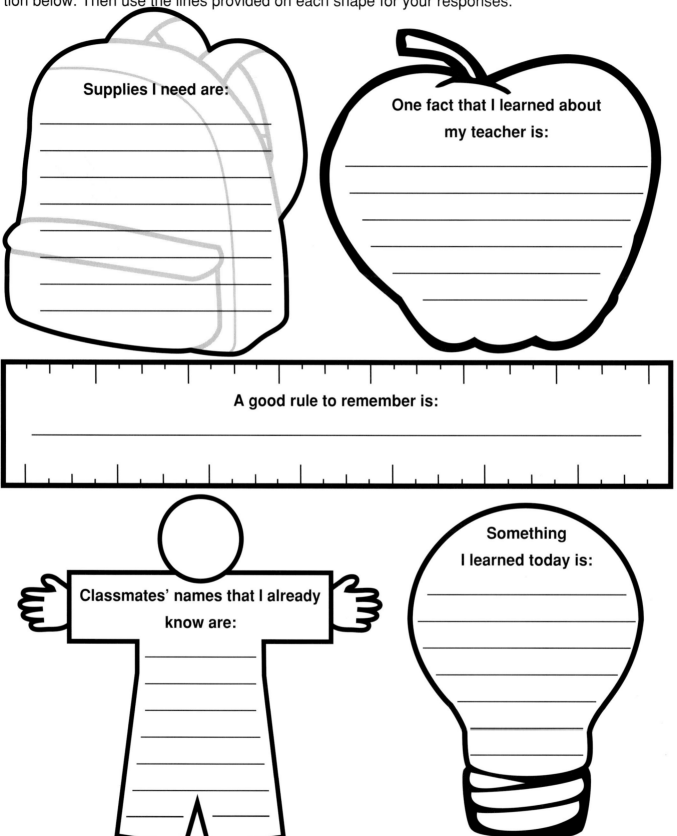

Supplies I need are:

One fact that I learned about my teacher is:

A good rule to remember is:

Classmates' names that I already know are:

Something I learned today is:

Note To The Teacher: Duplicate and distribute one copy of this sheet to use at the end of the first day of school. Instruct each student to complete the sheet as directed and take it home to share with his/her parents.

BULLETIN BOARDS

A Bulletin-Board Bonanza

Bulletin boards are vital to a classroom and can add much more than a nice decorative touch. Bulletin boards can be used to display student work, dispense information, and serve as interactive teaching tools. Create distinctive displays in your classroom by trying some of the following suggestions.

File It For Next Year

Before you take down a bulletin board, photograph it! Then store the photo in an appropriately labeled folder or album. You'll have a wonderful collection of bulletin-board ideas from which to choose in the future, plus a handy reference of all your completed displays.

Perking Up Your Background Paper

Allow the theme of your bulletin board to inspire your choice of background paper. Gift wrap comes in a variety of designs, patterns, and colors that can enhance a bulletin-board display. For example, cover a board with birthday wrap to feature your students' birthdays. Or add some sparkle to a seasonal display with a background of holiday wrap. Create other interesting displays with the following background-paper materials:

* newspaper
* calendar pages
* wallpaper
* plastic tablecloths
* road maps
* fabric
* colored cellophane
* bedsheets

Beautiful Borders

Looking for just a touch of color to add to a bulletin board with a solid-colored background? Accomplish this by creating colorful borders! Choose any material from the list above. Trace several strips of precut border onto your choice of material. Laminate the strips for added durability before cutting them out, if desired. Interesting borders can also be made using doilies, cupcake liners, dried leaves, die-cut shapes, and student-decorated adding-machine tape.

Distinctive-Lettering Designs

A bulletin board's title can be a work of art in itself. Add pizzazz to your board's letters by cutting them from any of the materials below using pinking shears or other specialized scissors.

* wallpaper samples
* greeting cards
* foil
* posters
* corrugated cardboard
* sandpaper
* newspapers
* magazine pages
* paper bags

Clue your students in on some of the exciting units they will study during the school year. From construction paper, cut a different, large geometric shape for each subject area. Then label each shape with titles of some upcoming units. Whether you're starting off the school year or preparing for Open House, this board will ensure that your classroom is in great shape!

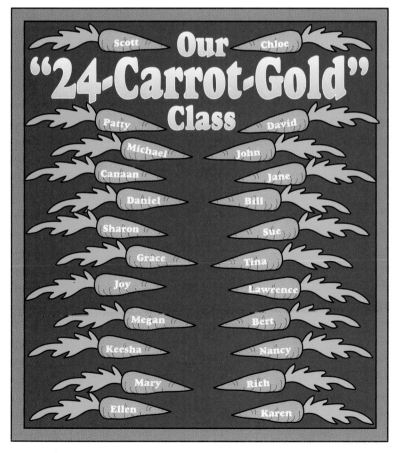

Display these carrots in your classroom, and "every-bunny" will hop over to take a peek. Using the patterns on page 34, trace and cut out a carrot from orange construction paper and a carrot top from green construction paper for each student. Label each carrot with a different student's name; then arrange the carrots on the board as shown. Adjust the "carrot-gold" number in the title to match the number of students in your classroom. If desired, save these carrots and post them with rabbits around your classroom door during the spring with this greeting: " 'Some-bunny' Has A Great Class!"

Set the stage for a "spooktacular" Halloween filled with reading and writing. Read aloud a picture-book mystery, such as *The Mystery Of King Karfu* by Doug Cushman (HarperCollins Pubs., Inc.) or *Piggins & The Royal Wedding* by Jane Yolen (Harcourt Brace & Co.). Afterward challenge each student to write her own mystery story. Display the resulting stories along with an enlargement of the hoot owl on page 35, pumpkins, colorful leaves, and a tree cut from brown bulletin-board paper as shown. To extend this bulletin board into November, just change its title to "Look 'Whoooo's' Thankful!" and display Thanksgiving stories written by your students.

Your students will have a heyday with this simple art project! Just give each student an 8 1/2" x 11" sheet of black or dark-blue construction paper, glue, and a handful of hay, straw, or raffia. Have the student create a fall scene by gluing his pieces of straw in place on the sheet of paper. Display your students' creations along with a haystack and pitchfork cut from construction paper as shown.

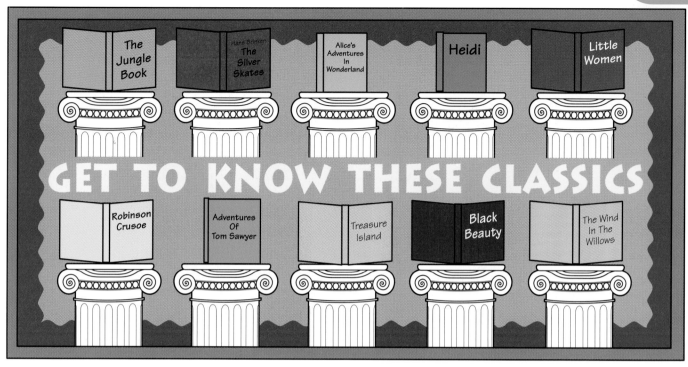

Show some class with this classy bulletin board. Discuss with your students what makes a book a classic; then provide them with an extensive list of classic books. Have each student choose a book from the list to read. Afterward direct each student to report on his book by designing a book jacket. Duplicate a copy of the pattern on page 36 on white construction paper for each student; then use a black marker to enhance the details of each column. Display the book jackets atop the columns as shown.

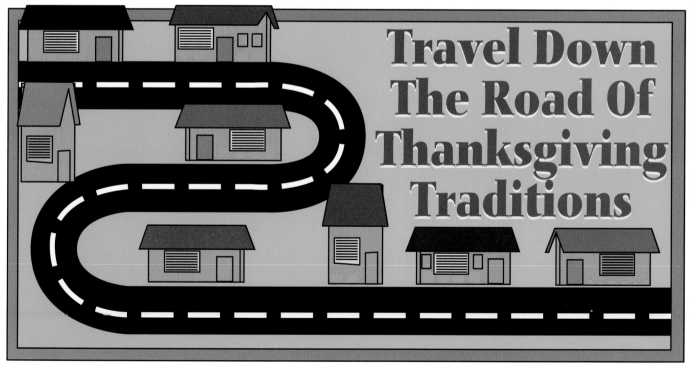

Sharing family traditions related to Thanksgiving will be quite an adventure with this bulletin board. Give each student an index card on which to bring in a favorite recipe or a description of a family tradition. Next direct her to use markers, crayons, and construction paper to decorate a paper lunch bag so that it resembles her home. Instruct her to cut out a window from the front of her house and tape her card to the back of this opening so that the card is visible from the front. Then post the bags along a winding road as shown. Students will want to travel from house to house looking for ideas to make their holiday even more special.

Celebrate the holiday season by having your students create a bulletin board about joy and peace. Divide your students into four groups, giving each group its assigned task.

Group One: From white paper, cut a semicircle with a diameter that's two-thirds the length of your board. Paint the semicircle with green and blue paint so that it resembles the world.

Group Two: Enlarge, decorate, and cut out a copy of the dove pattern on page 34.

Group Three: Cut out large letters for the board's title.

Group Four: Cut red paper so that it resembles a flowing ribbon. Write the word "Peace" on it four times in succession.

Give each student a copy of the dove pattern from page 34 on which to write a personal wish for joy or peace. Assemble the board as shown.

Enjoy a holiday board that is "tree-mendously" fast and fun to create. Cover a board with white paper; then draw the skeleton of a large pine tree on the white paper with a brown marker. Add green boughs to the tree by directing a student to paint them on with a semidry paintbrush. Have your students make paper ornaments and personalize them with their names. Staple the ornaments to the tree after it dries.

Usher in the Hanukkah season with a board that features bright blue dreidels and a large Star of David. Cover and title a board as shown, positioning a dreidel in each corner and a large Star of David with a menorrah in the center. Discuss the history and symbolism of Hanukkah with your students. Afterward give each student a copy of the star pattern on page 37. Have the student write his name in the center of the star and a fact about this holiday on each of the star's six points. After each child has decorated his star, add it to the board.

End the calendar year with a year-in-review bulletin board. Have your students bring in magazine covers and front pages of newspapers related to important events of the past year. Divide your students into groups; then give each group a different magazine cover or front-page article and an index card on which to summarize that assignment. If the given assignment reflects a current or ongoing situation, challenge that group to also predict how that situation could be resolved during the upcoming year. Display the index cards and their corresponding magazine covers or front pages in an attractive arrangement on the board.

Spread some warmth after winter break with a bunch of bundled-up penguins that broadcast the generosity and servant spirit of others. After winter break, have each student write an essay about a person who did something nice for him during the holidays. Make several enlargements of the penguin from the notecard on page 37. Decorate the penguins and display them along with your students' essays on a snowflake-bordered board as shown. Afterward give each student a copy of the penguin-shaped notecard from page 37 on which to write a special thank-you note to his person.

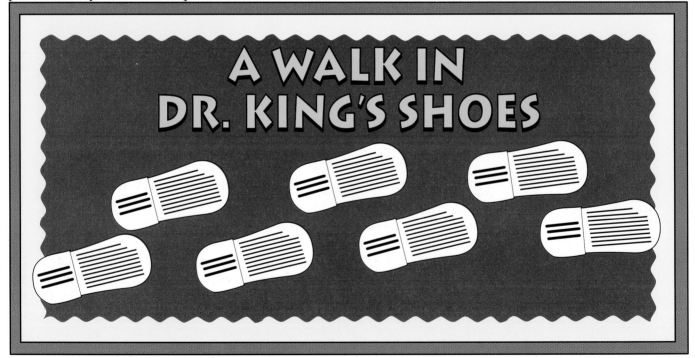

Celebrate Martin Luther King, Jr., Day with this student-created display. Divide your class into six groups. Assign each group a different event from Dr. King's life: leading the Montgomery bus boycott, founding the Southern Christian Leadership Conference, delivering the famous "I Have A Dream" speech, receiving the Nobel Peace Prize, supporting the Voting Rights Act Of 1965, or being assassinated on April 4, 1968. Have each group research its assigned event and write a brief description of it on a copy of the shoe pattern from page 38. Then arrange each group's event in chronological order on a bulletin board as shown.

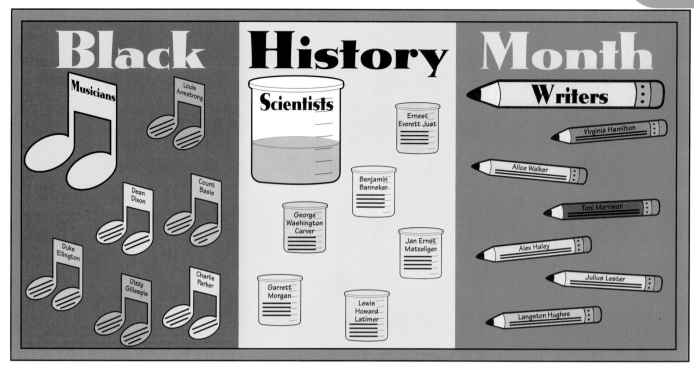

Commemorate Black History Month with a salute to famous Black Americans who have contributed to the development of American culture. Have each student choose a different Black American from the field of music, science, or literature to research. Direct the student to summarize that person's contributions in a sentence or two on a copy of a corresponding pattern from page 39. Post each student's summary on its matching red, yellow, or green section of the bulletin board as shown.

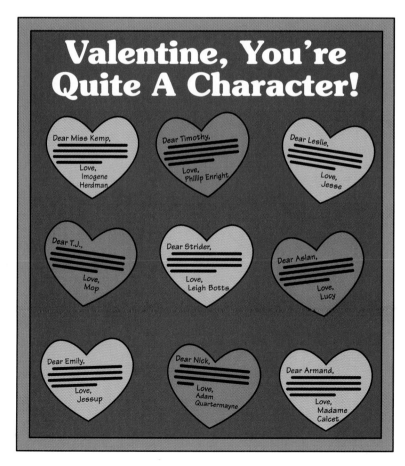

Celebrate Valentine's Day with story characters that your students admire. Have your students brainstorm a list of favorite characters from books they've read. Afterward ask each student to choose a character and have that character send a special valentine to another character from the same story. For example, Jesse in *Bridge To Terabithia* by Katherine Paterson (HarperCollins Children's Books) could send a valentine to Leslie. Or Lucy in *The Lion, The Witch And The Wardrobe* by C. S. Lewis (HarperCollins Children's Books) could send a valentine to Aslan. To make the valentine, have each student decorate a heart shape cut from red or pink paper. On the front of the valentine, ask the student to write his special message from one character to the other. On the back of the valentine, direct the student to write the title and author of the book from which his characters come. Display the completed valentines on a bulletin board, as shown, with some of the books they mention nearby.

Luck may not improve your students' writing skills, but writing *about* luck can certainly provide the practice! Discuss examples of superstitions that are said to bring bad luck: *stepping on a crack in the sidewalk* or *walking under a ladder.* Next brainstorm a list of good-luck charms, such as four-leaf clovers, rainbows, rabbits' feet, horseshoes, or the number 7. On a copy of the four-leaf clover pattern from page 40, challenge each student to write about either a superstition, a lucky charm, or a topic such as "The Luckiest Thing That Ever Happened To Me." After your students decorate and cut out their clovers, display them on a bulletin board with cutouts of good-luck charms as shown.

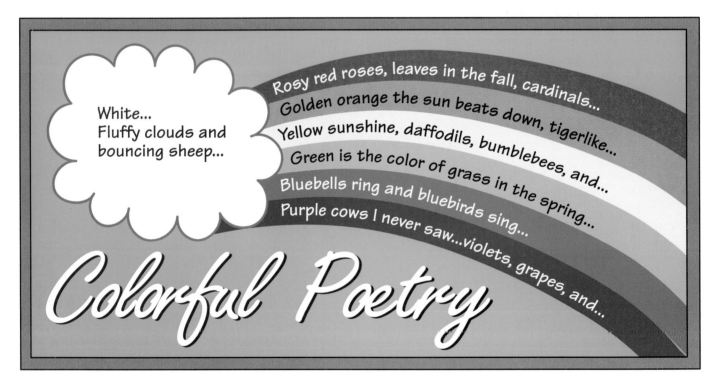

Integrate poetry into a springtime bulletin board. Read aloud several poems about color from *Hailstones And Halibut Bones* by Mary O'Neil (Doubleday). Afterward divide your students into groups; then have each group write its own poem about color. Next give each group a strip of wide-arched bulletin-board paper that matches the color in the students' poem. Direct each group to copy its poem in large letters onto the colored strip of paper. Assemble the strips on a bulletin board so that they extend from a large white cloud and represent a rainbow as shown.

Display your students' "egg-cellent" work on this springtime board. First cut a large basket from patterned gift wrap. Next have each student trace an enlarged copy of the egg pattern from page 41 onto white construction paper, cut out the shape, and—using a bottle of glue—draw a decorative pattern on the cutout. When dry, direct the student to color the spaces between the glue lines on his cutout with pastels or colored chalk. Spray the completed egg cutouts with a fixative such as hairspray. Then position the basket and eggs on a bulletin board as shown. Throughout the month, add to or change the good-work papers posted with the eggs.

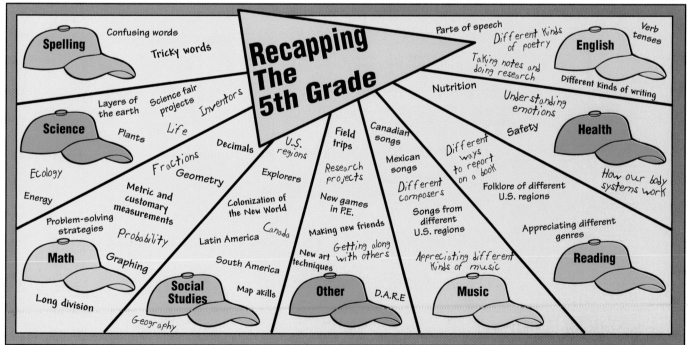

Conclude the school year with a bulletin board that allows your students to review a year's worth of learning. Cover a board with bulletin-board paper; then use yarn to divide the board into sections as shown. Cut out a sports pennant from construction paper, write the board's title on it with a black marker, and position the pennant in the center of the board. Enlarge and duplicate an appropriate number of baseball caps from the pattern on page 41. Color and program each cap with a different subject. During free time have your students use markers to write specific things learned about those subjects throughout the year in each section's space.

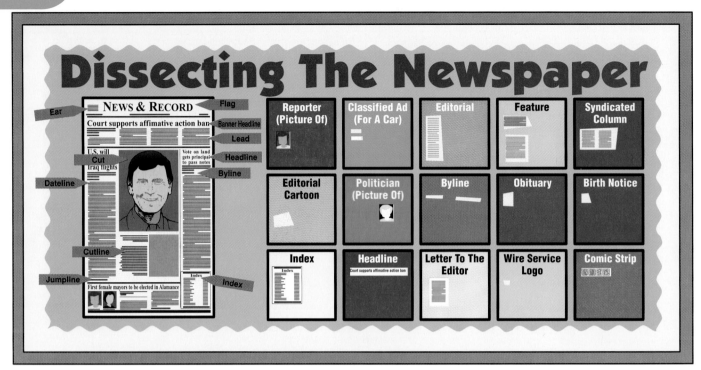

Examine the parts of a newspaper with a scavenger hunt that becomes an educational display. Collect newspapers in advance, one newspaper for each pair of students. Label and post the front page of a newspaper and 15 construction-paper signs as shown. Give each pair of students one newspaper, scissors, and glue. Explain how to use the newspaper's index to locate the topics on the signs . Have each pair search its newspaper to find an example of each topic, cut it out, and glue it to the appropriate sign. Require that only the top edge of a large example be glued to a sign so that other samples can be viewed simply by lifting one layer at a time.

Showcase the continuing efforts your students make to improve their skills. Create a range of mountain peaks by tearing a jagged edge along a sheet of gray bulletin-board paper. Staple the resulting mountain range onto a background of light-blue paper. Enlarge the goat pattern on page 42 and position it on the range's highest peak. Then add your students' work to the board in an attractive arrangement.

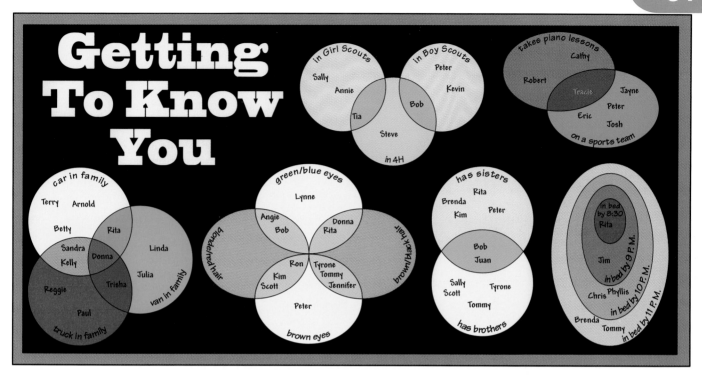

Challenge your students to learn more about one another with Venn diagrams. Draw and label a different Venn diagram on separate sheets of white construction paper, making the circles as large as possible and coloring them as shown. Wherever appropriate direct each student to sign her name in an appropriate circle on each diagram with a black marker. Then display the diagrams on a bulletin board as shown. Afterward pose questions that challenge your students to glean information from the diagrams—such as, "How many more students like peanut-butter-and-jelly sandwiches than ham-and-cheese sandwiches?"

When a student achieves a perfect score on a paper, show her how "tee-rific" that is by posting her paper on a special bulletin board. Cut a fairway from green bulletin-board paper, a flag and pole from red paper, a golf tee from brown paper, and a golf ball from white paper. Assemble the board as shown; then challenge all your students to try for a hole in one!

Math p. 42	Read Social Studies Ch. 2	Science p. 413, 1-10	Essay Due	None
Mon.	Tues.	Wed.	Thurs.	Fri.

We're Jammin' On Our Homework

Create a fun bulletin board that takes the guesswork out of what the daily class work or homework assignments will be. Cut a shelf from brown construction paper as shown. Decorate it with a red paper heart if desired. Cut five jar shapes from gray construction paper, topping each jar with a lid cut either from red paper or discontinued wallpaper samples. Affix a different Monday–Friday label to each jar; then position the jars on the shelf. Above each jar post a laminated sheet of white paper on which to write each day's assignment with a wipe-off marker. If desired, delegate the task of recording the assignments to a different student each week.

From Palette...

...To Portrait

Team this bulletin board with an art project that's related to making portraits. Cut a shape that resembles a palette from black paper. Paint or glue splotches of color to the palette as shown. Make several paintbrushes from construction paper and position them around the palette. Then, inside colorful frames, display your students' self-portraits or their student-made portraits of famous Americans or favorite story characters.

Apples

_____ , _____ , _____ , _____

_____ , _____ , _____

_____ , _____ , _____

_____ , _____ , _____

Apples

_____ , _____ , _____ , _____

_____ , _____ , _____

_____ , _____ , _____ , _____

_____ , _____ , _____

Awesome • Awesome

Awesome

Huge success deserves a big hip-hip-hooray from the class. Cover a bulletin board with red paper. Enlarge the patterns of the two hippos from page 43 on gray bulletin-board paper and position them on a board as shown. Each week reward any student who's shown improvement and/or made a top score in any subject area by posting his work on this attention-getting bulletin board. As a class write a chant that can be recited each week in recognition of the students whose papers are displayed on the board. This is a BIG way to encourage your students to be successful!

Good grades and good study skills usually go hand in hand. Enlarge and color the weight lifter and weights on page 44. Record the names of school subjects on the weights; then position the weight lifter and weights on the board as shown. As a class, brainstorm the types of study skills that produce good grades. Post the best responses on sentence strips in the spaces around the weight lifter. Refer to the board often—especially when your students have an upcoming test. If the advice on this board is taken, it should take some weight off your students' shoulders!

Patterns

Use with "Our '24-Carrot-Gold' Class" on page 21.

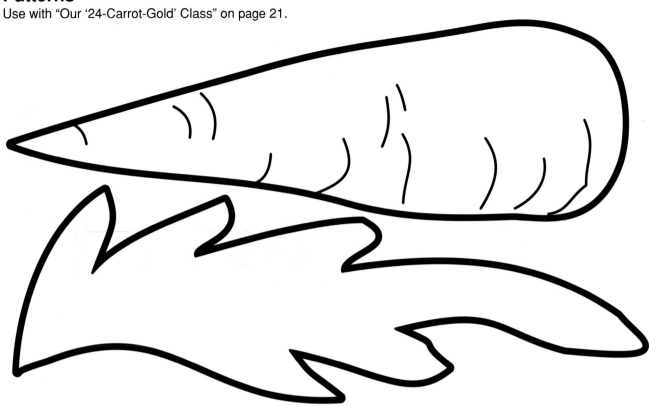

Use with "Joy To The World" on page 24.

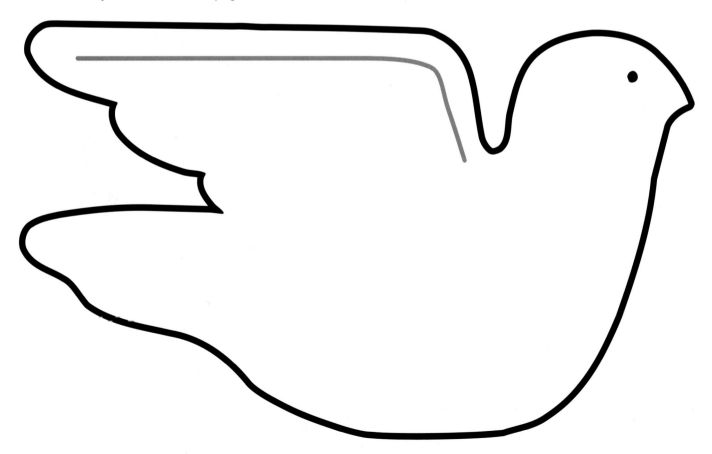

Use with "A Blizzard Of Blessings"
on page 26.

Pattern

Use with "A Walk In Dr. King's Shoes" on page 26.

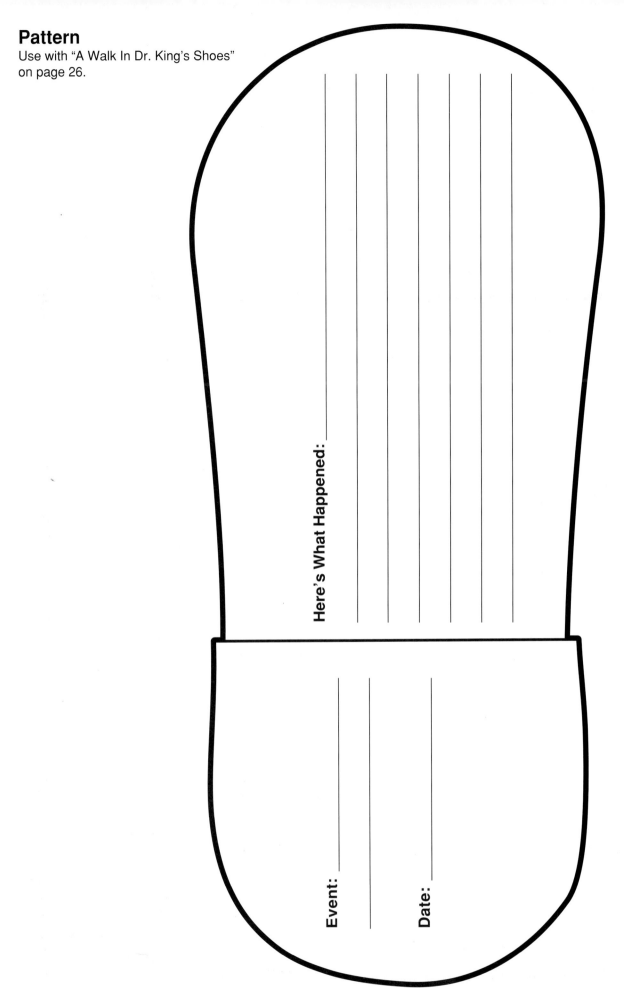

Here's What Happened:

Event:

Date:

Pattern

Use with "Lucky Charms" on page 28.

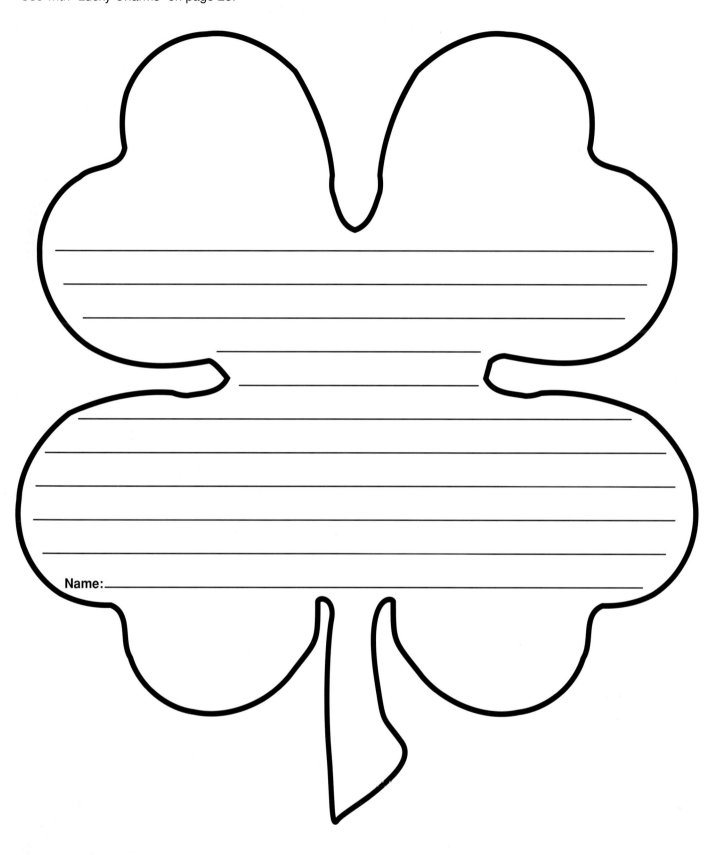

Name:

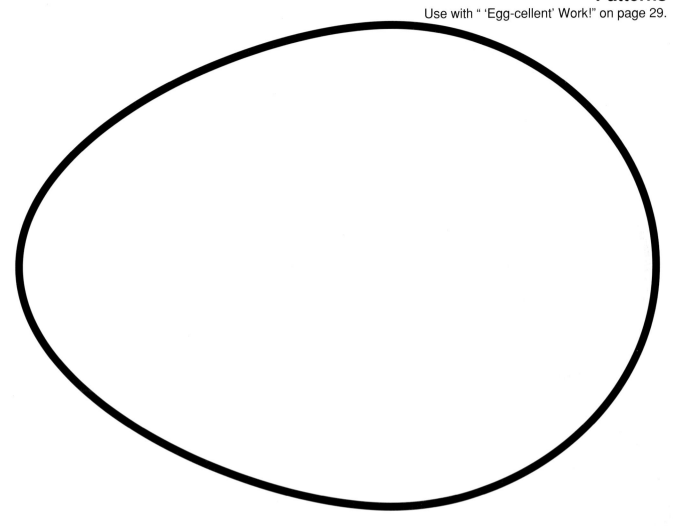

Use with "Recapping The 5th Grade" on page 29.

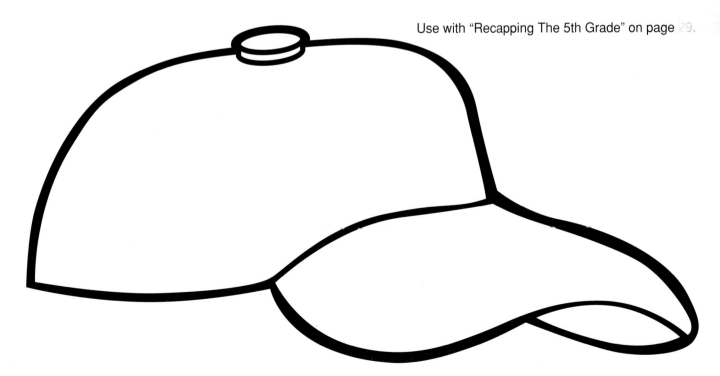

Pattern

Use with "Climbing Toward Peak Performances" on page 30.

CLASSROOM MANAGEMENT

CLASSROOM MANAGEMENT

EMERGENCY SUPPLY KIT

Individual teachers or grade-level teams will find this idea a lifesaver! Purchase a large plastic tub with a lid. Fill the tub with a variety of supply items that you never seem to have around when you need them such as:

- clear packing tape
- thank-you cards, notecards
- envelopes
- zippered plastic bags in various sizes
- safety pins
- brads and paper clips
- sewing needles and thread
- twine, yarn, string
- moist towelettes
- lotion
- liquid soap
- latex gloves
- antibacterial cream

Once a month check the box to see which items need to be replaced.

Quick Cleanups

Keep a pop-up dispenser of inexpensive baby wipes in your classroom for a quick and easy way to clean overhead transparencies. *(Be sure to get wipes without lotion.)* These handy wipes are also great for cleaning hands, faces, little messes, desk surfaces, and tabletops!

Borrower's Stash

A "Borrower's Stash" is a great idea for forgetful students. Fill a basket, box, or plastic tub with pencils, pens, scissors, protractors, and other items. Tie colorful ribbons to each item to easily identify it as belonging to the classroom *stash*. Place the *stash* on top of a file folder containing loose-leaf paper in an easy-to-reach spot in the classroom. Tell your students that the items belong to the classroom and are for their use when they've forgotten to bring an item or have run out of a particular supply. The ribbons will serve as gentle reminders for students to return items to the *stash* when finished so the supplies will be available when needed by other students.

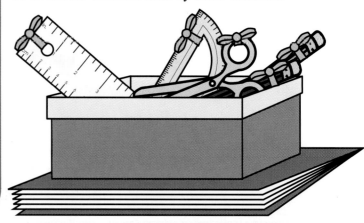

See-Through Organizers

Do you have several labeled supply boxes that don't contain what the labels indicate? Solve this problem by using plastic, see-through containers with lids. Now you will be able to find those manipulatives, glue bottles, scissors, or calculators quickly and easily!

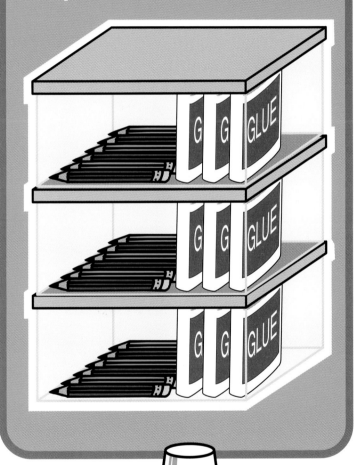

Classroom Supply Shower

Here's a great way to stock your classroom with supplies early in the year. Invite your students and their parents to a "Classroom Shower." A few weeks before the event, send home an invitation explaining the purpose of the shower. Then post a "Wish List" in the classroom so students can sign up for what they'd like to bring as a classroom gift. Be sure to balance your list with inexpensive items as well as the more costly items needed for classroom activities. Recruit parent volunteers to help decorate the classroom, plan games for the students, and provide refreshments. During the shower, open your classroom gifts and take time to enjoy the refreshments.

Keeping Track Of Supplies

Keep track of grade-level supplies with this simple trick. Have each teacher at your grade level choose a different color nail polish and use it to mark dots on those items that are shared throughout the year. These simple color dots will help ensure that protractors, geoboards, scissors, and other supplies get returned to the right rooms by the end of the day, week, month, or year. If a teacher moves away, have the new teacher use the same color nail polish as the previous teacher. This alleviates the confusion of having the previous teacher's name on classroom supplies.

Conduct Record

Keep track of student behavior with this timesaving idea. Duplicate one "Conduct Card" (see page 54) for each student. Keep the cards alphabetized in a binder or folder. When a student misbehaves or disrupts the class, have him fill in one row on the card. Then check the card to make sure the student's entries are appropriate. Briefly discuss the situation with the student, then date and initial the appropriate line. After two incidents, make a copy of the card and send it home with the student asking the parent for assistance in correcting the inappropriate behavior. This method helps the student take responsibility for her actions as well as providing a means of documenting the incident and communicating with parents.

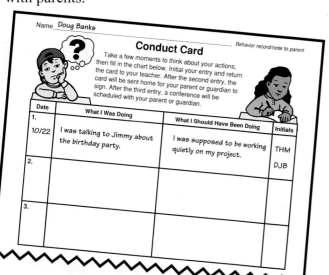

Sweet Rewards

Looking for a unique way to monitor class behavior? Obtain a clear, glass or plastic fishbowl and purchase a one-pound bag of M&M's®. Each time your class demonstrates good behavior—such as using lunchroom manners, walking quietly in line, and receiving good reports at special events—have a student add five M&M's® to the fishbowl. When the fishbowl is filled with the last five candies, celebrate with a special snack party including the bowl of M&M's®.

Shark Report

Use this effective idea for increasing open communication with your students. Duplicate a supply of the "Shark Report" form on page 55; then stack the forms next to a fishbowl in your classroom. When a student feels that the "sharks are circling"—he's having trouble with a particular subject, project, assignment, or friend—have him fill out a "Shark Report" and place it in the fishbowl. Check the bowl daily and respond to each student's report in writing or with a conference.

TEACHER ASSISTANT

Reward positive student behavior with this great idea. Each week select a different student to be your special assistant. Make the assistant responsible for passing out and collecting papers, gathering lesson materials, taking the lunch count, and any other classroom job. Your students will get a self-esteem boost—and you'll have the assistance of a valuable classroom aide.

Put It In Writing!

Need an easy way to help settle student arguments? Have each student take time out to cool off and write down exactly what happened, including emotions and events that led up to the incident. Chances are good that by the time each student has recorded his version of the story, tempers will have cooled. If the students still need your intervention, read each student's account of the situation, then discuss the versions with the students involved. Not only does this strategy help clarify the situation, it allows each student involved to tell his side of the story.

It all started when Sally called me a...

BALL TOSS

Use this quick and easy trick whenever you want to make it clear whose turn it is to talk. Buy an inexpensive sponge ball and keep it handy throughout the day. Whenever a discussion becomes too lively, toss the ball to a student and explain that only the person with the ball has permission to speak. That student now has the floor to ask a question or make a comment without any interruptions from the other students. When he is finished speaking, have that student pass the ball back to you so you can then toss it to another student. Continue in this manner until everyone has had a chance to speak.

SUMMER BIRTHDAYS

Wondering what to do about students whose birthdays fall during the summer? Try celebrating with birthday-and-a-half parties. At the beginning of the school year, duplicate one copy of the "Happy Birthday-And-A-Half!" card on page 55 for each student with a summer birthday. Fill in each card with the date your class will be celebrating that student's birthday-and-a-half (six months after his actual birthday). For example, if a student's birthday is on June 20, then write on the card that the class will celebrate his birthday on December 20. Distribute the completed cards so that everyone can look forward to a birthday celebration at school!

HAPPY BIRTHDAY-AND-A-HALF!

Ryan Scarborough
(Student's Name)

Because your birthday fell during the summer months, the class will celebrate your birthday on __December 20__, which is six months after your real birthday!
(Date)

©1997 The Education Center, Inc. • The Mailbox® Superbook • Grade 5 • TEC454

Party Booklet

Keep track of party successes with a party booklet. Each time you hold a class party, take notes on the foods served, games played, and art projects made. Include only the successes. Add to the booklet all year; then give it to next year's room parent. This idea-filled booklet will offer suggestions for both the novice and the veteran room parent!

Hot-air popcorn was quick and easy for the Behavior Party at the end of the week. Very little mess to clean up, and no greasy fingers!

GRADE A HOMOGENIZED MILK

Holiday Breakfast

Classroom parties don't always have to be at the end of the day. For a change of pace, plan a holiday breakfast—serving breakfast foods or featuring cakes and cookies that are appropriate for the time of the year. After the breakfast have students help clean up from the party. No more rushing around at the end of the day to put everything in order by yourself!

Monthly Folders

This monthly file-folder system is sure to make planning ahead a cinch! Label a folder for each month of the school year; then store the folders in a file box. Place appropriate activities, holiday reproducibles, and "to-do" lists in each folder. Also include in each folder preaddressed birthday cards for each student as well as a calendar for the month—marking birthdays, holidays, workdays, and deadlines. At the beginning of each month, simply pull the appropriate folder to give you a quick update on that month's activities.

NOVEMBER
OCTOBER
SEPTEMBER

MONTHLY FOLDERS

Good–Neighbor Reports

Update absent students on missed activities with this simple note-taking system. Duplicate a supply of the reproducible on page 56 to keep handy in the classroom. Each day a student is absent, assign a classmate to fill out a "Good-Neighbor Report." Instruct the selected student to be concise and specific when writing up that day's assignments. At the end of the day, have the recorder put the completed sheet in a three-ring binder labeled "Good-Neighbor Reports." Briefly look over the completed sheet to be sure no assignments were left off the sheet. Praise the recorder for a job well done, or give some pointers on how to write better notes next time. Direct each student returning from an absence to read the appropriate reports to find out which assignments he missed and what he needs to complete.

SHOE BAG LUNCH COUNT

Lunch counts will be a shoo-in with this easy tip! Hang a plastic, over-the-door shoe divider on the wall or on a closet door in your classroom. Label each pocket with a different student's name. Then cut out one 2" x 6" strip of yellow poster board and one 2" x 6" strip of red poster board for each student. Label each yellow strip "Bag Lunch" and each red strip "School Lunch." Place the strips in an empty pocket or in a container placed near the shoe bag. As each student enters the room every morning, instruct him to place the appropriate strip in his pocket. You'll know at a glance who is absent for the day—and taking the lunch count will be a breeze!

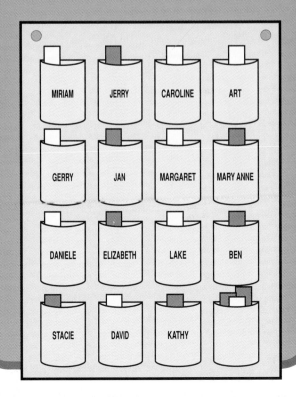

MIRIAM | JERRY | CAROLINE | ART

GERRY | JAN | MARGARET | MARY ANNE

DANIELE | ELIZABETH | LAKE | BEN

STACIE | DAVID | KATHY

Journal Responses

Simplify responding to student journals by using sticky notes! Every week give each student two sticky notes for flagging one page in his journal that he wishes you to read and respond to for that week. On one of the notes, have the student do two things: explain why he chose that particular entry for you to read, and indicate whether he wants you to comment on his mistakes in grammar, content, or sentence structure, etc. When you read his entry, use the blank note for your response. As you respond, quote a favorite line or phrase the student used in his writing or make a positive suggestion or remark about some aspect of his entry. You'll find that having the student highlight a specific entry for you to read gives the student some privacy and helps decrease your workload.

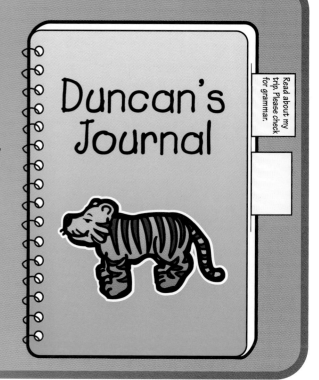

Duncan's Journal

Read about my trip. Please check for grammar.

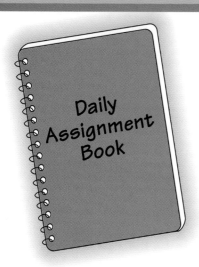

Daily Assignment Book

Study Buddies

Everyone can use a buddy! Divide your class into study-buddy pairs. Then explain that it will be each study buddy's responsibility to make sure that his partner has written down his assignments correctly at the end of each day, update his partner on missed assignments after he returns from an absence, and help his buddy study for tests and work on classroom assignments. Students will learn responsibility for themselves as they help their classmates.

Science	4/10/98	Sam

Heading Checkers

Identifying students' work is a snap with this simple tip. Model for students how you would like them to head their classroom assignments; then assign one student in each row or group of students to be a Heading Checker. Have the Heading Checker collect the papers from her row or group and quickly check to see that each student has put the name, date, and subject in the correct place. Reward each group that has perfect headings for a week with a special treat. In a short time, your students will be heading their papers accurately with very little effort on your part.

Cleanup Crew

Wish you had a simple way to have a clean room at the end of the day? Here's the solution you've been waiting for! Assign each row or group of students in your classroom a different area of the classroom to clean and tidy up at the end of each day. Since this is a group effort, the job will be done in no time and you will end up with a tidy room ready for the next day's activities. Change each group's designated area each week, month, or grading period.

Successful Seating

Do you find yourself at the beginning of each year trying to remember the seating arrangement that worked best the previous year? Keep track of successful seating formations by making a diagram of each arrangement throughout the year. Be sure to include centers, furniture, and other items that may affect a seating's layout. You may even want to visit other teachers' classrooms and make diagrams of their successful seating arrangements. Keep the diagrams in a file or notebook. Refer to the file each time you are in need of a change—and avoid making moves that may have hidden complications!

My Desk

Activity Table

Center 1

Center 2

Monday's Child

Looking for an easy way to form cooperative groups, organize chore rotation, or manage class movement? Divide your students' desks into five rows or groups; then name each row or group after each school day—Monday, Tuesday, Wednesday, Thursday, and Friday. Inform your students that each Monday, the students in the Monday group will be the first to put supplies away, line up, and go outside. Each Tuesday the Tuesday group will do everything first and so on. Whenever you need to form cooperative groups or assign classroom responsibilities, simply call for one student from each group, or call up an entire group.

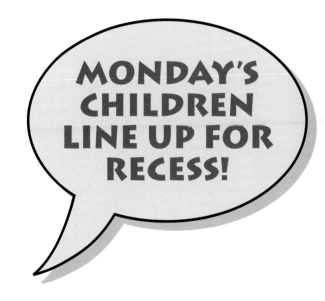

MONDAY'S CHILDREN LINE UP FOR RECESS!

Conduct Card

Take a few moments to think about your actions, then fill in the chart below. Initial your entry and return the card to your teacher. After the second entry, the card will be sent home for your parent or guardian to sign. After the third entry, a conference will be scheduled with your parent or guardian.

Date	What I Was Doing	What I Should Have Been Doing	Initials
1.			
2.			
3.			

Dear Parent,

We need your assistance to maintain a positive learning environment in our classroom. Please sign and return this card by ___/___/___ with any suggestions or comments you may have concerning the situation. Thank you in advance for your help.

Sincerely,

_____
Teacher's Signature

Parent suggestions/comments: _____

_____

_____

_____

_____

_____
Parent's Signature

Note To The Teacher: Duplicate one copy of this page for each student and use with "Conduct Record" on page 48.

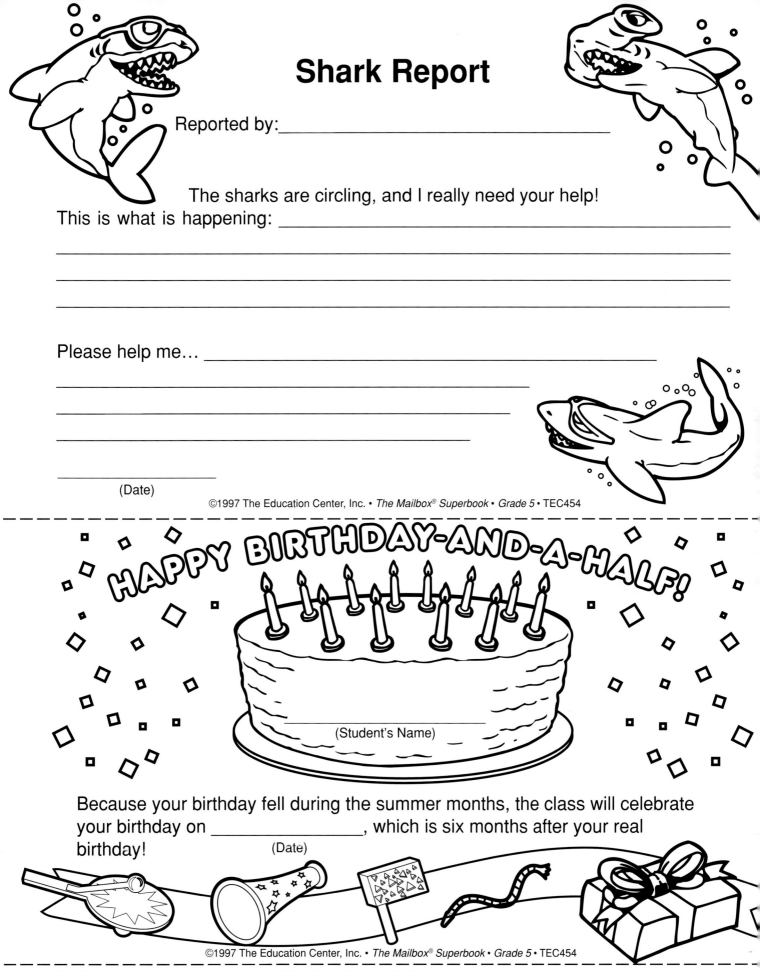

Shark Report

Reported by: _____

The sharks are circling, and I really need your help!

This is what is happening: _____

_____

_____

_____

Please help me... _____

_____

_____

_____
(Date)

©1997 The Education Center, Inc. • *The Mailbox® Superbook • Grade 5* • TEC454

HAPPY BIRTHDAY-AND-A-HALF!

_____
(Student's Name)

Because your birthday fell during the summer months, the class will celebrate your birthday on _____, which is six months after your real birthday!

(Date)

©1997 The Education Center, Inc. • *The Mailbox® Superbook • Grade 5* • TEC454

Note To The Teacher: Duplicate a supply of the "Shark Report" to use with "Shark Report" on page 48. Duplicate on colorful paper one copy of the "Happy Birthday-And-A-Half!" card for each student with a birthday that falls during the summer vacation. Use the cards with "Summer Birthdays" on page 50.

55

Good-Neighbor Report

Be a good neighbor by keeping track of today's activities for your absent classmates. Take careful notes on the chart below. Be sure to include page numbers, assignment directions, and any special instructions about an assignment given by your teacher.

Subject	Assignment
READING 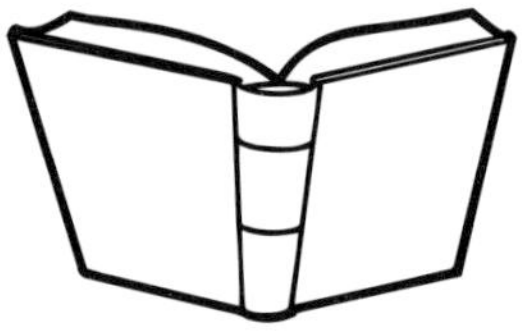	
LANGUAGE ARTS/ WRITING 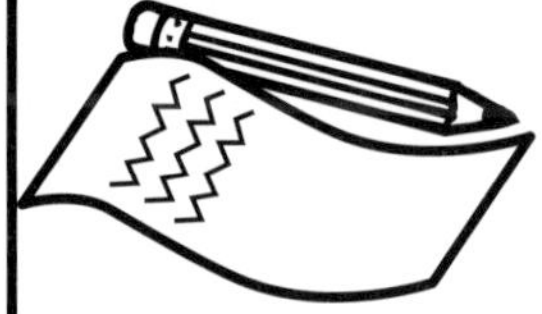	
SCIENCE 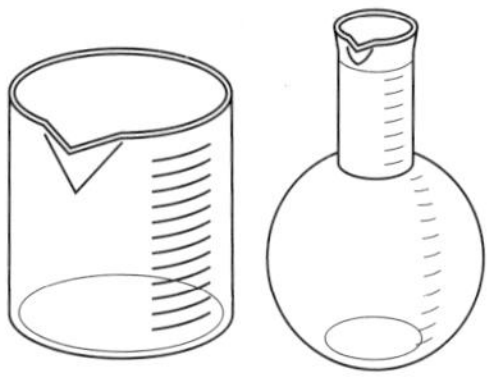	
SOCIAL STUDIES 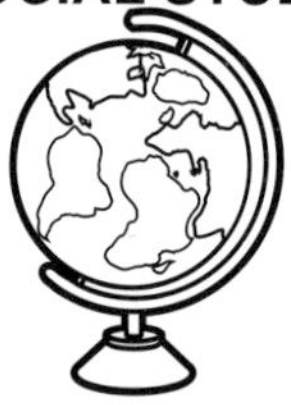	
MATH 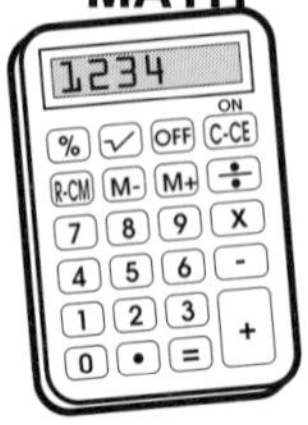	
OTHER ASSIGNMENTS/ ACTIVITIES 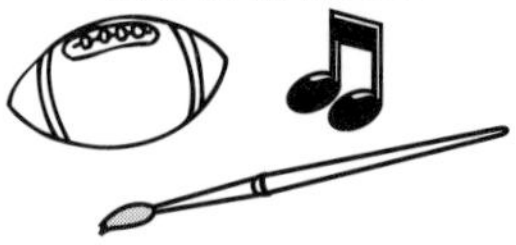	

Note To The Teacher: Use this reproducible with "Good-Neighbor Reports" on page 51.

STUDENT MOTIVATION
SELF-ESTEEM &
CHARACTER BUILDING

Motivating Students

Be A Topper!

Motivate your students to take pride in their schoolwork with these topper awards. Duplicate several copies of the certificate pattern at the top of page 64 on colorful paper. Have your school's principal sign each certificate; then store the certificates with your report cards. At the end of each grading period, fill out a topper certificate for each student who maintained or improved his grades from the previous grading period. Present each topper with his certificate and a special pencil or bookmark on the day you hand out report cards.

Thumbs-Up!

This motivation idea gets two thumbs-up! Duplicate and distribute one copy of the patterns at the bottom of page 64 for each student. Instruct the student to decorate his thumb patterns any way he wants; then have him cut the patterns apart along the dotted line. Direct the student to tape the two thumb patterns back-to-back. Next collect and laminate the patterns. Return each pattern to its owner and instruct him to keep it on the corner of his desk. Explain to each student that the thumbs-up side should be facing up when his work is caught up, and the thumbs-down side should be facing up when he still has work to do. Students will have a constant reminder throughout the day of their unfinished assignments.

Quick Check

Use this quick tip to keep your students motivated to complete their work on time. When lining up for lunch, a special class, or recess, call students to line up using the names from the last set of papers that students turned in to you. Any student who has not turned in that assignment can turn it in to you then if it is complete or make a note to finish the work later. You should soon have students who are eager to turn in their work on time every time!

We Really Did It!

Help your students remember to bring all the items they need for special classes with this idea. Use a computer program such as The Print Shop® Deluxe to design a banner that reads "We Really Did It!" Display the banner in the classroom. Each day that the entire class brings all the needed materials (including homework) to their special class, select a student to color one letter on the banner. When all the letters of the banner are colored, reward the class with a special treat.

We Really Did It!

Cooperative Display

This no-fuss bulletin board will help your students learn to work cooperatively. Divide your class into groups of four or five students; then divide a bulletin board into sections equal to the number of student groups. Assign each group a different section of the board; then explain that each group should decorate its section based upon something the class is currently studying. Explain that you will evaluate each group's section based on creativity, neatness, and its relevance to the selected unit of study. Emphasize to your students the importance of working together and sharing responsibilities. When the board is finished, you'll have an attractive display and some insight into what your students learned about that unit.

Group Study Time

Watch cooperation among your students grow by routinely scheduling times for groups to work together on the same assignment. For example, each Monday make the weekly spelling assignments and allow the groups time to complete the activities. Then on Thursday, permit the groups to study together for Friday's spelling test. As the groups are working, point out which groups are modeling your expectations for staying on task and helping one another. After the Friday spelling test, average each group's test scores; then reward the groups that averaged a score of *B* or higher with an inexpensive treat.

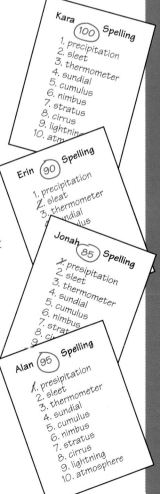

Putting In Your Two Cents

Make sure all your students get opportunities to contribute to discussions with this quick motivation tip! When working in cooperative groups, give each group member two pennies. Explain that when a student has something to add to the discussion, he must place one penny in the center of the group. After a student contributes both pennies, he cannot speak again until every other group member has put in his two pennies. This simple idea will help students become better listeners and ensure that every student always gets to put in his two cents!

Building Self-Esteem

Slips of paper reading:
- smile.
- I admire Sam because he is smart.
- I like the way Sam always draws his trees.
- ...m is always helpful.
- I trust S...

Sending Smiles

Boost your students' self-esteem with this simple idea. Display a transparency of your class list or write each student's name on the chalkboard. Then duplicate copies of page 65 and distribute one to each student. Have every student write a positive comment about each of his classmates on a different line of his reproducible. Emphasize that each sentence should be specific. Meanwhile write each student's name on a different envelope. Post the envelopes on the chalkboard; then instruct each student to cut apart his sentences and place them in the appropriate envelopes. Distribute the envelopes to their recipients and happily wait for the smiles to appear!

Look What We Did!

Give your students some bragging rights with this idea for building self-esteem. Purchase a decorative journal with blank pages or bind your own using construction paper and drawing paper. Title the journal "Look What We Did!" and place it in a special area of the classroom. Tell your students that the journal is for recording class and individual student accomplishments or recognitions throughout the year (see the illustration). Explain that accomplishments or recognitions earned at school, at home, in sports, or for any other part of their lives can be listed in the journal. Further explain that a student may write an entry in the book for himself or for a classmate and that he should date each entry. At the end of each month, read aloud any additions made to the journal. What a great way to give accolades and have your students pat themselves and their classmates on the back!

September
Matt scored a goal in soccer. 9/7
John S. hit his first triple in baseball. 9/15
Miss Adcock got a new kitten. 9/17
Barbara's parents won a new car. 9/21
Shana got a 100 on her social studies test. 9/25
Eddy won the class spelling bee. 9/30

Teacher's Helpers

Reinforce students' responsibilities and boost their self-esteem while you get valuable classroom help. Each day designate a different student to be your special helper. Have that student distribute papers, take the lunch count, and run errands as needed throughout the day. Program slips of paper with different classroom rewards as shown. Place the rewards in an envelope labeled "Thanks For Your Help!" At the end of each day, allow your special helper to draw a slip of paper from the envelope as a reward. Your students will feel good about themselves, and you'll get the help you need!

15 minutes at the library

10 minutes of free time

Heartfelt Adjectives

This activity is a great morale booster. Give each student a 9" x 12" sheet of colored construction paper. Direct the student to cut out a large heart shape and write her name in large letters along the left edge of the cutout. Collect the hearts and redistribute them, making sure that no student gets her own cutout. Have each student use a thesaurus to find positive adjectives that describe the person whose cutout she was given. After she writes the adjectives on the cutout, allow her to share what's written on the heart shape with the class. Then post the heart cutouts on a bulletin board titled "Adjectives With Heart."

pleasant
honest
intelligent
jovial
Julia

Postcard Express

The next time one of your students does something worth bragging about, send the message home via postcard express! At the beginning of the year, give each student two large blank index cards. Instruct him to decorate one side of each card any way that he chooses. Have the student turn over each card and neatly print his home address on the right half of the card. Collect the cards and store them in your desk. When a student does something special, simply write a brief message explaining what he did on the left half of one of his cards and drop it in the mail. What a great way to get both a student and his parents to feel very proud!

Jonathan Jones
8 Harbor Way
Jonesville, KS 12345

Bubbling Personalities

You'll have the self-esteem of your students bubbling over after this activity! As a class, brainstorm a list of words that can describe someone's personality. Then have several student volunteers choose one word from the list and give an example of something that a person with that personality might do. For example, a student choosing the word *courageous* could say, "A courageous person will stand in front of the class and give an oral report." Next duplicate copies of page 66 and distribute one to each student. Instruct him to complete the page as directed. Afterward collect and display your students' work on a bulletin board titled "Our Bubbling Personalities."

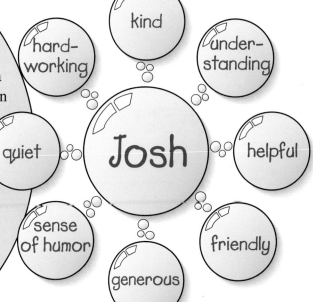

kind
hard-working
under-standing
quiet
Josh
helpful
sense of humor
generous
friendly

Building Character

Hats Off To You!

Encourage your students to perform random acts of kindness with this motivating bulletin board. Cover a bulletin board with bright-colored paper; then title the board "Hats Off To You!" Next cut out several hat shapes—such as baseball caps, cowboy hats, and top hats—from construction paper. Position the hat cutouts along with markers near the bulletin board. Each time a student notices a classmate demonstrating kindness to another student or teacher, invite him to write a sentence on a cutout telling what the student did, sign his own name on the cutout, and then post it on the bulletin board. Students will be encouraged to look for kindness in themselves as well as others.

Teamwork

Looking for a way to encourage peer cooperation? Divide your class into teams of four or five students. Have each team select a team name, write it on a sheet of construction paper, and illustrate the paper. Explain that each team will be working toward becoming "Team Of The Week." Further explain that the team earning this recognition is eligible for bonus privileges—such as being at the front of the lunch line, receiving extra free time, or getting to hold the class pet. Point out that in order to win, a team's members will need to work together. Give each team up to five points a day for keeping an assigned area of the room clean, winning a review game, or turning in homework assignments. Keep a running total of each team's points on a designated area of the chalkboard or on a special bulletin board decorated with illustrated team nametags. At the end of each week, declare the team with the most points the "Team Of The Week."

Kindness Is...

What exactly is *kindness*? Have each student define the term in the lines of his own poem about kindness. First read aloud *Kindness* by Jane Moncure (Child's World, Inc.; 1996), a picture book of simple acts that demonstrate kindness. Then challenge each student to write on a sheet of loose-leaf paper ten sentences, each one telling about a different act of kindness. Give each student one sheet of drawing paper and colored pencils or crayons. Instruct the student to edit his ten sentences and neatly copy them onto the drawing paper. Have the student add illustrations and title his poem "Kindness Is..." Allow each student to share his poem with the class. Afterward collect the poems and bind them into one class book for your reading corner. If desired, read aloud other books in this series for lessons on courage, self-control, or success.

Let's Discuss It!

Instead of arguing about their conflicts, challenge your students to discuss them! Cover a shoebox with decorative paper; then cut a slit in the top of the box and place it on your desk. Whenever a student has a problem or conflict with another classmate that he cannot solve himself, invite that student to write about it on a sheet of paper and place it—unsigned—in the covered box. At the end of each day, read a few of the papers aloud; then, as a class, discuss possible solutions. You'll be teaching your students that discussion is a great method for solving problems.

Learning Buddies

Initiate friendships and teach responsibility with learning buddies. Pair your fifth-grade class with a class of first or second graders. Work together with that classroom teacher to pair each of your students with one of the younger students. Then schedule a class time each week for the learning buddies to work together. For each visit, plan an activity—such as reading a picture book, completing an art project, or playing an educational game—that the buddies can work on together. Your students' sense of responsibility will grow to be just as wide as their smiles!

Brave As A...

Being courageous is not always easy, so seize every opportunity to build this character trait in your students. Read aloud Brave As A Mountain Lion by Ann Herbert Scott (Houghton Mifflin Company). This picture book tells the story of a boy named Spider who needs courage to compete in the school spelling bee. He gains courage by thinking that he is as brave as a mountain lion and as clever as a coyote. As a class, brainstorm situations in a fifth-grade student's day when courage might be needed. Record students' responses on the board. Explain that although it's not always easy to be brave, it's usually worthwhile. Then discuss the difficulty as well as the benefit of each situation listed on the board to help students understand the rewards of tough challenges.

I need courage...

to stand up in front of the class.

to not misbehave.

when I get a bad grade.

This Topper Award
is presented to

_____

for maintaining or improving grades.

_____   _____
Principal   ### Teacher

_____
Date

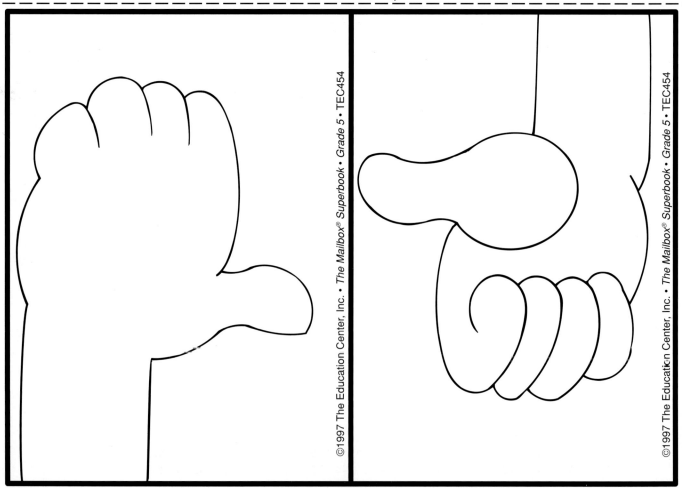

Name _____   *Building self-esteem*

     # Sending Smiles

Everyone likes to receive compliments, so why not give them? Use the sentence starters below to write one complimentary sentence about each of your classmates. Be specific so that the person will know exactly what you mean.

Example: I admire <u>the way Susan offers suggestions to help her team complete projects.</u>

I respect _____

I admire _____

I applaud _____

I appreciate _____

I enjoy _____

I like _____

I trust _____

I respect _____

I admire _____

I applaud _____

I appreciate _____

I enjoy _____

I like _____

I trust _____

I respect _____

I admire _____

I applaud _____

I appreciate _____

I enjoy _____

I like _____

I _____

I _____

I _____

I _____

I _____

I _____

I _____

Bonus Box: Choose one statement from above and send its message to that student in a greeting card made from construction paper. Then illustrate, sign, and deliver the card to that classmate.

©1997 The Education Center, Inc. • *The Mailbox® Superbook* • Grade 5 • TEC454

Note To The Teacher: Use with "Sending Smiles" on page 60.

My Bubbling Personality!

How bubbly is *your* personality? Write your name in the center bubble below. Then think about words or phrases that describe your personality and write each one inside a different large bubble surrounding your name. On another sheet of paper, use the words from the bubbles to write a paragraph telling about your personality.

I'm giddy, sparkling, and effervescent!

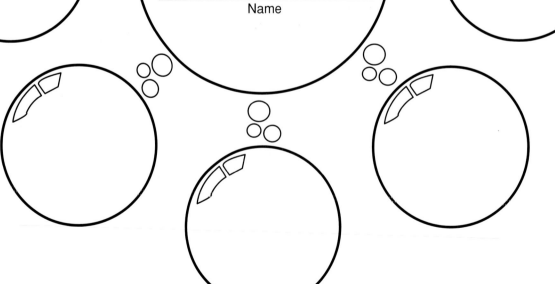

Name

Note To The Teacher: Use with "Bubbling Personalities" on page 61. Have each student cut out his paragraph and paste it on a bubble shape cut from blue construction paper. Post all the bubbles on a bulletin board titled "Our Bubbling Personalities."

WORKING
WITH
PARENTS

WORKING WITH PARENTS

PARENT-SURVIVAL GUIDE

Help each parent overcome the challenges of a new year by creating a personalized parent-survival guide. Before the beginning of school, duplicate important school and classroom information to include in the guide (see the examples below). Also include a brief welcome letter that includes background information about yourself. Next enlist the aid of your students in assembling the guide by following the steps below.

1 Give each student a 12" x 18" sheet of light-colored construction paper and a copy of each page in the guide.

2 Direct the student to fold the construction paper in half, labeling the front to make a cover as shown.

3 Have him decorate his cover with colorful illustrations of appropriate grade-level, survival-type items. Laminate the folders if desired.

4 Have each student design a table of contents; then have him bind the pages of his book using staples or a hole puncher and brads.

5 Allow each student to take the book he assembled home and present it to his parents.

Table Of Contents

Welcome Letter .... page 1
Staff Directory .... page 2
School Floor Plan .... page 3
Daily Schedule .... page 4
Materials List .... page 5
Policy .... page 6

How To Survive 5th grade

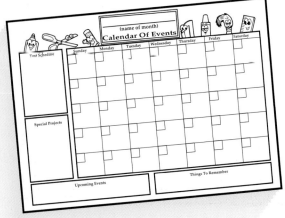

(name of month)
Calendar Of Events

Month At A Glance

Inform parents about upcoming events with a monthly at-a-glance calendar that's a perfect communication tool. At the beginning of each month, distribute a copy of the calendar on page 77 to each student. Discuss the month's upcoming special events, assignments, projects, and tests with your class. Direct each student to program his calendar with the information you discussed and to add any other necessary reminders to his parents. Then have each child take the calendar home and encourage his parent to place it in a prominent place for easy reference. Both parents and students should appreciate this monthly reminder to help plan the days ahead.

A Peek At Parents

Create camaraderie among parents by having them reminisce about their own school days. A week or so prior to Open House, generate ten parent-survey questions on the topic of school-time memories at a brainstorming session with your students. Expect questions such as, "What was your favorite subject?" or "What did you enjoy the least about school lunches?" Send the survey home. After each parent returns the survey, compile the information by first having each student cut her survey into question strips. Then collect the strips and separate them into ten different piles.

Next divide students into ten groups. Give each group a set of question strips, a large sheet of chart paper, a ruler, a pencil, and colored pencils or markers. Instruct each group to construct a bar graph as shown. Have each group share its graph; then display the graphs around the room. Both students and parents should get a kick out of this peek at the past!

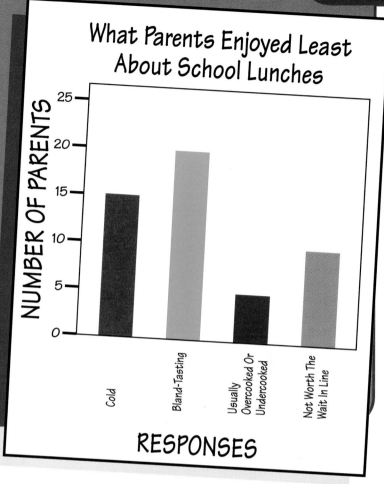

Getting To Know You

With such busy schedules at the beginning of the year, parents often have little time to get to know their child's teacher. So why not organize a special get-to-know-you album to help with this task? Purchase an inexpensive scrapbook or photo album. Then fill its pages with captioned photos of your home and family members, pets, favorite vacations and activities, and so on. (Make sure the photos you use are not keepsakes, unless they are duplicates.) Use various materials—such as colorful markers, paper cutouts, ribbons, and stickers—to add decorative details to each page. Share the album with your students; then send it home with a different student each day. Your students will be thrilled to share this special book about their new teacher, and their parents will appreciate learning more about you.

Valuable Volunteers

Parents can certainly be valuable resources for your classroom—from helping with art activities or science projects to sharing books with children. Some parents might have talents, hobbies, or occupations they could share with the class. Follow the steps below to put these valuable volunteers to work for you and your students!

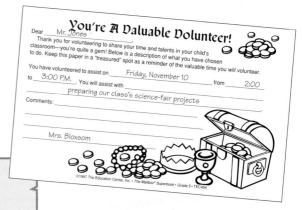

You're A Valuable Volunteer!

Dear _____ Mr. Jones _____,

Thank you for volunteering to share your time and talents in your child's classroom—you're quite a gem! Below is a description of what you have chosen to do. Keep this paper in a "treasured" spot as a reminder of the valuable time you will volunteer.

You have volunteered to assist on _____ Friday, November 10 _____ from _____ 2:00 _____ to _____ 3:00 P.M. _____. You will assist with _____ preparing our class's science-fair projects _____

Comments: _____

_____ Mrs. Bloxsom _____

©1997 The Education Center, Inc. • The Mailbox® Superbook • Grade 5 • TEC454

 1. Duplicate one copy of "Trackin' Down Treasures" at the top of page 78 to send home to each parent.

 2. Have each child ask his parent to indicate an area in which to help.

 3. Collect and compile all the information from the returned forms.

 4. Schedule designated times each week or month for different parent volunteers.

 5. Send home the bottom half of page 78 as a reminder to each parent of the appointed time.

 6. Follow up each parent's visit by having students sign a thank-you card to send to each visitor.

Everyone involved will reap the rewards of these valuable volunteers!

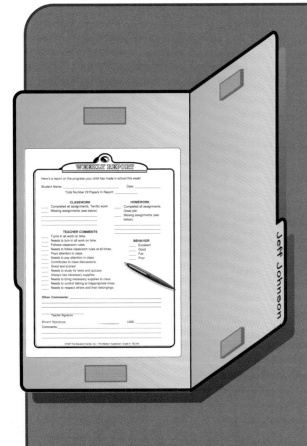

Don't Forget Your Briefcase!

Looking for a way to inform each parent of the progress his child is making and send papers home safely? Then have each student construct a "personal briefcase." Obtain a file folder for each student; then write each student's name on the tab of a different folder. Give each student his folder and have him decorate it. Collect the folders—laminating them for durability if desired; then attach two Velcro® strips onto the inside flaps of each folder as shown.

Next make multiple copies of the "Weekly Report" on page 79. If desired, also duplicate copies of "Missed Assignments" and "Incomplete Work" on page 80. Each time you send papers home, fill out a report—including a report on missed or incomplete work—for each student; then staple it to the inside flap of his folder. Request that each parent read and discuss the report with his child, then sign and return it in the folder the following day. Collect each student's folder and store it until the next round of papers is ready to go home.

RAFFLE RALLY

Motivate your students and parents to return important papers to school by holding a monthly raffle. Each time a student returns an important note, form, or paper, put a slip of paper labeled with his parent's name in a designated container. Then at the end the month, draw a name from the container. Reward the lucky parent with a prize—such as a book, small plant, baked good, or gift certificate donated by a local restaurant. Also reward the student with a special treat. Both students and parents should readily respond to the raffle, and you'll benefit from getting your papers back on time!

Mrs. Richard's Raffle Ralley

Mr. Alan Anderson

Audio Newsletters

Keep each parent informed about current classroom happenings with an *audio newsletter* composed and personally recorded by her child. In advance, ask each parent to send in a blank cassette tape labeled with her child's name; then follow the steps below.

1. Set up an area of the room with a tape player, a microphone, a headphone set, and a storage box for students' tapes.

2. At the end of each month, duplicate a copy of "'Class-ified' News" on page 81.

3. Have the class brainstorm a list of that month's happenings; then give each student time to write a summary of each section's happenings.

4. After each student has written her report, have her record it on her tape, and take her tape home to share with her parent.

Remind the student not to rewind the tape, so that each successive report will follow the previous one. Between tapings, see that the returned tapes are stored in the designated storage box. At the end of the year, each student will be delighted at taking home a self-made memento of a busy year.

"This is Tammy Thompson reporting live from Mrs. Slater's fifth-grade class on September..."

OPEN HOUSE

Super Sign-Up Sheet

Take advantage of Open House night in your class to establish a volunteer list for use throughout the current school year. Call attention to the sign-up sheet by placing it and several pens next to a colorful display of photos of the previous year's classroom activities. At this display, also include an outline of the special events slated for the current school year. Invite parents to sign up to help you with these events during the year. Then consult the handy volunteer list each time you need some extra help.

5th-Grade Fun!

Students On Center Stage

Step out of the spotlight on Open House night by having your students present important information to parents via videotape. Assign each student a different classroom procedure to discuss on the video. Tape your students' presentations; then show the informative video during Open House. You'll be pleased with the turnout you get when parents find out their children will star in the video!

Open House Raffle

Encourage parental attendance at Open House by holding a raffle. Decorate your room for the event with carnations and inexpensive plants. Also purchase some inexpensive edible treats. Have each parent who attends Open House fill out a nametag and drop it in a decorated box. At the conclusion of the Open House, draw names and present the carnations and plants to the winning parents. Provide the child of each winning parent with a small edible treat. In addition, further express your appreciation to the parents who attended Open House by having a student hand out thank-you cards with candies attached to them (see the reproducibles at the top of page 82).

OPEN HOUSE RAFFLE

Thanks For Coming

Express to parents how appreciative you are of their attendance at Open House with personalized postcards. Ask parents who attend Open House to sign an attendance sheet before they leave. The next day, send a brief message via postcard to those parents, thanking them for attending Open House. Also express your enthusiasm about the upcoming year and the opportunity to work closely with them. In addition, send postcards to the parents who were unable to attend Open House, inviting them to visit the classroom sometime during the year. What a simple and easy way to strengthen your relationship with parents!

Dear Mr. and Mrs. Lundein,
Thanks for coming to Open House. I look forward to working with you and Gregory to make this a great school year!
Sincerely,
Mrs. Mary Smith

Mr. and Mrs. Lundein
4322 Armadillo Way
Abilene, TX 41249

USA 20¢ FREEDOM OF CONSCIENCE... AMERICAN RIGHT

Parent Packets

Supply parents with packets of materials that will help their children have a more successful year. Prior to Open House, record each child's name on a large manila envelope. Then have each child decorate his envelope with a self-portrait. Instruct each child to write a letter to his parents welcoming them to Open House, and place it in his envelope. Have each child stuff his envelope with important papers such as school policies, classroom rules and procedures, study tips, and other important information. In the packet, also include a copy of the "Student Information Card" at the bottom of page 82 for parents to complete and return. Then place each student's envelope on his desk so his parents can review its contents during Open House.

Unusual Welcome

Welcome parents to Open House with the help of some student dummies. Have each student bring in a long-sleeved T-shirt or jacket to use in making a model of herself. Give each student a paper plate to decorate so that it resembles her face. Also have each student trace and cut out a pair of construction-paper hands. Next direct the student to place a coat hanger inside the shirt or jacket; then help the student attach the hanger to her chair, adjusting the shirt so that it covers the back of the chair. Instruct each student to tape her paper-plate head to the top of the hanger. To complete the model, have her position each of the garment's sleeves on top of her desk and tape the paper hands inside the sleeves. If desired, use yardsticks to raise the hands of several of the dummies. Parents and students alike will get a kick out of the resulting model classroom!

PARENT CONFERENCES

Coffee, Tea, And Conference!

Warm up to parents on conference day by providing them with cookies and a fresh pot of coffee or tea. Cover a small table with a decorative tablecloth; then place two thermal carafes—one filled with coffee and the other with hot water—on the table. Stock the table with tea bags, packets of hot chocolate, plastic spoons, foam cups, cream and sugar, and napkins. Invite parents to enjoy the refreshments while they await their scheduled time with you. What a great way to welcome parents!

Portfolios That Prove Your Point

Conferences provide parents with valuable information about their child's progress in school. Be sure you are prepared to provide specific examples that support any comments you make regarding a child's progress. To do this, prepare a portfolio of each child's work and a list of the comments you plan on making. Use sticky notes to mark specific examples to which you wish to refer during the conference. By showing specific examples, parents can more easily understand your concern and willingness to help their child!

NAME THAT PARENT

Avoid confusion with names on conference day by having each child make personalized nametags for her parents. Several days before the scheduled conference date, provide each student with an adhesive nametag to decorate for each person attending her conference. On conference day, display the nametags on a table just outside your classroom. Post a note asking each parent to find his nametag as he arrives. Provide extra nametags and a marking pen in the event that additional visitors come to a conference. Don't forget to wear a nametag yourself!

Bill Willett

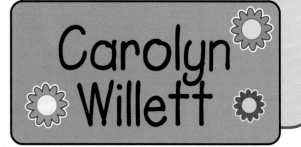

Carolyn Willett

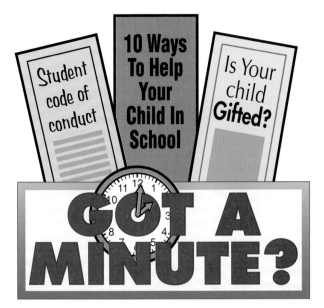

GOT A MINUTE?

Provide parents who arrive early for scheduled conferences with interesting reading material to help pass the time. Prior to conference day, make copies of class newsletters, outlines of school policies, home-learning activities, and articles about learning disabilities, cooperative discipline, gifted programs, and other topics of interest. Also include several order forms for children's books and children's magazines for young readers. Parents will appreciate the opportunity to do something constructive while they wait.

Plan Ahead For Success

Lay the foundation for a successful conference with a little advance planning. Prior to conference day, write down several positive comments about each child that you want to share with his parents. Also record each child's strengths in specific subject areas and note any areas in which the child needs additional practice. List any questions you want to ask the child's parents and jot down suggested actions to be taken for improvement. Get advance input from parents by sending home a copy of the survey on page 83 for parents to complete and return. Compile the input and suggestions received from each parent survey with your notes for each conference; then refer and respond to them along with your other written comments at conference time. Conclude the conference by developing a plan to address any outlined concerns, being sure to set a date for evaluating the progress of the plan.

Liz is a good listener. She always comes to class prepared.

Staying On Schedule

Veteran and novice teachers alike know that sticking to a conference schedule is not always easy. Adhere to your schedule by posting a sign on your door that asks each parent to knock when it is his scheduled conference time. Inform each parent of your procedure at the start of the conference and explain that if additional time is needed, you can schedule another conference as soon as possible. What a great way to ensure that your schedule stays on track and parents are not left waiting too long!

WELCOME PARENTS!

Please knock if it is past your scheduled conference time. For your convenience, we want to adhere to the schedule as closely as possible.
Thank you,
Mrs. Kreger

Child-Teacher Conferences

Ease your students' fears about upcoming parent conferences by conducting your own child-teacher conferences. Prior to your scheduled parent-teacher conferences, hold an individual conference with each of your students. At each conference, discuss that child's grades and mention the comments you plan to make to her parents. Allow each child to ask questions and express any concerns she has. Students will feel less anxious about your upcoming meetings with their parents when they know what you plan to discuss with them.

While You're Here

Individualize parent-teacher conferences by having each child design a personal classroom-tour brochure for his parents to use on conference day. Direct each child to design a colorful brochure that contains a special note to his parents explaining what he specifically wants them to view while in your room. For example, parents could be asked to view work or any special projects recently completed by the class. This personal touch will make your visitors feel even more welcome in your classroom.

Scheduling Solution

Parents' work and child-care schedules often make it difficult to schedule conferences at convenient times. Make this task easier by asking for parental input before scheduling any conference. One week prior to the conferences, send home a note requesting parents to suggest several workable conference times. From the responses, select a time from each parent that best fits your conference schedule. Send a confirmation form to each parent honoring one of the specific times he suggested (see the forms on page 84). Allowing parents flexibility in scheduling conferences is just one more way you can keep the lines of communication open.

Conference Request

Dear _Mrs. Willett_ ,

I have scheduled you for a parent-teacher conference at the following time:
Date: _Friday, November 16_
Time: _1:45_ to _2:15_

Please complete the information at the bottom of this form; then return the form to school tomorrow. If the time scheduled above is n[ot] convenient for you, please suggest several alternate times.

Sincerely,

Mrs. Cox

Teacher's Signature

©1997 The Education Center, Inc. • The Mailbox® Superbook • Grade 5 • TEC454

Student's Name : _Jake Willett_

✓ Yes, I will attend the conference at the time and date listed above.

____ No, I cannot attend a conference at that time.

I would rather schedule a conference for :
Date: _____
Times: (please list more than one) _____ to _____ o[r]
_____ to _____, or _____ to _____

Parent's Signature : _Mrs. Willett_
Daytime phone: _348-5645_
Evening phone: _348-8890_

☆ ☆ ☆ ☆ See you then!

©1997 The Education Center, Inc. • The Mailbox® Superbook • Grade 5 • TEC454

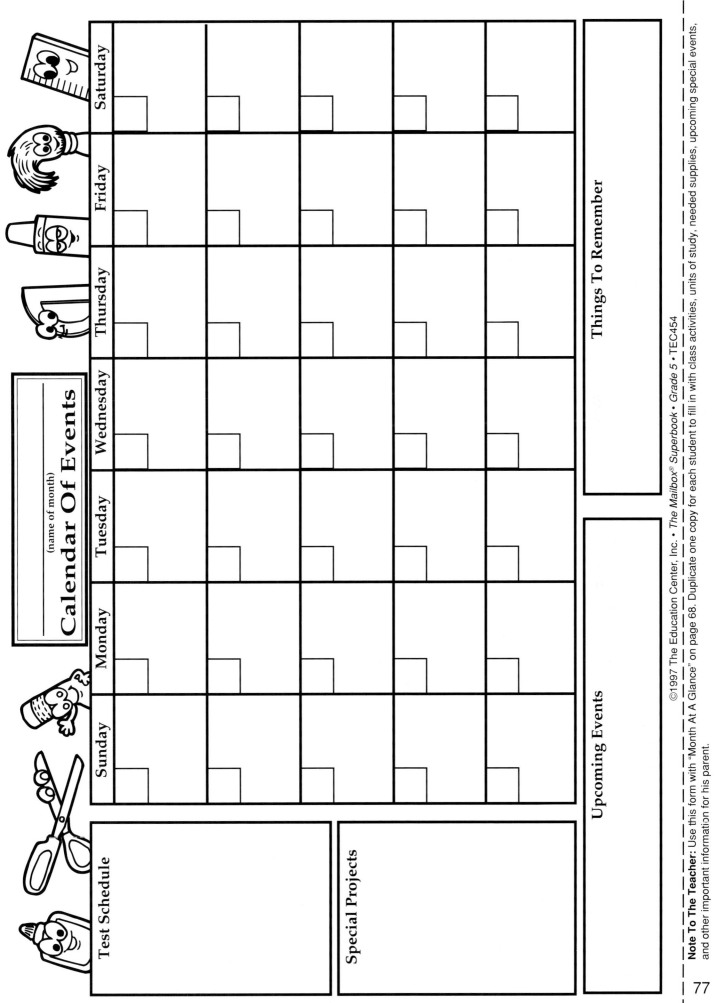

Calendar Of Events
(name of month)

Sunday	Monday	Tuesday	Wednesday	Thursday	Friday	Saturday

Test Schedule

Special Projects

Upcoming Events

Things To Remember

Note To The Teacher: Use this form with "Month At A Glance" on page 68. Duplicate one copy for each student to fill in with class activities, units of study, needed supplies, upcoming special events, and other important information for his parent.

Trackin' Down Treasures

Dear Parent,

We're trackin' down some hidden treasures—the skills and talents of our classroom parents! Please complete the information below and return it to school as soon as possible.

Parent's name: _____

Child's name: _____

Phone number: _____

Occupation: _____

Talents/interests: _____

_____

Convenient day and time for me to assist: _____

I would like to assist in the area(s) of:

- art projects
- field trips
- holiday parties
- making projects at home
- providing supplies and materials
- providing treats
- teaching a special interest/talent
- tutoring students
- special student projects
- other: _____

You're A Valuable Volunteer!

Dear _____,

Thank you for volunteering to share your time and talents in your child's classroom—you're quite a gem! Below is a description of what you have chosen to do. Keep this paper in a "treasured" spot as a reminder of the valuable time you will volunteer.

You have volunteered to assist on _____ from _____

to _____. You will assist with _____

_____.

Comments: _____

_____

_____

Note To The Teacher: Use both forms with "Valuable Volunteers" on page 70. Duplicate one copy for each parent volunteer.

WEEKLY REPORT

Here's a report on the progress your child has made in school this week!

Student Name: _____   Date: _____

Total Number Of Papers In Report: _____

CLASSWORK
_____ Completed all assignments. Terrific work!
_____ Missing assignments (see below).
_____
_____
_____

HOMEWORK
_____ Completed all assignments. Great job!
_____ Missing assignments (see below).
_____
_____
_____

TEACHER COMMENTS
_____ Turns in all work on time.
_____ Needs to turn in all work on time.
_____ Follows classroom rules.
_____ Needs to follow classroom rules at all times.
_____ Pays attention in class.
_____ Needs to pay attention in class.
_____ Contributes to class discussions.
_____ Great test scores!
_____ Needs to study for tests and quizzes.
_____ Always has necessary supplies.
_____ Needs to bring necessary supplies to class.
_____ Needs to control talking at inappropriate times.
_____ Needs to respect others and their belongings.

BEHAVIOR
_____ Excellent
_____ Good
_____ Fair
_____ Poor

Other Comments: _____
_____
_____

_____
Teacher Signature

Parent Signature: _____   Date: _____

Comments: _____
_____
_____

Note To The Teacher: Use this form with "Don't Forget Your Briefcase!" on page 70. Duplicate one copy for each student.

79

Incomplete Work

_____ date

Dear Parent,

_____ needs to complete the following assignments:

_____

_____

_____

This work is due by: _____

Your help and support are greatly appreciated.

Sincerely,

_____
teacher signature

_____
parent signature

Please sign and return.

Missed Assignments

_____ date

Dear Parent,

_____ needs to complete the following assignments:

_____

_____

_____

This work is due by: _____

Your help and support are greatly appreciated.

Sincerely,

_____
teacher signature

_____
parent signature

Please sign and return.

MISSED ASSIGNMENTS

Note To The Teacher: Use with "Don't Forget Your Briefcase!" on page 70.

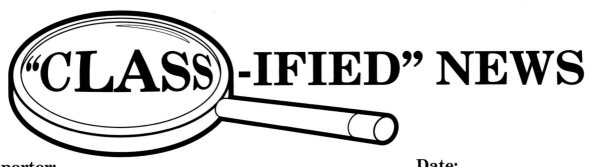

"CLASS-IFIED" NEWS

Reporter: _____ **Date:** _____

Currently Working On...

Spotlight On Special Events

Take Note!

Holiday Happenings

Subject Summaries

Project Pride

Birthday Bashes

Note To The Teacher: Use this form with "Audio Newsletters" on page 71. If any heading is inappropriate for your classroom, simply white-out that heading and replace it with one that better meets your needs.

Thanks For Coming To Our Open House!

YOUR ATTENDANCE REALLY "MINT" A LOT TO US

Thank You For Attending Our Open House!

FEEL FREE TO DROP BY ANYTIME!

Note To The Teacher: Use with "Open House Raffle" on page 72 or whenever you have an Open House. Duplicate several copies of these thank-you notes; then have students color them. Use clear tape to attach a mint or gumdrop to the circle on each corresponding card. Then have a student volunteer give one card to each person who attends Open House.

Student Information Card

First Name _____ Last Name _____ Middle Initial _____

Birthdate _____ Home Phone _____

Address _____

City _____ State _____ ZIP Code _____

Mother's Name _____ Father's Name _____

Mother's Work Phone _____ Father's Work Phone _____

Emergency Contact _____ Emergency Number _____

Comments: _____
_____
_____

Note To The Teacher: Use with "Parent Packets" on page 73. Duplicate one copy of this form for each child in your class. Request that the child's parents fill out the form at Open House. Then keep the cards for future reference.

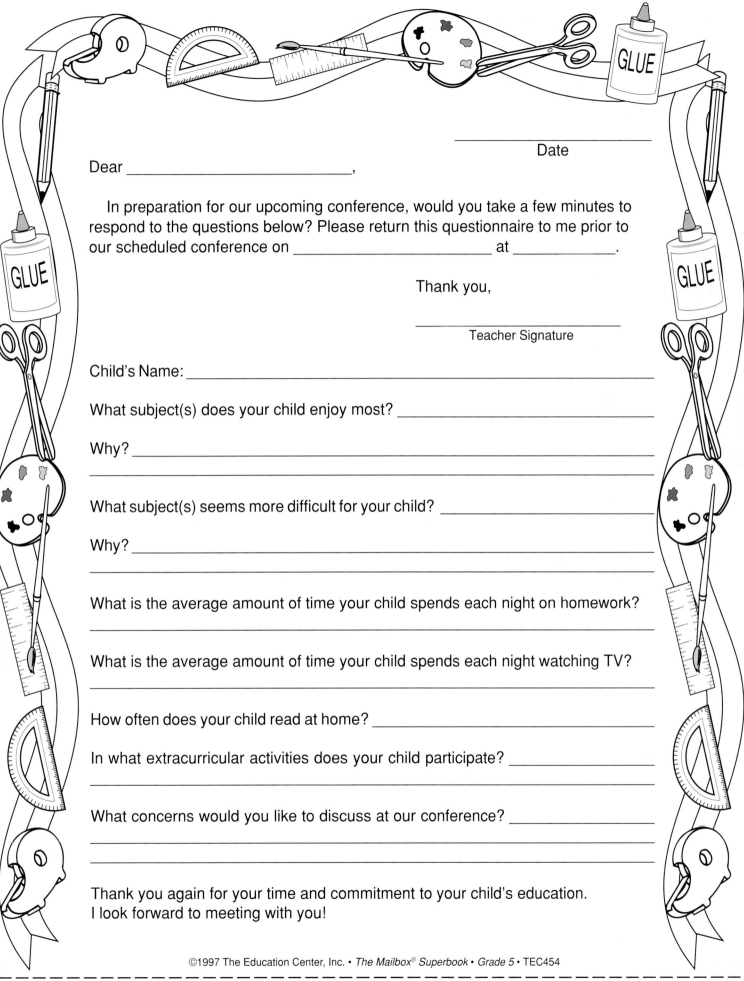

_____ Date

Dear _____,

In preparation for our upcoming conference, would you take a few minutes to respond to the questions below? Please return this questionnaire to me prior to our scheduled conference on _____ at _____.

Thank you,

_____
Teacher Signature

Child's Name: _____

What subject(s) does your child enjoy most? _____

Why? _____
_____

What subject(s) seems more difficult for your child? _____

Why? _____
_____

What is the average amount of time your child spends each night on homework?
_____

What is the average amount of time your child spends each night watching TV?
_____

How often does your child read at home? _____

In what extracurricular activities does your child participate? _____
_____

What concerns would you like to discuss at our conference? _____
_____
_____

Thank you again for your time and commitment to your child's education.
I look forward to meeting with you!

Note To The Teacher: Use with "Plan Ahead For Success" on page 75.

Conference Request

Dear _____,

I have scheduled you for a parent-teacher conference at the following time:

Date: _____

Time: _____ to _____

Please complete the information at the bottom of this form; then return the form to school tomorrow. if the time scheduled above is not convenient for you, please suggest several alternate times.

Sincerely,

☆ Teacher's Signature

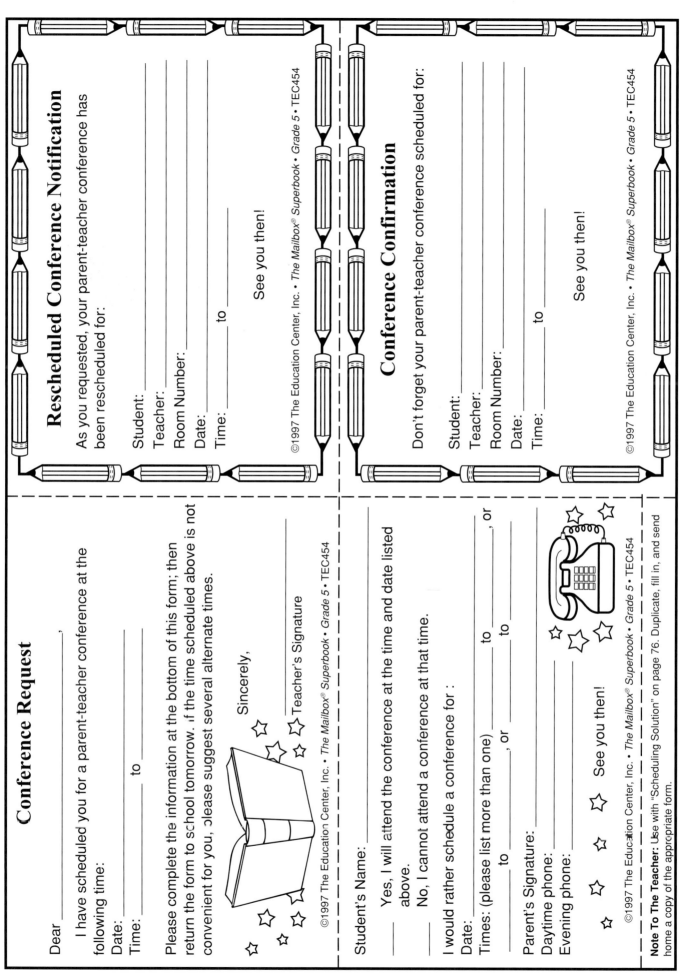

©1997 The Education Center, Inc. • *The Mailbox® Superbook* • *Grade 5* • TEC454

Rescheduled Conference Notification

As you requested, your parent-teacher conference has been rescheduled for:

Student: _____

Teacher: _____

Room Number: _____

Date: _____

Time: _____ to _____

See you then!

©1997 The Education Center, Inc. • *The Mailbox® Superbook* • *Grade 5* • TEC454

Student's Name: _____

____ Yes, I will attend the conference at the time and date listed above.

____ No, I cannot attend a conference at that time.

I would rather schedule a conference for :

Date: _____

Times: (please list more than one) _____ to _____, or

_____ to _____, or

Parent's Signature: _____

Daytime phone: _____

Evening phone: _____

☆ See you then!

©1997 The Education Center, Inc. • *The Mailbox® Superbook* • *Grade 5* • TEC454

Note To The Teacher: Use with "Scheduling Solution" on page 76. Duplicate, fill in, and send home a copy of the appropriate form.

Conference Confirmation

Don't forget your parent-teacher conference scheduled for:

Student: _____

Teacher: _____

Room Number: _____

Date: _____

Time: _____ to _____

See you then!

©1997 The Education Center, Inc. • *The Mailbox® Superbook* • *Grade 5* • TEC454

ARTS & CRAFTS

Arts & Crafts

Back-To-School Pencil Toppers

Top off your students' first day of school with this art project.

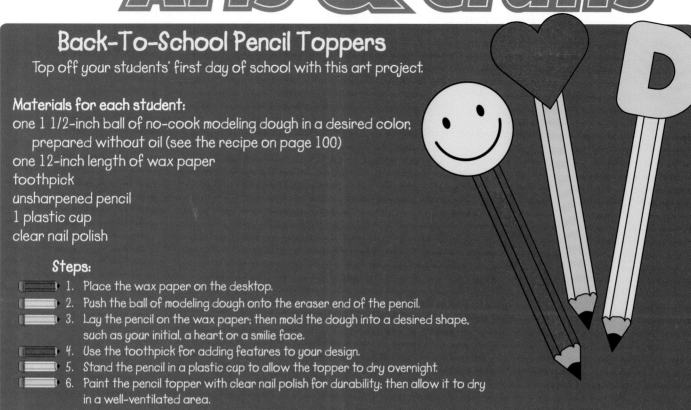

Materials for each student:
one 1 1/2-inch ball of no-cook modeling dough in a desired color,
   prepared without oil (see the recipe on page 100)
one 12-inch length of wax paper
toothpick
unsharpened pencil
1 plastic cup
clear nail polish

Steps:
1. Place the wax paper on the desktop.
2. Push the ball of modeling dough onto the eraser end of the pencil.
3. Lay the pencil on the wax paper; then mold the dough into a desired shape, such as your initial, a heart, or a smilie face.
4. Use the toothpick for adding features to your design.
5. Stand the pencil in a plastic cup to allow the topper to dry overnight.
6. Paint the pencil topper with clear nail polish for durability; then allow it to dry in a well-ventilated area.

First-Day Picture Frames

Preserve your students' memories of the first day of school with this picture-perfect craft. During the first day of school, take a photograph of each student. Then give the student his developed photograph along with the materials listed below to create a framed first-day-of-school memory.

Materials for each student:
several old puzzle pieces that have been spray-painted different colors
three 3 1/2" x 5" tagboard cards
glue
scissors
ruler
hot glue gun
black permanent marker

Fifth Grade With Mrs. Adcock

Steps:

1. Cut away the interior from one tagboard card to make a frame with a one-inch border.
2. Glue the puzzle pieces around the border's perimeter.
3. After the glue has dried, have an adult hot-glue a second tagboard card to the back of the frame at the bottom and sides only, leaving the top open for inserting the photo.
4. Use the permanent marker to write the date or other words, such as "Piecing Together A New Year" or "Picture-Perfect Student," on the frame.
5. Make a stand for the frame by cutting away a corner from the remaining tagboard card. Fold the card in half; then glue the uncut half to the back of the frame.
6. Insert your first-day photograph, cutting it to fit if necessary.

Corny Cobs

Kids love to hear and tell jokes—the cornier the better! Combine their love for jokes with this art idea for a great fall display. Post your students' completed work on a bulletin board titled "Corny Cobs Corner" and enjoy a few chuckles together!

Materials for each student:
1 copy of page 102
one 9" x 12" sheet of yellow construction paper
one 4 1/2" x 6" sheet of green construction paper
pencil
scrap pieces of different-
    colored construction paper
crayons or colored pencils
clear tape
scissors
stapler

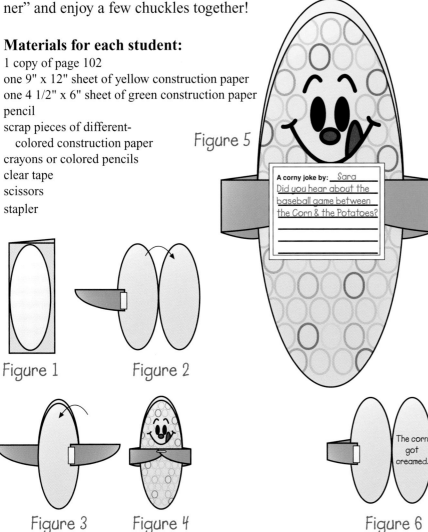

Figure 1

Figure 2

Figure 3

Figure 4

Figure 5

A corny joke by: _Sara_
Did you hear about the
baseball game between
the Corn & the Potatoes?

Figure 6

The corn got creamed.

Steps:

1. Fold the yellow construction paper in half vertically.
2. Cut out the corncob pattern; then position the pattern along the fold line of the yellow construction paper and trace it. Cut out the tracing (see Figure 1).
3. Cut out the arm pattern; then trace it twice on the green construction paper. Cut out the tracings.
4. Tape the squared-off end of the corncob's left arm to the back of the top cob (see Figure 2).
5. Tape the squared-off end of the corncob's right arm to the back of the bottom cob (see Figure 3).
6. Decorate the corncob with kernels using scrap pieces of construction paper and crayons or colored pencils. Overlap and then staple the ends of the arms together in front of the cob (see Figure 4).
7. Write a joke on the square-shaped pattern and tape it to the overlapped section of the cob's arms (see Figure 5).
8. Open the corncob and write the answer to the joke inside (see Figure 6).

Spiced Apples

Fall is apple-pickin' time! Celebrate this occasion with an old-fashioned project that will leave your classroom smelling like fresh-baked apple pie. Enlist help from your grade mothers in gathering the needed supplies for this project, or ask local stores to donate the supplies. Give each student one small, red apple; about 50 whole cloves; and one 30-inch length of 1/2-inch-wide decorative ribbon. Instruct each student to cover his apple with cloves by pushing them into the apple one at a time in an attractive arrangement. Next have him tie the ribbon around his apple as if he were wrapping a present, double-tying the bow on top as shown. Position the completed apples around the classroom as attractive air fresheners. Or, if desired, have your students knot the ends of the ribbon to form closed loops for hanging the apples.

3-D Haunted House

These haunted houses will make a frighteningly attractive Halloween display!

Materials for each student:
one 9" x 12" sheet of brown construction paper
one 12" x 18" sheet of white construction paper
scrap pieces of construction paper
crayons or colored pencils
scissors
glue stick

Figure 1

Figure 2

Steps:

1. Cut a house shape from the brown construction paper.
2. On the house draw a door and a few windows. Add other details as desired.
3. Cut along the top and bottom edges of the door and windows; then cut down the middle of each one, folding back along the lines so that the flaps fold open (see Figure 1).
4. Glue the house onto the white construction paper. (Do not glue the flaps of the windows and doors.)
5. Cut out one creepy creature from scrap pieces of construction paper to fit in the door and each window. Leave a tab of undecorated paper at the bottom of each character for gluing (see Figure 2).
6. Fold open the windows and door; then affix the creatures inside by gluing the tab of each creature to the back of a window or door.
7. Color a Halloween scene around the house using crayons or colored pencils.

Two-Sided Mask

Target antonyms with this Halloween mask project. As a class brainstorm several pairs of adjectives that are antonyms—such as *happy* and *sad*, *grotesque* and *beautiful*, or *serious* and *humorous*. List students' responses on the chalkboard. Instruct each student to select one adjective pair; then have him draw a rough sketch of two different faces—one that portrays each adjective—on drawing paper. Next give each student a brown-paper grocery bag with no writing on it (or turn a bag with writing on it inside out), paints, crayons, markers, scissors, paste, and assorted craft materials. Instruct each student to refer to his sketches to draw and create faces illustrating his pair of adjectives, showing one face on one side of the bag and the second face on the other side of the bag. Have your students slip the bags over their heads and turn, one at a time, to share both sides of their masks with the class. Your students will not only be displaying their artistic talents and strengthening their vocabulary skills—but having fun, too!

Native-American Story Belts

What would Thanksgiving be without discussing Native Americans? Native Americans strung *wampum*, polished shell beads, into belts. Some wampum belts were used by Native Americans to document information exchanged among tribes and important public events. Guide each student through the steps below to make her own wampum belt that illustrates the important events in her life. Then allow each student to wear her belt while she shares the illustrated events with the class.

Materials for each student:
two 3" x 18" strips of oaktag
hole puncher
assorted colored yarn
clear tape
colored pencils or markers
scissors
ruler

Steps:
1. Tape together the two strips of oaktag end-to-end. Measure the oaktag strip to fit your waist, cutting away any excess (see Figure 1).
2. Use colored pencils or markers to illustrate the important events in your life on the belt.
3. Punch holes about one inch apart along the outer edges of the belt's perimeter.
4. Thread and wrap a length of yarn through the holes and around the edges to create an edging for the belt. Knot the ends (see Figure 2).
5. Tie several lengths of yarn to both ends of the belt. Braid the lengths; then use them to tie the belt around your waist.

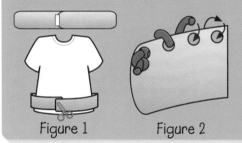

Figure 1   Figure 2

Thanksgiving Placemat

Thanksgiving brings to mind family dinners and nicely decorated tables. Have each student make a woven placemat for a colorful, artistic addition to his Thanksgiving celebration.

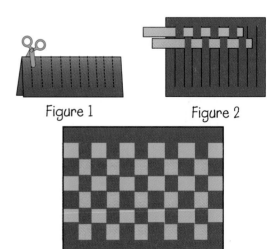

Figure 1   Figure 2

Materials for each student:
one 12" x 18" sheet of brown construction paper
two 9" x 12" sheets of construction paper in two different colors
ruler
pencil
scissors
glue

Steps:

1. Fold the brown sheet of construction paper in half lengthwise. Starting at the fold, cut strips one inch in width, stopping your cuts one inch from the edges. Unfold the paper (see Figure 1).

2. Use a ruler to measure 1" x 12" strips on both of the 9" x 12" sheets of construction paper. Cut them out. Weave the strips over and under the slats of the brown paper, alternating colors (see Figure 2).

3. Use small dabs of glue to secure the strips to the brown paper.

Hanukkah Stained-Glass Window

The six-pointed Star of David is believed to have been a decoration on King David's shield. It has since become a symbol of the Jews. Guide each student through the steps below for making a stained-glass window featuring the Star of David to display during Hanukkah.

Materials for each student:
1 copy of the Star of David pattern on page 103
two 6" x 6" black construction-paper squares
two 6" x 6" squares of wax paper
1 old yellow or gold crayon
glue
scissors
plastic knife
hole puncher
string or yarn
tape
pencil

Figure 1

Figure 3

Figure 2

Setting up the pressing station: In a safe location, cover a tabletop with a towel; then place an iron and a supply of newsprint nearby.

Steps:

1. Cut out the Star of David pattern; then trace the star in the center of one black square.

2. Cut out the interior of the star tracing so that the star's border is uncut (see Figure 1).

3. Place that black square on top of the second black square and trace the star pattern. Repeat Step 2 with the second star tracing.

4. Trace the star pattern onto one wax-paper square.

5. Use the plastic knife to shave the crayon onto this star tracing (waxy side up). Place the shavings slightly beyond the star's border to ensure complete coverage when melted. Cover the shavings with the second wax-paper square waxy side down (see Figure 2).

6. Melt the crayon shavings between the two wax-paper squares by placing a sheet of newsprint over them, then pressing the newsprint with a warm iron at the pressing station.

7. Glue the stained-glass window between the two black squares, making sure the star patterns are aligned (see Figure 3).

8. Tape the creation to the inside of a classroom window. Or hole-punch the top corner and tie a length of string through the hole for hanging the design.

Kwanzaa Harvest-Basket Collage

Kwanzaa is an African-American holiday based on the traditional African festival of the harvest of the first crops. Have your students celebrate by making a harvest-crop collage. Discuss some of the fruits and vegetables grown in Africa, such as bananas, plantains, yams, cassava, coconuts, and dates. Give each student an 18" x 24" sheet of manila paper, scissors, glue, and magazines to cut up or a supply of paint-chip samples from a local paint store. Instruct each student to draw a large basket containing outlines of African fruits and vegetables on his paper. Then direct the student to cover each fruit and vegetable, collage-style, by gluing on small colored squares cut from the magazines or paint chips. Suggest that students use different shades of color to give the effect of light and dark shadings. Display the completed collages around the classroom.

Tiny-Tree Trimming

For as long as people have brought evergreen trees into their homes, they have decorated them with candles, cookies, paper, and more. Guide each student through the steps below to make and trim his own miniature Christmas tree.

Materials for each student:
1 copy of the cone pattern on page 103
1 large paper or plastic cup
ten to twelve 1 1/2" x 12" strips of green construction paper
one 6" x 9" sheet of green construction paper
clear tape
glue
scissors
assorted decorative craft materials, such as glitter, trims, stickers, and beads
ruler
pencil

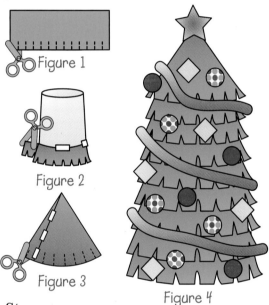

Figure 1

Figure 2

Figure 3

Figure 4

Steps:

 Cut approximately 3/4-inch-long slits about 1/4 inch apart along one long edge of each strip of green paper (see Figure 1).

 Turn the cup upside down. Tape or glue one strip, cut edge down, around the bottom edge of the cup. Trim away any excess. (See Figure 2.)

 Tape or glue another strip above the first one, overlapping it slightly. Trim to fit.

 Continue taping or gluing the strips in this manner until the entire cup is covered.

 Cut out the cone pattern and trace it onto the 6" x 9" sheet of green construction paper. Cut out the tracing.

 Form the cone and secure it with tape. As in Step 1, cut slits in the base of the cone (see Figure 3).

  Secure the cone to the top of the cup with tape. Then decorate the tree as desired (see Figure 4).

Christmas Wreath

When it comes to Christmas, this holiday wreath says it all! Hang the completed wreaths from the ceiling for everyone to read and enjoy.

Materials for each student:
1 wire coat hanger
red and green construction paper
scissors
markers
1 length of ribbon
glue or clear tape
1 length of yarn
decorative craft materials, such as glitter, trims, and stickers

Steps:

1. Pull and shape the coat hanger to create a circle (see Figure 1).
2. Trace your hand 12–15 times on red and green construction paper. Cut out each tracing.
3. On one side of each hand cutout, write a word or phrase that represents the meaning of Christmas or names a gift that cannot be purchased.
4. Tape or glue the hands at the wrists around the wire, positioning the cutouts so that they completely cover the hanger and show the writing on each hand.
5. Complete the wreath by adding a ribbon bow, glitter, or other decorative items.
6. Tie a length of yarn from the top of the hanger for hanging.

Figure 1

Bird Feeder

These bird feeders will keep your students' feathered friends around all winter long!

Materials for each student:
1 scrap piece of wood
2–4 long nails
hammer
2 screw eyes
two 24" lengths of cord or heavy string
tempera paint
paintbrush

Steps:

 Hammer the nails partway into the piece of wood.

 Use paint to decorate the bird feeder.

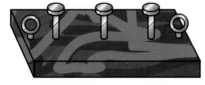

 After the paint has dried, screw one screw eye into each end of the bird feeder.

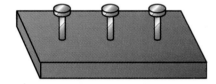

 Loop a length of cord through each screw eye and tie it around a tree branch.

Stick pieces of fruit or bread on the nails; then wait for the birds to appear.

A Puzzling Christmas Card

Is searching for a unique Christmas craft leaving you puzzled? Have your students create these puzzling greeting cards to give as gifts. Give each student a 9" x 12" sheet of oaktag, a ruler, scissors, a Ziploc® bag, and colored pencils or crayons. First instruct each student to measure and mark 1 1/2-inch points along all the edges of the oaktag. Then direct her to connect the dots vertically and horizontally to form 1 1/2-inch blocks. Have the student turn over her oaktag and illustrate a Christmas scene or message. Tell the student to color as much of the area as possible. Next laminate the picture for durability, if desired; then direct the student to cut the picture into blocks, using the lines on the back as a guide. Finally have each student place the block-shaped cutouts in a Ziploc® bag and send it on to its recipient. All that person has to do is assemble the puzzle to receive his holiday greeting!

Wintry Scenes

Get your students into a wintry spirit with this simple art activity. For each student, mix together equal parts of shaving cream and thick craft glue in a paper cup. Distribute a 9" x 12" sheet of blue construction paper, one cup of the glue mixture, and a paintbrush to each student. Instruct the student to draw a wintry scene on the construction paper first with a pencil, then fill in the drawing with the glue mixture. (If desired, substitute old Christmas cards featuring wintry scenes for the blue construction paper and have students just add the snow.) Allow the scenes to dry; then display them around the classroom, creating a winter wonderland.

Holiday Note Clip

Have your students make these handy note clips to hold their special Valentine's Day cards.

Materials for each student:
1 copy of the heart pattern on page 103
1 spring-type clothespin
one 2" x 4" piece of red craft foam or poster board
red tempera paint
paintbrush
fine-tipped white paint pen
craft glue
scissors
pencil

Steps:

1 Paint the clothespin red. Allow it to dry.

2 Cut out the heart pattern and trace it three times on the red foam or poster board. Cut out the tracings.

3 Use the paint pen to draw a broken line near the outer edge of each heart. Add other details as desired.

4 Glue the three hearts to the clothespin as shown.

Bank On It!

Every student needs a place to store his pot of gold, and these St. Patrick's Day banks will certainly fill the bill! Have each student bring in an empty cocoa can or other sturdy container. Then give each student a cup filled with green tempera paint, a paintbrush, different-colored paint pens, scissors, and one copy of the St. Patrick's Day patterns on page 104. Direct each student to paint the sides of his container green and cut out the patterns. After the paint has dried, have the student use the paint pens to trace the patterns on the sides of his bank, decorating them as desired. Then suggest to your students that the end of the rainbow must be your classroom!

Quilled Cards

Quilling will turn your students' plain Valentine's Day cards into masterpieces! Give each student a sheet of white construction paper; a supply of 1/4-inch-wide red, pink, and purple construction-paper strips; glue; scissors; and a toothpick. Have each student fold his white construction paper to form a greeting card. Provide pinking shears for each student to trim the edges of his card, if desired. Then demonstrate how to decorate the card by wrapping a strip of construction paper halfway around a toothpick, sliding it off, and gluing it—standing on edge—to the card to form different designs. Direct each student to hold each piece briefly after gluing until the glue starts to set. Suggest that each student glue the strips on his card in heart, flower, or scroll shapes. Also have him experiment with wrapping the strips tightly and loosely around his toothpick. Allow the glue to dry; then have each student pen a Valentine's Day note to a friend inside his card.

Spring Paperweight

To prevent students' papers from being carried away by spring breezes, have each student create a personal paperweight for her desk! Provide each student with a small rock (about three or four inches long), acrylic paint, a paintbrush, craft glue, and assorted craft materials. Instruct the student to decide what kind of paperweight to design; then have her paint the rock accordingly. Allow the paint to dry. Next have the student create three-dimensional details for her design, attaching them with craft glue. Allow students to place their paperweights on their desktops. What a great springtime pick-me-up!

Cookie-Cutter Magnets

Brighten up your classroom by having students make these springtime magnets. Display the completed magnets on the chalkboard or the side of a file cabinet.

Figure 1

Materials for each student:
craft foam (or poster board) in spring colors
scissors
craft glue
1 flower-shaped cookie cutter (optional)
1 disc-shaped magnet (or self-adhesive magnet)
pencil
permanent markers

Steps:

1. Press the cookie cutter into the craft foam, or use the pencil to lightly draw or trace a simple flower shape on the foam (see Figure 1).

2. Cut out the shape.

3. Use craft-foam scraps and permanent markers to add details—such as the other parts of a flower, a bee, or a butterfly—to your flower (see Figure 2).

4. Glue the magnet to the back of your flower.

Figure 2

Your students' moms will find lots of uses for this classy Mother's Day gift!

Materials for each student:
one 5" x 8" index card
several 5" x 7" sheets of blank paper
one 18" length of 1/4" ribbon
one 7" x 10" piece of fabric
craft glue
paintbrush
scissors
stapler

Steps:

1. Stack the blank pages one on top of the other; then fold the stack in half, greeting card–style.
2. Fold the index card in half greeting card–style; then insert the blank pages.
3. Staple the pages and card together along the fold lines to create a book (see Figure 1).
4. Lay the fabric on your desktop, printed side down. Open the book and lay it flat so that its spine is centered over the piece of fabric. Cut the fabric as shown in Figure 2.
5. Apply glue to the spine of the book using a paintbrush and press the book onto the fabric.
6. Fold each flap of fabric, one at a time, onto either the front or back cover of the book. Secure each flap with glue. Cut away any excess fabric. (See Figure 3.)
7. Glue the first blank page of the notebook to the front cover and the last blank page to the back cover, concealing the fabric edges.
8. Glue the length of ribbon horizontally around the book's cover. Allow the glue to dry; then tie the ends of the ribbon into a bow. (See Figure 4.)

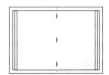

Figure 1

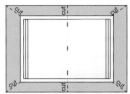

Figure 2

Figure 3

Figure 4

Mother's Day Planters

Help each student plant a smile on her mother's face with this Mother's Day project!

Materials for each student:
1 half-gallon plastic milk jug
1 plant
single-hole puncher
2 cups of potting soil
four 24" lengths of 1/4-inch-thick macramé cord

sharp scissors or an art knife
permanent markers
water
ruler

Steps:

1. Create a planter by using the sharp scissors or an art knife to cut off the bottom four inches of the half-gallon jug. (Have an adult complete this step for students.)
2. Punch a hole one inch below the top edge of each of the four corners of the planter. (Students may need assistance with this step.)
3. Using the markers, decorate the outside of the planter with appropriate Mother's Day messages and illustrations. Set the planter aside until the marker ink has dried.
4. Place two cups of potting soil in the planter.
5. Poke a hole in the center of the soil; then carefully place the plant in the hole, positioning it at the same depth as it was in its last container. Press the soil gently, but firmly, around the plant.
6. Water the plant.
7. Knot one end of each 24-inch length of cord; then thread each cord through a hole. Gather all the cords' ends together and tie them in a knot.
8. Present the planter to your mom, or an appropriate mother figure, for Mother's Day.

End-Of-The-Year Frame

Capture lasting memories of the school year by having each student make a photograph frame that's perfect for year's end.

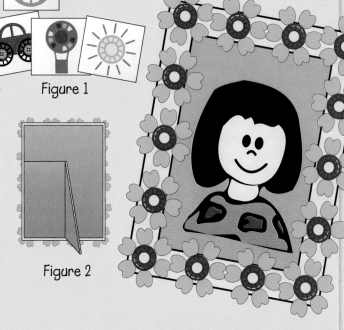

Figure 1

Figure 2

Materials for each student:
2 end rollers from cash-register tape (or 2 markers or highlighters)
2 different colors of acrylic paint
paintbrush
three 3 1/2" x 5" tagboard cards
glue
scissors
ruler
hot glue gun
assorted craft materials
1 photograph

Steps:

1. Cut away the interior from one tagboard card to make a frame with a one-inch border.

2. Create a design within the border by applying paint to the end of the roller or marker and pressing it onto the frame (see Figure 1).

3. After the paint has dried, glue on different craft materials—such as buttons or ribbon—to add a finishing touch.

4. Have an adult hot-glue the second tagboard card to the back of the frame at the bottom and sides only, leaving the top open for inserting the photo.

5. Make a stand for the frame by cutting away a corner from the remaining tagboard card. Fold the card in half; then glue the uncut half to the back of the frame. (See Figure 2.)

6. Insert a favorite photograph, cutting it to fit if necessary.

Chip Clip

This chip clip will come in handy at summer picnics, at camp, and even for next school year's lunchbox.

Materials for each student:
1 spring type clothespin
one 3/4" x 6" craft stick
acrylic paint
paintbrush
paint markers
craft glue

Steps:

1. Paint the craft stick a solid color. Allow the paint to dry.
2. Decorate one side of the craft stick using paint markers.
3. When those designs are dry, glue the clothespin to the back of the decorated stick.
4. After the glue is dry, you'll be ready for summertime snacking.

World-Class Pencil Holder

Locating pencils will be a thing of the past with these top-notch containers.

Materials for each student:
1 empty frozen-juice can
used postage stamps (can be found at
   hobby stores)
glue
decorative cording
Mod Podge®
paintbrush
scissors

Steps:
1. Wash and dry the juice can.
2. Glue the stamps to the can collage-style, overlapping them so that they cover the entire can.
3. After the glue has dried, use the paintbrush to apply Mod Podge® over the stamps. Allow it to dry.
4. Glue decorative cording around the top and bottom edges of the can.

Bubble Art

These simple bubble pictures burst with color! Give each student a 12" x 18" sheet of white construction paper, several different-sized plastic lids, a pencil, and colored pencils. Instruct him to fill the construction paper with circles by tracing the different-sized lids, overlapping the circles in several places. Explain that the tracings should look as if bubbles have blown across their papers. Then have each student use colored pencils to color the circles. Further explain that these colors should blend where two or more bubbles overlap. Suggest that each student add depth to his picture by experimenting with light and dark colors. Your students will bubble over with excitement as they work!

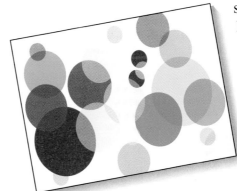

Decorative Bookmark

Motivate your students to read with these decorative bookmarks. Give each student a 2" x 6" piece of white poster board, an eight-inch length of ribbon, scissors, glue, and a hole puncher. Provide discontinued wallpaper books for your students to peruse. Instruct each student to cut out any interesting wallpaper designs that she sees and glue them on her blank bookmark in an attractive arrangement. After the glue has dried, laminate the bookmark for durability. Next have each student punch a hole at the top of her bookmark and attach the ribbon as shown.

Eggshell Art

These notecards are an "eggs-cellent" way to brighten someone's day!

Materials for each student:
washed and dried crushed eggshells (about a handful)
one 5" x 8" sheet of colored construction paper
watercolors
paintbrush
fine-tipped black marker
glue

Steps:

 Fold the construction paper in half, greeting card-style.

 Use the black marker to outline a simple shape—such as a heart, a butterfly, or a flower—on the front of the card.

 Spread a thin layer of glue within the outline of your shape; then cover the glued area with crushed eggshells.

 After the glue has dried, paint the eggshells with watercolors. Let them dry.

5 Open the card and write a note to a friend.

Balm Babies

This simple art project is sure to soothe your students!

Materials for each student:
one 10" helium-quality balloon
funnel
plastic spoon
1 sheet of newspaper
1/2 cup flour, sand, or salt
unsharpened pencil
1 black permanent marker

Steps:

1 Cover your work surface with newspaper.

2 Insert the funnel into the balloon; then spoon as much flour, sand, or salt into the balloon as possible (see Figure 1).

Figure 1

3 Use the unsharpened pencil to pack the filler down into the balloon (see Figure 2).

Figure 2

4 Gently squeeze the balloon to force out the excess air; then tie the end of the balloon in a knot. Draw a smilie face on the balloon using a black permanent marker.

5 Knead the balloon whenever you feel tense or stressed. Now don't you feel better?

Shoebox Marionette

Dramatize lots of favorite stories with this lovable student-made puppet.

Materials for each student:

1 empty shoebox
8 toilet-tissue tubes
1 paper-towel tube cut in half
scrap pieces of oaktag
six 36" lengths of yarn
scissors
pencil

stapler
crayons or markers
assorted craft materials,
  such as yarn, construction
  paper, and glitter
ruler

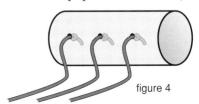

Steps:

1. Discard the shoebox lid; then decorate your shoebox with crayons and assorted craft materials to look like a character, an animal, or a person.
2. Use a pencil to poke six small holes in the shoebox: two at the top, two at the bottom, and one on either side (see Figure 1). Do not push your pencil all the way through. Lay the decorated box on your work surface facing upward.

figure 1

3. Use your pencil to poke three holes in each half of the paper-towel tube (see Figure 2). Do not push your pencil all the way through. Put the tubes aside.

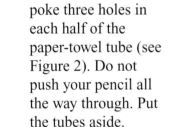
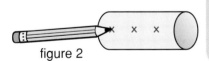

figure 2

4. Make two hands and two feet for your marionette using oaktag scraps; then staple each hand and foot to the end of a different toilet-tissue tube (see Figure 3).

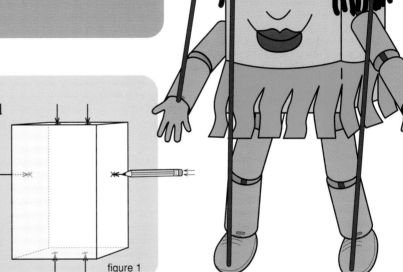

figure 3

5. Tie a large knot at the end of a length of yarn. Thread the unknotted end of the yarn through the hole on the left side of the box and also through a toilet-tissue tube and the tube connected to the left hand. Then knot the yarn.
6. Repeat Step 5 with the hole on the right side of the box, another tube, and the tube connected to the right hand.
7. Use your pencil to poke one hole in the toe and heel of each foot.

8. Tie a large knot at the end of a length of yarn. Thread the unknotted end through the heel of the left foot and the attached tube, through a second toilet-tissue tube, and through the holes at the bottom and top of the left side of the marionette's body.
9. Repeat Step 8 with the right foot, another tube, and the remaining holes.
10. Tie a large knot at the end of a length of yarn. Thread the unknotted end through the hole in the toe of the left foot. Repeat this step with the remaining length of yarn and the right foot.

11. Thread each of the yarn ends through a hole in the paper-towel tubes as shown in Figure 4. Adjust the lengths of yarn; then secure each length with a knot. (Allow about 12 inches of yarn between the top of the marionette and the paper-towel tubes.)

figure 4

ART ESSENTIALS

Easy-To-Do Recipes For A Variety Of Art Supplies

These easy-to-make arts-and-crafts recipes are just what your students need to create their own masterpieces.

Homemade Play Dough

Use homemade play dough in place of expensive store brands for your next class project.

1 cup flour
1/2 cup salt
2 teaspoons cream of tartar
1 cup water
1 teaspoon vegetable oil
food coloring

Mix the dry ingredients. Then add the remaining ingredients and stir. In a heavy skillet, cook the mixture for two to three minutes, stirring frequently. Knead the dough until it becomes soft and smooth. Stir up several colors and store them in icing tubs.

No-Cook Modeling Dough

Begin your next modeling project with a batch of this no-cook dough that's a snap to make!

2 cups flour
1 cup salt
water
food coloring or tempera paint
2 tablespoons vegetable oil (optional)

Mix the ingredients together. Add oil if you do not want the dough to harden.

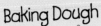

Baking Dough

Bake this dough in the oven after your students use it to create their art projects.

2 cups flour
1 cup salt
water

Mix enough water with the dry ingredients to make a dough. Give each student a portion of the dough with which to work. After students create their master-pieces, bake the dough at 300° for about an hour—longer for thicker objects.

To-Die-For Dye

Use this simple method of dyeing to yield an abundance of bright and colorful art materials.

1/3 cup rubbing alcohol
food coloring
items to be dyed (beans, rice, macaroni, seeds, etc.)
waxed paper

Pour the rubbing alcohol into a container; then add food coloring to obtain the desired color. Drop the materials to be dyed into the liquid and let them soak for a few minutes. Finally spoon the mixture onto waxed paper to dry. The alcohol evaporates quickly, leaving the dyed objects ready for art.

Papier-Mâché

Stir up a quick-and-easy batch of papier-mâché to fan your students' 3-D creativity!

1 part liquid starch
1 part cold water
newspaper strips

Mix equal parts of liquid starch and cold water. Tear strips of newspaper, and dip each strip into the mixture before applying it to a form of chicken wire, rolled newspaper, or an inflated balloon.

Salt Paint

Add an icy touch to winter pictures with salt paint.

2 teaspoons salt
1 teaspoon liquid starch
several drops of tempera paint

Mix the ingredients together and apply with a paintbrush. Then allow the painting to dry.

Shiny Paint

Give your next painting project a wet look with this easy recipe.

1 part white liquid glue
1 part tempera paint

Mix equal parts of liquid glue and tempera paint; then apply with a brush. Shiny paint provides a wet look even when its surface is dry.

Pattern
Use with "Corny Cobs" on page 87.

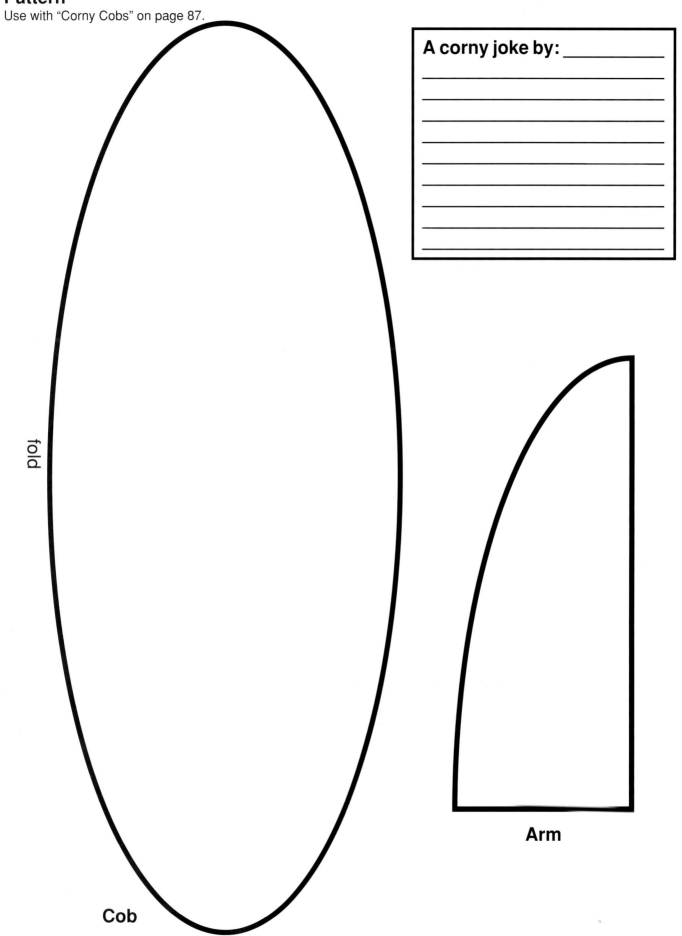

A corny joke by: _____

fold

Cob

Arm

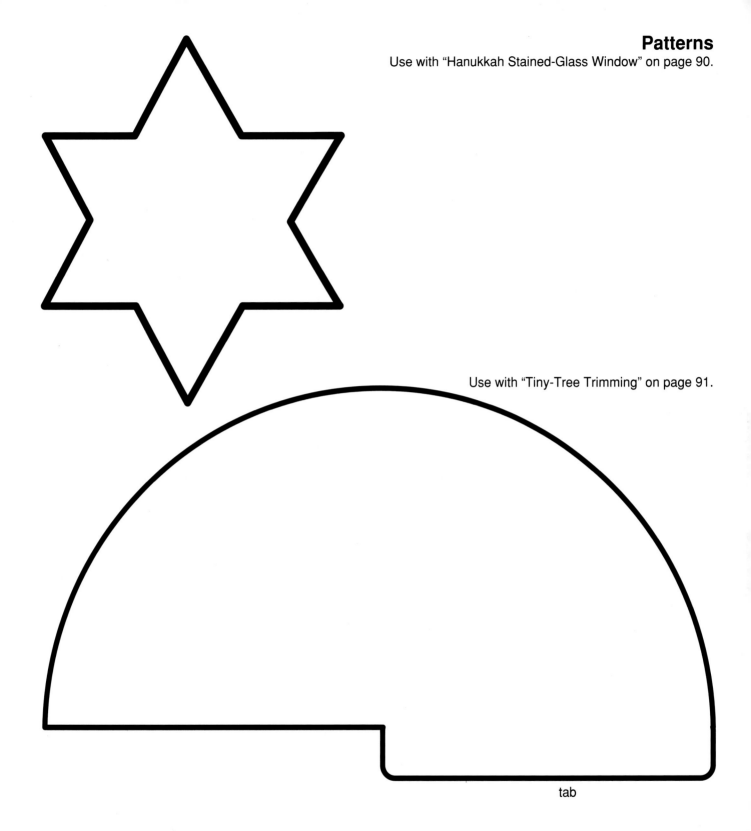

Use with "Tiny-Tree Trimming" on page 91.

tab

Use with "Holiday Note Clip" on page 93.

Patterns
Use with "Bank On It!" on page 93.

CENTERS

Reading And Writing CENTERS

Book-Cover Summaries

For this creative-writing center, photocopy the front of several eye-catching book covers with intriguing titles from your classroom or school library and place them in a center. Select books representing the various genres of literature—mystery, fantasy, science fiction, adventure, realistic fiction, and historical fiction. Instruct each student to select one book cover, look at the title and cover illustration carefully, and then write a brief summary of the book that might appear on the back cover. So that students will be as creative as possible, explain that a summary does not have to be about the actual book. Also explain that a student would not have to have read the book before writing a summary of it. Post the directions at the right at the center and anticipate some interesting recaps!

Directions:
1. Select one book cover from the center.
2. Look carefully at the book cover. Think about what the cover represents and what its title means.
3. What type of book is it? A mystery? An adventure? A fantasy? Or other?
4. Read a few actual book-cover summaries to see how other authors write a summary.
5. Select character names, settings, and events for your summary. Be creative!
6. Write a brief one- or two-paragraph summary about what you think your book is about.
7. Proofread your work to check for complete sentences, correct punctuation, and proper spelling.

WHAT'S NEXT?

Motivate your students to be clear and concise when writing directions with this writing-center idea. Photocopy several simple sets of directions—such as those for a recipe, for playing a children's game, for filling out an order form, or for setting a digital clock. White-out two or three steps from each set of directions; then make one copy of each set of directions for each student. Place the copies in the center along with an answer key containing the missing steps. Instruct each student to think about the sequence of events before and after each missing step. Have the student complete each set of directions by filling in the missing steps; then direct him to use the answer key to check his answers.

Author's Inspiration Station

Put all of a story's elements at your students' fingertips with this center idea. Duplicate page 112; then color each story-element column a different color and laminate the page. Post the chart in a writing center and instruct each student to pick one story element from each column to use in writing a story. This center will offer a quick remedy for any of your young authors who suffer from writer's block!

CHARACTERS	PLOT	SETTING	THEME
Scout Max Flash	Two characters search for the missing one.	The wilderness	Acting without thinking often brings trouble.

WHO? WHAT? WHEN? WHERE? WHY?

Use this great center idea to introduce your students to the five Ws of a newspaper article—Who? What? When? Where? and Why? Stock the center with fairly current newspapers, index cards, highlighter pens, and pencils. Instruct each student to look through the newspapers and cut out one interesting news article. Have the student read the article and use a highlighter pen to mark the article's five Ws. Next instruct the student to write the article's headline at the top of an index card, then write the article's five Ws on the index card. Post the cards on a bulletin board titled "News In Brief."

A Wall Of Words

All you need to set up this center is a blank wall, a dictionary, black markers, and a supply of brick-shaped construction-paper patterns (see the top of page 113). Have each of your students follow the steps below to contribute to a wall of words—one brick at a time!

1. Keep a running list of unfamiliar and interesting words.
2. Take one brick pattern for every word on the list.
3. Use a black marker to write a different word from the list on each brick.
4. Find a definition in the dictionary for each word, and write its definition on the appropriate brick.

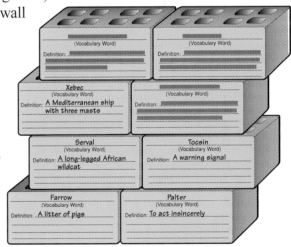

Tape the completed bricks to your classroom wall to create a wall of words. Also post a sheet of white poster board near the word wall on which students can record their names, the date, and the words they've contributed. At the end of the week, recognize students who added words to the wall that week to encourage continued use. Then watch your students' vocabularies grow along with the wall!

STORY COLLAGES

Students will delight in bringing the novels they've read to life when visiting this literature center. Stock the center with construction paper, old magazines, scissors, markers, and glue. Instruct each student to find magazine pictures that represent characters, events, and settings from the class novel currently being read. (This center also works well with novels students are reading independently.) Have the student cut out the selected pictures and glue them collage-style to a sheet of construction paper. Direct each student to write the novel's title at the top of the collage, and to write a brief sentence explaining it at the bottom of the collage. Display the finished products in or near the center or around the classroom.

Tuck Everlasting

The Ferris wheel represents the life cycle. The characters are Mae, Tuck, Winnie, Jesse, and Miles.

Report-Card Time

Your students will love the chance to be the ones filling out the report card! Duplicate and place in a center one copy of the "Report Card" reproducible at the bottom of page 113 for each student. Have each student select a historical figure from your current unit in social studies. Stock the center with reference materials for the appropriate historical period of time as well as with drawing paper, crayons, and markers. If possible, put a CD-ROM of a multimedia encyclopedia in a computer; then place the computer at or near the center. Instruct each student to complete one report card for his chosen historical figure and also draw a picture of that individual. Display both the student's report card and his accompanying illustration on a bulletin board or wall space near the center.

EVERYBODY'S A CRITIC

This center idea will provide you and your students with a great reference of student-recommended books.

To set up the center:

1. Gather a three-ring binder and select a student volunteer to design a cover for it.

2. If desired, purchase plastic page protectors and tabbed dividers.

3. Divide the notebook into sections by genre—such as mystery, adventure, realistic fiction, humor, fantasy, and science fiction.

4. Duplicate a class supply of the student book review form on page 114.

5. Place the decorated binder and forms in a center near your classroom library.

Each time a student reads a book, have him critique the book by completing a form and placing it in the appropriate section of the three-ring binder. Suggest that your students consult the notebook of reviews to help them decide what to read next.

Tape It!

Ever feel that you need to clone yourself when it comes to reteaching lessons or catching students up when they've been absent? Here's a simpler solution! Make a recording—audio or video—of yourself teaching a simple reading or language-arts lesson. Be sure that the lesson you select to tape is simple and clear. Place the tape in a center along with any necessary assignment directions. Whenever a student returns from being absent or just needs a quick review of that lesson, point him toward this center!

Creative Card Center

Here's a center that you'll want to keep going all year long! Gather a generous supply of drawing paper, markers, paper lace, stencils, rubber stamps, ink pads, stickers, and envelopes. If you have old greeting cards, clip the fronts of the cards (to recycle their great illustrations) and include them at the center as well. Allow students to visit the center whenever they have special occasions in their lives that can be commemorated by making special handmade greeting cards. Also assign individual students or student pairs to create birthday and holiday cards for members of your school's staff—such as the principal, the secretary, the resource teachers, the librarian, the cafeteria staff, and the custodians. Move over, Hallmark®!

Categories Galore!

This easy-to-create center will require your students to do lots of creative thinking! Fill a shoebox with approximately 30 small household or school-related items—such as a pencil, a soup-can label, a piece of candy, a candle, a piece of chalk, and a crayon. Challenge students to visit the center and try to put the items in the box into categories. Tell them that each category created must contain at least five items. Have students list the name of each category and its specific items on a sheet of paper. Challenge each student to see who can come up with the most categories. Periodically change the items in the box and have students create new lists.

IMAGINARY VACATION

Bon voyage! Give your students a short vacation with this center idea! Decorate a center area with travel posters. Also stock the center with travel magazines, scissors, glue, and large index cards. Instruct each student to select, cut out, and mount on an index card a picture of a vacation spot he'd like to visit. Help him focus on his picture's details to draw conclusions about what he could do there. Tell the student to fill out the back of the index card like a postcard, addressing it to a friend or family member. Then direct the student to write a brief message to that person. Explain that the message must include details of his experiences at this place. Be prepared for some interesting reading!

Dear Joe,
This is a picture of the Statue of Liberty. I saw it from a ferry boat. Tomorrow we are going to tour Ellis Island, where many immigrants were allowed to enter the United States early in this century.

Your friend,
Ben

Joe Smith
123 Pine Lane
York, PA 17365

THE PRICE IS ALMOST RIGHT

Use this game/center idea to reinforce your students' estimation skills. Stock a center with several mail-order catalogs, pencils, scrap paper, calculators, game pieces, dice, and a laminated copy of the gameboard on page 115. Duplicate the rules below and post in the center. Then watch your students "come on down" to this fun math center every chance they get!

Rules/Directions (for 2–4 players):
1. Each player gets one game piece, one sheet of scrap paper, a pencil, a calculator, and a catalog.
2. Roll the die to see who goes first.
3. The first player rolls the die and moves his/her game piece that number of spaces on the gameboard. Follow the directions in the space on which you land.
4. The object of the game is to estimate the exact answer as closely as possible without going over.
5. Use the catalogs and mental math to round prices and estimate answers.
6. For each problem, record on your sheet of scrap paper the difference between your estimate and the exact answer. (Use a calculator to determine exact answers and to find differences, but not to find estimates.)
7. The person with the closest estimates wins! To determine which player has the closest estimates, each player finds the total of his recorded differences. The player with the smallest total is the winner!

Spend It Wisely

This simple and easy center will make good use of the numerous sales brochures you receive in the mail. Or you can collect several sales flyers from various stores. Attach a shopping list to each flyer consisting of ten items featured in the flyer. Include the brand name and the desired quantity of each product on the shopping list. Instruct each student to find the correct total for each list. For another activity, place the correct amount of play money for each shopping list in individual unmarked plastic sandwich bags. Direct the student to select a bag, count the money inside, and find the matching shopping list. What smart shoppers your students will become!

Lock It Up!

Here's a "safe" and easy way to encourage students to practice math skills. Attach a combination lock to a locked box or a small safe. Create math exercises with answers that match the numbers of the combination. Direct students to solve all the problems, then check their answers by trying to "crack the safe." (Students will know right away if their answers are correct!) Place stickers or candy inside the locked box or safe as a reward for students who successfully open the lock. This center can be enjoyed throughout the year with each new math concept. And if you purchase a lock with a programmable code, you can use this center over and over without having to change locks.

Recycle That Junk Mail

Searching for a practical use for all those catalogs that keep piling up at school and at home? Gather a variety of catalogs for clothing, home decor, hobbies, crafts, furniture, party supplies, and books. Before placing them in the center, staple an index card to the front of each catalog. On each index card write a different shopping scenario. For example:

You are furnishing a new apartment and need to buy furniture. You have saved $2,500 for these purchases. Using this catalog, select the items you would like to purchase. Try to get as close to $2,500 without going over this amount as possible. On a separate sheet of paper, record each item you purchase and its price. Then add the prices of all the items together to find the grand total of your shopping spree. At the bottom of the same sheet, briefly describe why you chose to buy these particular items.

As a challenge, have students fill out a photocopy of the catalog's order form. This will give each student more practice in adding in sales tax and shipping-and-handling costs, as well as in following directions.

CENTER OF THE UNIVERSE

Use this easy-to-set-up center to complement a study of the universe or of science fiction. Equip the center with construction paper, old magazines, scissors, glue, tape, and one copy for each student of the reproducible on page 116. If desired, decorate the center with hanging stars, planets, and moons. Instruct each student to create an alien by cutting parts of several different faces from magazine photos and combining them Into one face. Have him glue his final version of the face onto a piece of construction paper. Next instruct the student to complete one copy of the "Alien Profile" sheet in the center. Direct him to tape the profile to the bottom of his alien creation. Display each student's alien on a bulletin board or wall titled "Aliens—Up Close And Personal."

SHOPPER BEWARE

Your students will enjoy this mind-stretching center. Save your store receipts for several weeks. Ask your students to also save and bring in receipts from the grocery store, drugstore, hardware store, etc. (Be sure that none of the receipts contain credit-card numbers.) When you have a good number of receipts—and a wide variety—bundle them in groups of five or six. Make sure that each receipt within a bundle is from a different store. Instruct students at the center to select a bundle of receipts. Tell them to examine the receipts carefully, noting the types of stores and the items purchased. Provide scrap paper and pencils for students to use to take notes as they examine the receipts. Explain that students should use their notes to help them draw conclusions about the shoppers who purchased the items. Post the list of questions shown below at the center. Direct each student who uses the center to answer the questions about each different receipt in the bundle. Afterward have him summarize his thoughts in a paragraph on a separate sheet of paper.

Shopper Questions:
1. Is the shopper male or female?
2. Does this person live alone or with a family?
3. What are this person's likes and dislikes?
4. What is this person's job or hobby?
5. When does this person do his/her shopping?
6. What other conclusions can you draw based on the bundle of receipts?

Story Elements

Directions: Select one story element box from each column. Use each element to help you write a story. Feel free to add more to each element. For example, you may want to add an extra character or setting.

CHARACTERS	PLOT	SETTING	THEME
Scout Max Flash	Two characters search for the missing one.	The wilderness	Acting without thinking often brings trouble.
Junior Princess Mr. Shortcut	Someone has stolen the president's car.	A character's backyard	Better late than never.
Willy Jones The Witch Wendy Walsh	The characters are on an arctic adventure.	An underwater hideout	Honesty is the best policy.
Gus Caesar The Shadow	The characters have a wonderful vacation in a surprising place.	Another planet	You can't judge a book by its cover.
Clancy Miss Fancy Sunny	The characters find a treasure and decide what to do with it.	An ice palace	The best things in life are free.

Note To The Teacher: Use this reproducible with "Author's Inspiration Station" on page 106.

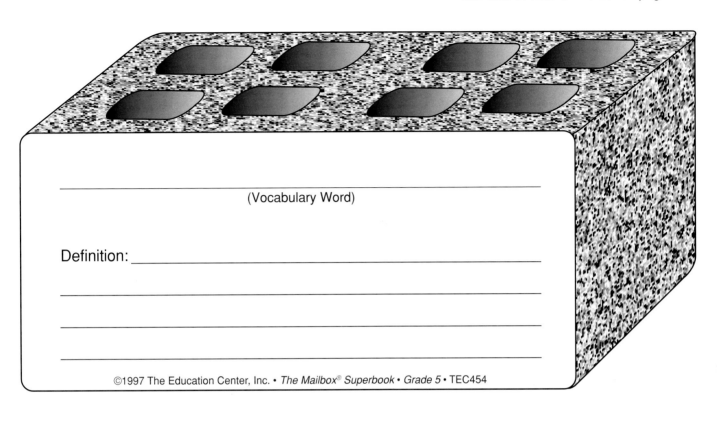

(Vocabulary Word)

Definition: _____

_____

_____

_____

©1997 The Education Center, Inc. • *The Mailbox® Superbook* • *Grade 5* • TEC454

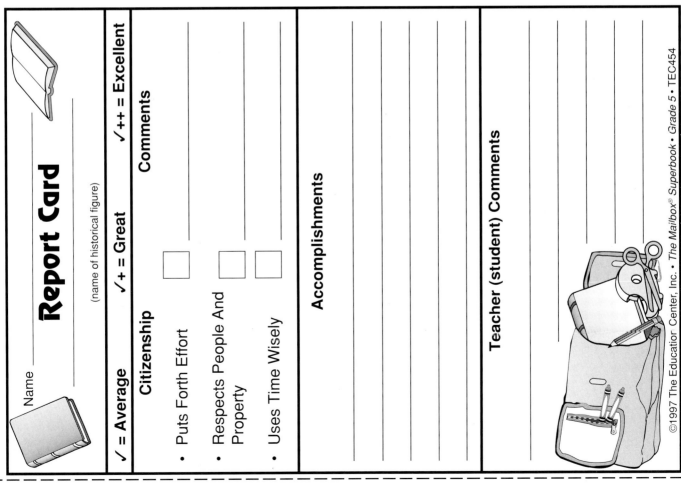

Report Card

Name _____

(name of historical figure)

✓ = Average   ✓+ = Great   ✓++ = Excellent

Citizenship   **Comments**

• Puts Forth Effort   ☐

• Respects People And   ☐
  Property

• Uses Time Wisely   ☐

Accomplishments

Teacher (student) Comments

©1997 The Education Center, Inc. • *The Mailbox® Superbook* • *Grade 5* • TEC454

Book Review

I recently read a book titled

_____.

This book had approximately _____ pages, and it took me about _____ days to read it. The main character is a _____ named _____.

This book contains several events. The first thing that happens is _____

_____

_____.

The next thing that happens is _____

_____.

This is followed by _____

_____.

You'll have to read the book to find out what happens next. The ending **will/will not**
(circle one)
be a surprise. There **is/is not** another book that continues this story.
(circle one)

This book would be enjoyed by people who_____

_____.

I would/would not recommend this book to my classmates. I got this book from the
(circle one)
classroom library/school library/home.
(circle one)

_____
(Student Critic)

_____
(Date)

Note To The Teacher: Use with "Everybody's A Critic" on page 108.

You're An Heir! Move Ahead 3 Spaces.

Bankrupt! Lose A Turn.

Held Up By A Bank Robber! Re-turn To Start.

Find an item in your catalog that you can't use. If someone gave you 13 of that item, how much money would you get when you returned them?

Purchase a great outfit for yourself. Be sure not to spend more than $145.

Find cool outfits for the four members of your band. You have $444 to spend.

Find the most ex-pensive item in your catalog. How much would four of that item cost?

Find an item that costs less than $10. How many of that item can you pur-chase for $100?

Find an item in your fa-vorite color. If you buy six of that item, how much will it cost?

Find the last item in your catalog. If you have $135 to spend, how many of that item can you buy?

Find the least expen-sive item on the first two pages of your cata-log. How many of this item can you buy if you have $100?

Find an item that makes life easier. Buy one for each of your ten friends. Don't spend more than $100.

Buy a gift for your dog and a gift for your cat. Estimate the difference between the two prices.

You have $67 to spend. Find three toys to buy.

You need to buy a gift for each of your eight brothers! You have $108 to spend.

Find gifts for each of your teachers. Don't spend more than $50.

Purchase three items that would be great to use outdoors.

START

You've Won The Sweep-stakes! Roll Again!

You're An Heir! Move Ahead 3 Spaces.

Held Up By A Bank Robber! Re-turn To Start.

Bankrupt! Lose A Turn.

FINISH

©1997 The Education Center, Inc. • The Mailbox® Superbook • Grade 5 • TEC454

Note To The Teacher: Use this gameboard with "The Price Is Almost Right" on page 110.

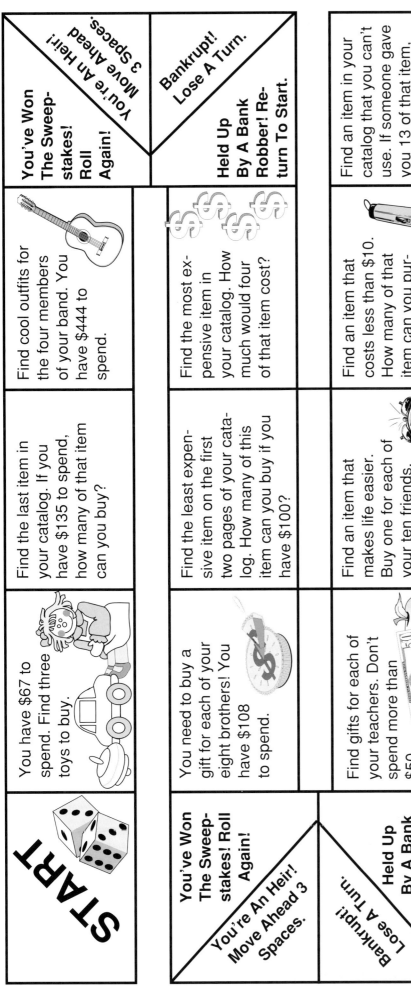
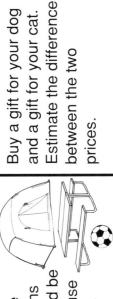

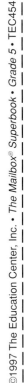

Alien Profile

Favorite
Food:

Favorite
Activity:

Favorite
Planet:

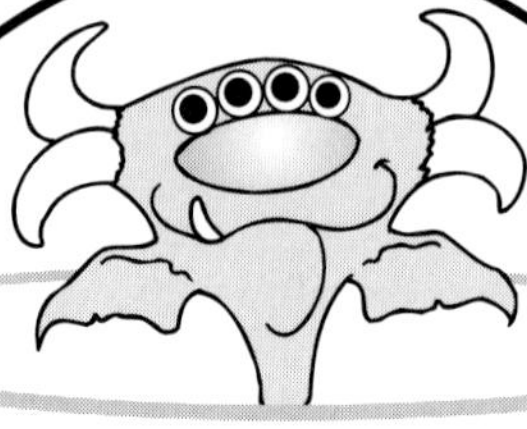

Plans For
The Future:

Favorite
Earthling:

Name: _____

Planet Of Birth: _____

Age: _____

Family: _____

_____

Something That
Makes Me Proud:

Three Words That Best Describe Me:

1. _____

2. _____

3. _____

One
Wish I Have:

Something I can do that earthlings
can't do!

Favorite Earth Attraction:

Note To The Teacher: Use this reproducible with "Center Of The Universe" on page 111.

GAMES

GAMES
For Any Subject

MAKE A MATCH

Here's a review game that will get your students up and moving in a hurry! In advance, make (or have students make) a set of review questions and answers by writing a review question on one slip of paper and its answer on another. Then follow the steps below to play the game.

1. Give each student a folded slip of paper that contains either a question or an answer.
2. On your signal, have each student quickly find the classmate whose paper matches his question or answer and then stand together in the front of the room. Declare the first pair to do so the winners.
3. Have all the pairs read their questions and answers aloud.
4. Collect the slips of paper and play another round.

roots, stem, and leaves

What are the main parts of a plant?

Money Hungry

Capitalize on students' interest in working with money the next time you review a unit with your class. Write review questions on slips of paper (or have students create the questions and put them on paper); then assign each question a monetary value according to its level of difficulty. Fold the slips of paper and place them in a container such as an old piggy bank. Divide your class into teams of three to five students and have them take turns drawing questions from the container. For every correct answer, reward each team play money equal to the monetary value of its question or keep a running total of the values on paper. Declare the team with the most money at the end of the game the winner.

$10.00 QUESTION

Identify the adverb in this sentence:

She had to leave for the airport soon.

TRUTH OR CONSEQUENCES

The next time you use a class game to review for a test, add a fun twist to it that will get your students' hearts a-pumpin' and the oxygen a-flowin'! Before playing the game, write several fun-to-do consequences on slips of paper (see the suggested list) and place them in a paper bag. Divide your students into teams; then begin asking review questions of each team. If a team gives an incorrect response (doesn't tell the truth), instruct one of the team members to draw a slip of paper from the consequences bag. Then have the whole team perform that stunt. As a variation, collect an object from each student before starting the game. Whenever a team answers a question correctly, allow one team member to reclaim his object!

Fun-To-Do Consequences
- run in place for ten seconds
- do five jumping jacks
- touch your toes as you spell your name aloud—backward— five times
- hop on one foot five times
- walk in place as you count backward from 100 to 85
- stand on your tiptoes as you count by threes from 0 to 33

BUILD IT!

Piecing together bits of information will be loads of fun with this science or social-studies review game! Prior to playing the game, have groups of students cut apart posters, pictures, or maps related to a current unit of study to serve as puzzle pieces. Divide your class into teams of four to six students. Explain that the object of the game is to be the first team to collect all the puzzle pieces. For example, appropriate puzzle pieces for a review of the solar system could be individual pictures of the nine planets, the Sun, the Moon, a constellation, a comet, and a meteor. Then ask Team 1 the first review question, allowing about 15 seconds for an answer. If the members of Team 1 answer correctly, allow them to choose one puzzle piece. Continue play in the same manner by asking the other teams, in turn, a question. But if the members of a team answer incorrectly, do not allow them to choose a puzzle piece; just repeat the same question for the next team.

Vary the game by mixing all the puzzle pieces—plus some extras—in one large envelope from which the teams draw after answering a question correctly. Allow a team to "steal" a puzzle piece from a team giving an incorrect answer if its members answer the same question correctly. As another variation, stipulate that the puzzle pieces be letters that spell key vocabulary words; then challenge each team to acquire the letters needed to spell an entire word before being declared the winner.

Ideas For Cut-Apart Puzzles

➤ a map of the 13 colonies
➤ a map of the U.S. regions
➤ sections of the periodic table
➤ parts of an airplane or rocket
➤ categories and examples of solids, liquids, and gases
➤ the three main types of rocks with examples of each type
➤ groups of vertebrates and invertebrates
➤ examples of different parts of speech
➤ different families of basic math facts

Words	Category
guide words, pronunciation key, entry words	parts of a dictionary
ten millions, tenths, hundreds	place value of numbers
beautiful, gorgeous, stunning	synonyms
acute, obtuse, right	types of angles or triangles
Boston Tea Party, Sugar Act, Stamp Act	events leading to the American Revolution
veins, arteries, blood	parts of the circulatory system

Categories

Play this review game any time of the year, but especially keep it in mind for the end of the year. Prepare (or have your students prepare) clue cards for identifying different topics studied throughout the year. Stipulate that each card have three words or phrases on it that help identify a specific category (see the chart). Divide your class into teams of three to five players; then follow the steps below to play the game.

➤ 1. Say the words on one of the cards to the first team.
➤ 2. Allow that team's members about ten seconds to name a specific category.
➤ 3. If the first category named is not specific enough, allow the team an additional 15 seconds to revise its answer. For example, if the clues are *humerus, radius,* and *ulna,* and a team's guess is *bones of the body,* you could say, "Think of a more specific category," giving that team a chance to say "Arm bones."
➤ 4. If the named category is correct, give that team three points; if incorrect, pass the play to Team 2, giving them two points for a correct guess.
➤ 5. Should Team 2 answer incorrectly, give Team 1 another chance to win just one point for answering correctly. Then announce the next set of clues to a different team.
➤ 6. Play for a set amount of time; then declare the team with the most points at the end of that time the winner.

MATH GAMES

PLACE-VALUE LINEUP

Review place value with this interactive game. Divide your class into teams of 11 players. Give one player on each team a card labeled with a decimal point and each of the other players a card labeled with a different digit 0–9. (If teams with fewer players are needed, have each player hold more than one card.) Next call out a number requiring the use of all 11 cards. Have teams form that number by lining up in the appropriate order as quickly as possible. Declare the first team to correctly form that number the winner. Play additional rounds as time permits. To vary the game, write a number's word or expanded form on the board instead of saying the number aloud.

3 5 8 2 7 1 6 . 4 9 0

QUICK DRAW!

Review geometric shapes with this fast-paced drawing game. Divide your class into teams with an even number of players on each team. Number the players on each team; then supply each team with small sheets of scrap paper, a pencil, and—if desired—a ruler and a protractor. To play, call out a number and a geometric term (see the list). Have each player with that number take a sheet of scrap paper and the pencil and draw that shape as quickly as possible. If the player does not know what to draw, allow coaching from his teammates. After he completes his drawing, have him quickly run the paper to you. Give the first team to give you a correct drawing two points and other teams with correct drawings one point. Continue play in this manner until all the items have been drawn. Declare the team with the most points the winner.

Geometric Items To Draw: point, plane, line AB, ray CD, line segment EF, parallel lines, intersecting lines, perpendicular lines, acute angle CAB, obtuse angle EFG, right angle ABC, acute triangle, right triangle, obtuse triangle, equilateral triangle, square, rectangle, pentagon, hexagon, octagon, parallelogram, rhombus, trapezoid, shape with only one line of symmetry, shape with two lines of symmetry, shape with three lines of symmetry, rectangle with perimeter of 10 cm, rectangle with area of 10 cm², etc.

Tic Add Toe

Add a new twist to an old game the next time you review addition and subtraction facts. Pair your students; then have each pair draw a game grid on paper. Direct each player, in turn, to write a digit 0–9 instead of an *X* or an *O* in a row, column, or diagonal, explaining that the object of the game is to create an addition or subtraction sentence. Explain further that the player who places the third digit and completes the number sentence gets one point. For example, the player who places a 9 in the upper right corner of the grid that's shown would receive one point because 3 + 6 = 9. Allow students to play as many rounds as time permits; then declare the player with the most points the winner.

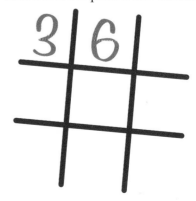

Basic-Facts Circle

Get your students moving with this fun review of basic multiplication and division facts! Write each of the following numbers on a different index card: 1, 2, 3, 4, 5, 6, 7, 8, 9, 10, 12, 14, 15, 16, 18, 20, 21, 24, 25, 27, 28, 30, 32, 35, 36, 40, 42, 45, 48, 49, 50, 54, 56, 60, 63, 64, 70, 80, 81, 90, 100. **Have your students sit in a circle; then pass out all the cards (some students will have more than one card).**

To play:

1. Direct each student to hold his cards so that the numbers face outward and are visible to every person in the circle.

2. Explain that you will call out a basic multiplication or division fact and that the two players having those numbers on their cards must get up and race to find the player holding the solution for that basic fact.

3. After finding the solution, instruct those two students to resume their places in the circle; then have each player pass his cards to the player on the right.

4. If a player is in charge of two or more cards and one of his numbers is called, tell him to have the player on his right hold and play his other cards until he sits down again.

5. If by chance a student holds both of the basic-facts cards, call out a different basic fact for that round and direct that player to trade one of his cards with another player so that fact can be used later.

6. Continue play by saying the next basic fact. To vary the game, call out a basic fact and have the player holding the answer card go and stand in the center of the circle. Or call out a number and challenge students to suggest possible equations that will equal that number.

"EQUIZ!"

Strengthen your students' skills in basic operations with this quick equation game. Write the digits 0–9 and draw a chart like the one below on the board; then pair your students. Have each pair of students copy a blank chart from the board on paper. To play, direct Player 1 to write down any five digits from 0–9 in the chart. Have Player 2 use as many of those five digits as he can—without repeating any digit—to form a correct number sentence and write it in the chart. Explain that the basic-operations symbols +, –, x, and ÷ can be used as often as needed, but that the = symbol can be used only once. Also explain that each player can earn one point—up to a maximum of five points in each turn—for every digit he uses correctly. Continue play by having Player 2 list five digits in the chart for Player 1 to use. End the game after a set amount of time or when both players have had an equal number of turns. Declare the team with the highest total points the winner.

Player	Digits	Equation	Points
1	1,2,3,5,0	1x2+3=5+0	5
2	3,6,2,4,8	6÷3+2=8-4	5
1	3,6,9,7,2	9-7=2	3

LANGUAGE-ARTS GAMES

Silly-Dilly Sentences

Help your students review the different parts of speech with a game that ends with building sentences. In advance, create a class set of game cards by writing a different adjective, adverb, verb, and noun on separate index cards. Shuffle the cards; then distribute the cards for Round 1, one card for each student.

To play:

1 Direct all students whose cards have nouns to go to one corner of the room, those with adjectives to a second corner, and so on with verbs and adverbs.

2 In turn, have every student in each group read aloud the word on his card so that the class can determine whether he has classified his word correctly or not.

3 Give each team one point for every correctly classified word.

4 Have the class reclassify any word that was grouped incorrectly; then direct the student holding that card to move to the correct group.

5 Play additional rounds as time permits; then declare the team with the most points the winner.

Continue the activity by forming smaller groups. Have four students (one from each of the four large groups) work together in a small group. Challenge each small group to use its four words, adding articles such as *a, an,* or *the* as needed, to create a silly—but complete—sentence for you to record on the board. As each group shares its sentence, be prepared to hear the resulting laughter!

BUILD-A-SENTENCE RELAY

Making complete sentences will take on a whole new perspective when students play this new game. Divide your class into teams of five to six students. Explain that the object of the game is to be the first team to write a complete sentence on the board. Direct the first player on each team to go to the board, write one word, and return to his team. In the same manner, instruct each remaining member of the team to contribute one word or punctuation mark to form a complete sentence. If a complete sentence—including its end punctuation—has been formed when the last team member takes his turn, have that team indicate that fact by sitting down. Declare the first team to complete the task the winner of that round. If a complete sentence has not been written after every team member has had a turn, require that team to play until they do have a complete sentence. Appoint a new player to start the next round, explaining that a different sentence must be written. If desired, add a challenge by requiring that the first player must write a word other than the first word of the sentence. Or have team members write the sentence backward, beginning with the first player writing the last word in the sentence!

The enormous shoe danced carefully.
   adj.   noun   verb   adv.

Team 1	Team 2
Saturdays are for	Mom told my

Shaping Up With Spelling

Give your students an aerobic workout with this spelling game that can be played inside or outside. Prepare for the game by having each student write a different spelling word on an index card. Collect the cards for later use. Next write the motions listed below on the chalkboard and practice them with your students. Divide your class into teams of six to eight students; then have each team stand in a line. (If necessary, move desks or tables out of the way.)

To play:

1 Divide the game cards that students made earlier into as many sets as you have teams. Then place each set facedown in a designated spot at an equal distance from each team.

2 On your signal, direct Player 1 on each team to run to the pile of cards, take the top card, run back to his team, and hand the card faceup to Player 2.

3 Instruct Player 2 to say the word aloud to Player 1; then have Player 1 spell the word aloud while performing the different motions assigned to each letter.

4 After spelling the word, direct Player 1 to take the card from Player 2 and sit down.

5 Instruct Player 2 to run to the pile and repeat the process with Player 3 on his team.

6 Continue play in this manner until every player on the team has spelled a word and sat down. Declare the first team to complete these tasks as directed the winner.

7 Play additional rounds by having the teams exchange their sets of cards.

Motions For Spelling A Word
First Letter: squat down
Second Letter: stand up
Third Letter: raise right arm
Fourth Letter: raise left arm
Fifth Letter: clap hands
Additional Letters: repeat each motion in the same order

DESCRIBE IT!

Need a game that provides students practice with using adjectives? Prepare for the game by distributing old magazines to your students. Direct each student to cut out pictures of objects and food items, then mount each picture on a different sheet of construction paper. To play the game, select one student to be It and have him stand behind you in front of the classroom. Next hold up a picture for class viewing in a way that prevents It from seeing the picture. Instruct It to call on five different classmates to suggest a specific adjective that describes the picture being held. Then have It try to guess what the picture is. If he succeeds, allow him to choose one of the five students who supplied adjectives to replace him as It. If he guesses incorrectly, allow him to call on five more students to offer different adjectives that might help him guess the word.

spring-timey

worm-eating

beaked

feathery

two-legged

SOCIAL-STUDIES GAMES

PACK YOUR SUITCASE!

"Travel" with your students to the capitals of the United States with this fun geography game that can double as a time filler. Display a U.S. map; then divide your class into two teams. Challenge each team to be first at naming the home state of each capital you announce. Start the game by designating one state capital as a departure point and another as the destination. Give one point to the first team that correctly names the home states of these two capitals. Next have each team imagine traveling in a straight line between the two capitals. Give one point to each team for correctly naming each state falling along this line.

To vary the game, direct students to cut out pictures of clothing from old magazines before beginning play. Also have each team cut out and decorate a construction-paper suitcase. Label the suitcase cutouts by teams and display them on a bulletin board titled "Pack Your Suitcase!" Place the magazine pictures in a pocket on the board. Each time a team wins a point (or accumulates a certain number of points), allow a student from that team to select an article of clothing and tape it to his team's suitcase. Declare the first team to get ten clothing items in its suitcase the winner of the game.

Picture-Perfect Map Terms

Check your students' understanding of map terms with this team game. Divide your students into teams of four. Number the members of each team; then follow the steps below.

To play:

▶ Call Player 1 on each team to a designated spot at the chalkboard.

▶ Select one map term (see the suggested list) and whisper that same term to each player at the board.

▶ Direct the players to illustrate that map term on the board. Do not allow the players to use words.

▶ When the members of a player's team think they know the term being illustrated, have Player 2 on that team run to the board and write the word underneath the drawing.

▶ Give one point to the first team that correctly identifies the term in that manner.

▶ If a team guesses the wrong term and the term has not yet been identified, allow that team to make another guess.

▶ Play Round 2 in the same manner, this time having Player 2 illustrate the new term while Player 3 runs to the board to do the writing and so on.

▶ End the game when all the terms have been reviewed. Declare the team with the most points the winner.

Suggested Map Terms:

gulf, bay, sound, strait, peninsula, cape, lake, river, mouth of a river, tributary, ocean, country, continent, state, island, delta, scale of miles, capital, international border, highway, city, airport

SUBSTITUTE TEACHER TIPS

SUBSTITUTE TEACHER TIPS

Survival Notebook

Don't leave your substitute in the dark about classroom procedures. Prepare a survival notebook containing a class list, a fire-drill procedure, a daily schedule, your discipline policy, a completed copy of page 129, and any other relevant information. Store the notebook in a visible location on your desk. You'll rest easy knowing the substitute is aware of classroom procedures—and she'll feel more confident about spending a day in your classroom!

Lesson-Plan Outline

Spend less time writing plans for a substitute by preparing a general lesson-plan outline on your computer. On the outline, include all the information about your class's schedule that remains the same, such as recess, lunch, and specialists' times, plus the times that you teach each subject. Whenever you need to make substitute plans, simply fill in a copy of your lesson-plan outline, adding the specific instructions for each subject. If you don't have access to a computer, print a supply of the outline and store the copies in a convenient location. This simple tip will save you a lot of time!

What's Your Name?

Not being able to call students by their names can frustrate a substitute and your students. Avoid this problem by having your students create decorative nametags for their desks. Give each student a large unlined index card; then have him fold it in half lengthwise so that it stands like a card tent. Have the student use a black marker to write his first name on both sides of the card. Allow him to decorate his card any way he chooses as long as his name is still clearly visible. Collect the nametags and store them with your substitute notebook. Instruct your substitute to have one student pass out the nametags for students to place on their desktops. At the end of the day, have the substitute collect the nametags so that they'll be ready to use the next time you have a substitute.

Mrs. Hubal Grade 5
Date

7:30–8:00	Attendance, lunch count, collect homework
8:00–8:45	Music
8:45–9:30	Reading
9:30–10:15	Writing
10:15–10:45	Recess
10:45–11:30	Grammar And Spelling
11:30–12:00	Lunch
12:00–12:20	D.E.A.R.
12:20–1:00	Science
1:00–1:45	Math
1:45–2:30	Social Studies
2:30	Dismissal

Picture Books To The Rescue!

Nothing captures the attention of a class like a good book! Compile a list of age-appropriate picture books that can be found in your school's media center. Keep a copy of the booklist in your substitute notebook along with instructions on how to access the books. After sharing a book aloud, suggest that the substitute choose one of the follow-up activities below and instruct each student to complete it. Your substitute will never be without an appropriate filler activity!

Follow-up activities

- Write a letter telling your teacher about the story using symbols (rebus).
- In a paragraph, explain why you think the author chose to tell this story.
- Write a 15-word telegram that summarizes the story.
- Divide each of two sheets of notebook paper into fourths. Illustrate 6–8 scenes from the book to create sequence cards. Cut apart the scenes; then challenge a classmate to sequence the events.
- Write a letter to a friend encouraging him to read the book.
- Write a paragraph describing the book's main character.
- Use a sheet of construction paper to create a new book jacket for the book.
- List five ways you could improve the story.
- On a sheet of graph paper, create a crossword puzzle about the story.
- Draw a comic strip based on one of the book's characters.

A Helping Hand

Let your substitute know that he has a helping hand close by! On a hand-shaped cutout, write the name of a teacher in a nearby classroom to whom the substitute can turn for answers to questions. Select a teacher who is familiar with your classroom procedures and make her aware that you are suggesting her as a helper. Laminate the hand and tape it to the front of your substitute notebook. This will make your substitute feel more comfortable, and you'll feel better knowing his day will run smoothly.

A Helping Hand! See Mrs. Adcock in Room 406 about any questions you may have.

How Did The Day Go?

Provide your substitute with a simple form that will tell you which lesson plans were actually accomplished in your absence. Duplicate several copies of "A Note From The Sub" at the top of page 130. Write the date you will be absent on each form; then clip the form(s) to the front of your substitute folder. Each note can serve as an invitation for your substitute to inform you of that day's happenings.

Faithful Elephants
by Yukio Tsuchiya

Handy Map

Help your substitute teacher navigate the school better by providing him with a labeled map. Make a copy of your school's fire-evacuation map. White-out any unnecessary information; then duplicate the edited map. Next highlight and label important locations in the school, such as faculty restrooms, the teachers' lounge, the cafeteria, special teachers' classrooms, and the media center. Store the map in your substitute notebook so that your substitute will be able to find his way around the school with ease.

Substitute Helpers

Help your substitute focus on implementing your lesson plans by designating a few student helpers to take care of the early-morning classroom routine. Train a few students to take the attendance, tally the lunch count, and perform any other morning tasks. List the names of those students inside your substitute notebook to let her know that she can call upon one or more of these students for assistance. That can be one less thing your substitute has to think about!

Where Is Everybody Going?

Is your classroom sometimes like Grand Central Station because of your students' many comings and goings? Imagine how confusing it must be for a substitute! Keep your substitute informed about which child needs to go to a resource room or other place throughout the day by duplicating one or more copies of the bottom half of page 130. On this sheet, record the name of every student who will leave your classroom for any reason during the day. Note the time that each child should leave and return, and his destination. Your substitute can feel secure in knowing where each child is, and the child won't be late because of trying to explain why he needs to leave the classroom.

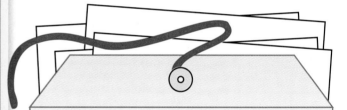

From _10:15_ to _10:45_ _Sara Genson_ goes to _Mrs. Bautel for math_
(Name of student)
He/She needs to take the following items: _math book, pencil, loose-leaf paper_

Substitute Stash!

Every teacher knows that the day doesn't always go as planned. Prepare your substitute for the unexpected by creating a valuable supply of educational activities just for the substitute's use. Duplicate a class set of a variety of fun reproducibles, games, and puzzles. Place these papers inside a labeled envelope or drawer. In your lesson plans, tell the substitute where to find this stash of ideas. Now your substitute will never be without an extra activity for your class if she needs it!

Sub Information Sheet

Name(s) Of:

Principal: _____

Secretary: _____

Nurse: _____

Counselor: _____

Assistant: _____

Parent Volunteer(s): _____

Special Teachers:

Resource Room: _____

AG: _____

Speech: _____

Music: _____

Art: _____

P.E.: _____

Librarian: _____

Other: _____

Times For:

Lunch: _____

Recess: _____

Bathroom Break: _____

Other: _____

Children With Special Needs:

Health: _____

Behavior: _____

Learning: _____

Procedures For:

Start of Day: _____

Lunch and Milk Count: _____

Attendance: _____

Homework: _____

Free-Time Activities: _____

Collecting Papers: _____

Lining Up: _____

Dismissal: _____

Fire Drill: _____

Tornado Drill: _____

Other: _____

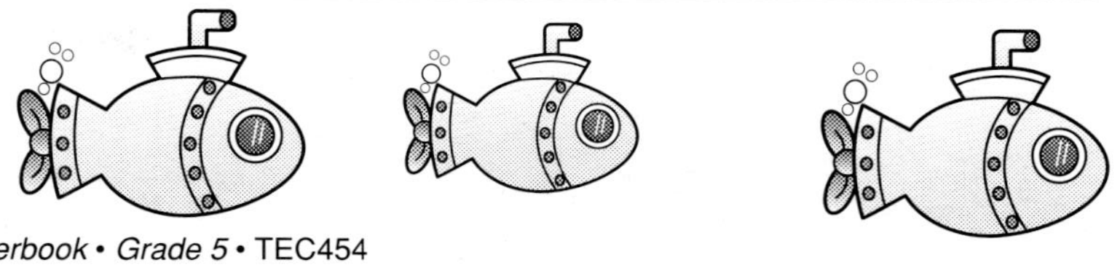

©1997 The Education Center, Inc. • *The Mailbox® Superbook • Grade 5 • TEC454*

Note To The Teacher: Use with "Survival Notebook" on page 126.

129

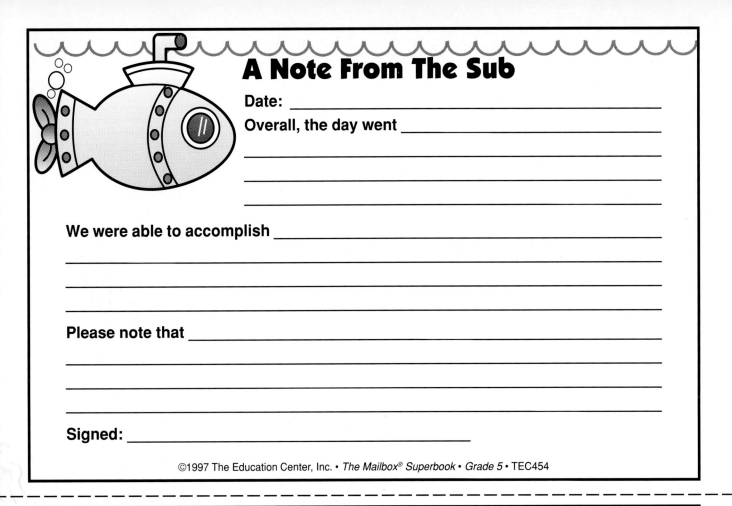

A Note From The Sub

Date: _____

Overall, the day went _____
_____
_____
_____

We were able to accomplish _____
_____
_____
_____

Please note that _____
_____
_____
_____

Signed: _____

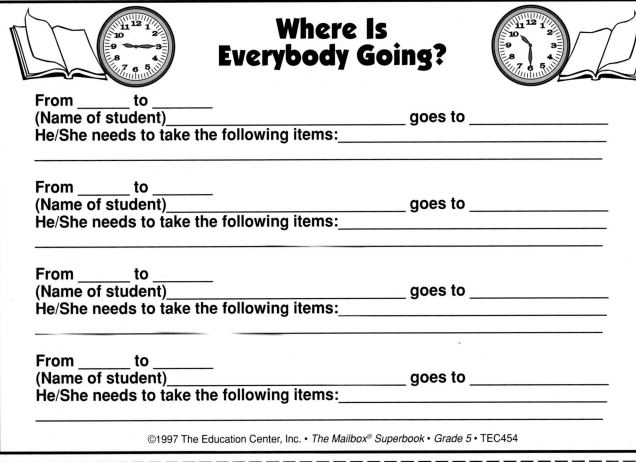

Where Is Everybody Going?

From _____ to _____
(Name of student)_____ goes to _____
He/She needs to take the following items:_____
_____

From _____ to _____
(Name of student)_____ goes to _____
He/She needs to take the following items:_____
_____

From _____ to _____
(Name of student)_____ goes to _____
He/She needs to take the following items:_____
_____

From _____ to _____
(Name of student)_____ goes to _____
He/She needs to take the following items:_____

Note To The Teacher: Use "A Note From The Sub" with the activity on page 127. Use "Where Is Everybody Going?" with the activity on page 128.

LANGUAGE ARTS

GRAMMAR

Sentence Signals

Here's a tip that's sure to get your students to recognize the four types of sentences in a snap! Write one example of each of the four types of sentences on the chalkboard—*declarative, interrogative, imperative,* and *exclamatory.* Have your students identify how each sentence is different from the others. Next designate a different corresponding signal or action for each type of sentence—such as clapping hands (declarative), snapping fingers (imperative), slapping hands against thighs (interrogative), and stomping feet (exclamatory). Have students practice the signals using the sentences on the board. Then display a transparency of 15 to 20 of the four types of sentences on an overhead projector. Cover all but the first two sentences. Challenge your students to identify each sentence by demonstrating its signal. For example, if you show a declarative and an interrogative sentence, have each student clap his hands, then snap his fingers. Continue the activity, increasing the number of different types of sentences shown each time.

Fishing For Fragments And Run-Ons

Set off with your students on a fun-filled fishing expedition to reel in sentence fragments and run-ons. Label a supply of index cards, each with a different sentence fragment or run-on. Shuffle the cards and place them facedown in a stack at a center. Invite two students at a time to the center to play a game of Fishing For Fragments And Run-Ons. Have the students follow the same rules used in playing the game of Go Fish, with students collecting pairs of fragments and pairs of run-ons. Declare the player who collects the most pairs the winner of the game.

Don ate four pieces of pepperoni pizza he was stuffed!

My dog, Sandy, knows lots of tricks she went to dog-training classes.

Searching For Subjects And Predicates

Send your students outside for a real-life lesson on subjects and predicates! First write a sample sentence on the chalkboard. Explain that a sentence has two parts: a *subject,* which names someone or something; and a *predicate,* which tells what the subject is or does. Have your students identify the subject and predicate of the sample sentence. Next have students take sheets of loose-leaf paper and pencils outside, sit in an area of the playground, and make observations about the happenings around them. Instruct each student to write five different sentences about whom and what he sees. Afterward return to the classroom and direct him to highlight the subject and predicate of each sentence with different-colored markers. Follow up the activity by having each student in turn write one of his sentences on the chalkboard. Instruct a different student to label that sentence's subject and predicate; then have the author of the sentence tell whether the parts were labeled correctly.

Four kids played a game of Four Square.
The teachers watched their students climb on the playground equipment.

Intriguing Interjections

Here's an activity that's sure to interject some fun into a lesson on recognizing and using interjections! Cut out several pictures from magazines of people whose facial expressions show different emotions—such as happiness, surprise, sadness, and concern. Display these pictures on the chalkboard. Explain to students that an *interjection* is a word or phrase used to express strong emotion. Next show your students each magazine picture in turn, having them create interjectory sentences for each one. Write your students' responses on the chalkboard, pointing out that a comma or an exclamation point is used to separate an interjection from the rest of the sentence (see the example at the left).

Next provide each student with a magazine, a 9" x 12" sheet of light-colored construction paper, scissors, glue, and a black marker or pen. Direct each student to find a magazine picture similar to the ones shown, cut out the picture, and glue it to his sheet of construction paper. Then instruct the student to draw a speech bubble on his paper that includes an interjectory sentence to accompany the picture. Have each student share his picture; then display the pictures on a wall area for student reference.

Amazing Adjectives

Open your students' eyes to the benefits of using descriptive words with this picturesque activity! Write a sentence on the board that contains several nouns, but no adjectives (see the example); then follow the steps below.

1 Direct students to close their eyes and visualize the sentences you will read.

2 Read aloud the sentence on the chalkboard; then after a minute, read it again, adding an adjective before each noun.

3 Have students open their eyes; then ask how their visualizations of the two sentences differed.

4 Discuss how the adjectives in the second sentence make it more descriptive and help create a more vivid picture in a reader's mind.

5 Have each student write the sample sentence on a sheet of loose-leaf paper, filling in a different adjective before each noun.

6 Collect the papers; then redistribute them, giving a paper to each student along with an 8 1/2" x 11" sheet of drawing paper and crayons or colored pencils.

7 Direct the student to copy the last sentence on the paper at the top of her sheet of drawing paper, then draw a picture of what she sees when she reads the sentence.

> The vast meadow was covered with emerald green grass and multicolored flowers.

Have each student share her sentence and drawing with the class. If desired display students' work on a bulletin board or wall space titled "Amazing Adjectives!"

Parts-Of-Speech Collage

Use this hands-on activity to combine reviewing parts of speech with a little bit of artistry! Divide students into teams. Assign each team a different part of speech—such as a noun, an adverb, an adjective, etc. Also supply each team with a magazine and newspaper, a 12" x 18" sheet of construction paper, scissors, and glue. Direct the team to search its magazine and newspaper for words and pictures that represent its part of speech. Instruct the team to arrange its words and pictures in collage fashion on the sheet of construction paper. If desired have each team add its own decorative examples to the sheet. After each team shares its collage, store it along with the others for future parts-of-speech lessons.

Super Sentence Grab Bag

Add an element of surprise to your next review of combining sentences. Write different sentences on separate slips of paper, repeating subjects and predicates on more than one slip. Make two slips for each student. Place the slips in a brown paper lunch bag. Then have each student pull two slips from the bag. Have each student, in turn, read her two slips, then combine the two sentences into one. For instance, if the student pulls the sentences "Maria ate a piece of apple pie at the carnival" and "Maria rode the roller coaster at the carnival three times," she might say, "At the carnival, Maria ate a piece of apple pie and rode the roller coaster three times." If necessary help students correct any problems with subject-verb agreement. With this quick review, combining sentences will be in the bag for your students.

Maria ate a piece of apple pie at the carnival.

Maria rode the roller coaster at the carnival three times.

Parts-Of-Speech Word Wall

If your students often hit a brick wall when it comes to identifying a vocabulary word's part of speech, try this simple activity. On a large sheet of bulletin-board paper, draw a brick-like wall pattern with one block for each student. Leave a blank space below the wall for a key. Create the key, designating a different color for each part of speech you are studying (for example, red = noun, blue = adjective, yellow = verb, etc.). Post the paper on a wall or bulletin board, placing a container of markers by it. Then, as your class reads a classroom story or novel, have each student write both a vocabulary word and the sentence in which that word was found within one of the blocks. After a lesson on the different parts of speech, have each student choose one word listed on the wall. Direct the student to identify the vocabulary word's part of speech (in the context of the recorded sentence) by shading the block the corresponding color in the key. Follow up the activity by giving each student a copy of "Packing Up Parts Of Speech" on page 149.

wisps
In the morning the chill was more pronounced, and he could see tiny wisps of steam from his breath.

Pitching Punctuation Marks

When it comes to punctuation, your students will be on the mark with this idea! Divide students into nine groups; then assign each group a different punctuation mark from pages 144–145. Give each group a large sheet of chart paper, a marker, and these instructions:

1. Look in your English or language-arts book to find the rules for using your assigned punctuation mark.
2. Find a sample word or sentence to accompany each rule and write them on chart paper.
3. Use your chart to teach the class the rules for using that punctuation mark.

Next write several sample sentences on the chalkboard, omitting all punctuation marks. Also label a supply of index cards, each with a different punctuation mark. Distribute one card to each student. Read aloud a sentence on the chalkboard, directing each student who has a card labeled with a punctuation mark that belongs in that sentence to stand. Instruct the students sitting in their seats to agree or disagree with those who are standing. Repeat this procedure with each sentence written on the chalkboard.

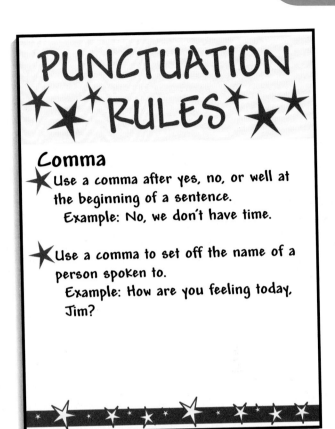

PUNCTUATION RULES

Comma

★ Use a comma after yes, no, or well at the beginning of a sentence.
   Example: No, we don't have time.

★ Use a comma to set off the name of a person spoken to.
   Example: How are you feeling today, Jim?

Telling Telegrams

Telegram

We're in sunny Florida stop Having a great time stop Been to beautiful beaches, super shopping centers, and marvelous museums stop Look forward to coming home stop Will bring lots of pictures stop See you soon stop The McLaurins

Reinforce students' use of ending punctuation with this telling idea! Write on the chalkboard several sample telegram messages such as the one shown. Share the messages with your students, explaining that a *telegram* is a message that is received over an electric transmission and is then written out on paper. Further explain that the message is usually made up of very short sentences that end with the word *stop* instead of a period. Guide your students to conclude that without the word *stop* ending a sentence, it would be difficult to read the message. Have your students brainstorm situations—such as during a vacation or an emergency situation—in which a telegram might be sent. Write your students' responses on the chalkboard. Then give each student a 5" x 7" index card. Direct the student to choose one of the situations discussed, then write a message on the front of the card using the word *stop* in place of each period. Pair your students; then have each student read his message to his partner. Direct the partner to copy the message on the back of his index card, replacing each *stop* with a period. Finally have the partners check each other's messages.

Quotable Quotes

Which topics do people talk or give advice about the most? Have your students identify these subject areas—such as *money, education,* and *happiness*—as you record them on the chalkboard. Then write several famous quotes on the chalkboard (see the examples at the right) and discuss their meanings with your students. Explain to students that a quotation mark is used to show a direct quotation (see reference page 144). Use the examples to explain the rules for using quotation and punctuation marks in a quoted sentence. Next give each student a sentence strip and a colorful marker, directing her to choose one of the topics listed on the board. Pair your students; then have each student in the pair dictate a quote about her topic to her partner. Instruct the partner to record and punctuate the quote on her sentence strip. Afterward have the students in each pair share each other's quotations with the class. Display the quotes on a wall or bulletin board titled "Our Most Quotable Quotes."

➤ Benjamin Franklin said, "A penny saved is a penny earned."

➤ "A book," says an old Chinese proverb, "is like a garden carried in the pocket."

➤ "Most folks are about as happy as they make up their minds to be," said Abraham Lincoln.

"Saving money," said Matthew, "is very important."

"A good education is the key to a bright future," said Marsha.

Who Said That?

Challenge your students to combine their favorite book characters with a little bit of imagination for a fun-filled lesson on writing quotations. Write the following quoted sentence on the chalkboard: " 'This jar of honey is simply delicious!' said Winnie the Pooh." Use the sentence to discuss with students the rules for punctuating quotations. Next ask students which word, besides *said,* could be used in the sentence to identify the speaker. Expect a response such as *exclaimed, cried,* or *shouted*. Record your students' responses on a large sheet of chart paper. Next direct each student to choose a favorite character from a book or movie and to think of something the character might say. Then have a student volunteer write a quote on the chalkboard, omitting the quotation marks and the speaker identification phrase. Next direct a different student to identify the speaker of that sentence by adding an identification phrase—using one of the words for *said* from the chart—and then punctuate the sentence. Finally have the original writer of the sentence tell if the quotation was identified and written correctly.

"Frobscottle," bellowed the BFG, "is the best drink in the world!"

"Wilbur is a terrific pig," remarked Charlotte.

Capitalization—It Rules!

What student doesn't enjoy hanging up decorative posters? Put this interest to use—and strengthen skills in capitalization—by having your students create posters highlighting capitalization rules. Using their English texts for help, have your students list various capitalization rules on the chalkboard. (Refer to the capitalization rules on page 146 if needed.) Divide your students into groups of four; then give each group a sheet of poster board and markers or colored pencils. Direct each team to pretend it has been asked by an educational company to design an eye-catching poster about capitalization rules that also features an example of each rule. After each team completes and shares its poster, invite other teachers to display one of the posters in his or her classroom

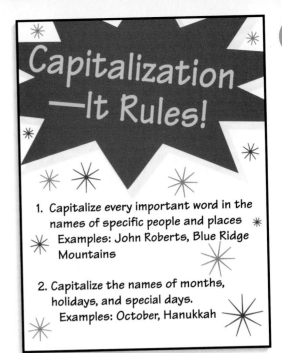

Capitalization —It Rules!

1. Capitalize every important word in the names of specific people and places
   Examples: John Roberts, Blue Ridge Mountains

2. Capitalize the names of months, holidays, and special days.
   Examples: October, Hanukkah

SPELLING

Tune In To Spelling

Keep your students tuned in to spelling each week with this fun and easy organizer. Provide each student with a file folder, a ruler, a pencil, scissors, and markers or colored pencils. Direct the student to write her name on the tab of the folder and "Tune In To Spelling" at the top of the folder. Next have the student draw a 3" x 3" square in the center of the folder, then draw a larger square around that square to create a television set as shown. Instruct the student to add details to and decorate the TV set; then have her cut along both vertical lines of the inside square.

Catherine Smith
Tune In To Spelling
vacuum
reliable

After introducing the week's spelling words, give each student a sentence strip. Then guide her through the steps below to complete the organizer.

1. Use a marker to divide the sentence strip into three-inch segments (front and back).
2. Write a spelling word in each segment.
3. Weave the sentence strip from the back of the top leaf of the file folder, up through the right slit, and down through the left slit.
4. Pull the strip across the screen to study each spelling word.

For added practice, duplicate a copy of the "Tune In To Spelling" contract on page 150 for each student. Direct her to keep the contract inside her folder along with any completed work.

WORD SKILLS

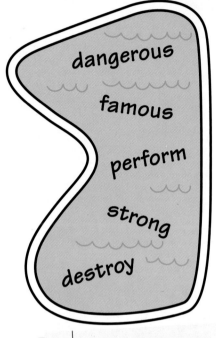

dangerous
famous
perform
strong
destroy

Dip Into
Synonyms And Antonyms

Get your students to take a dip into synonyms and antonyms while giving them practice with analogies. Draw two large swimming-pool shapes on the chalkboard. Fill the first pool with a list of vocabulary words that your students are currently studying. Fill the second pool with a synonym or antonym (see page 148) for each vocabulary word. Then use the words from the pools to write incomplete analogies on the chalkboard (see the examples below). Direct each student to complete each analogy using a synonym or antonym from the pool. Afterward have your students share their answers. Finally pair your students, having the pairs pool their knowledge to create more analogies using different synonyms and antonyms. To provide additional practice with synonyms, see the reproducible activity on page 151.

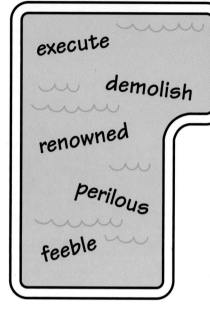

execute
demolish
renowned
perilous
feeble

Dangerous is to perilous as destroy is to _____.

Famous is to _____ as perform is to execute.

Hopping-Good Homophones

stare
stair
paws
pause

If you feel that dangling a carrot in front of your students will get them to use the right homophone, then try this activity! Gather a supply of index cards, one for each student. Write one commonly misused homophone (see page 148) on each card. Write a humorous fill-in-the-blank sentence for each word on a sheet of paper. (See the sample sentences below.)

Next mix up the cards and give a different card to each student. Read one of the silly sentences aloud. Have the student with the appropriate word card hop up and share that word. Extend the activity by having each student write a humorous story with a rabbit as the main character. Challenge the student to misuse as many homophones as possible in his story. Have each student exchange papers with a classmate; then have students correct one another's homophone mistakes.

Bernadette Bunny was sitting on the _____ steps eating a celery sandwich.

Rodney Rabbit held a piece of carrot candy in his _____.

Etymology—It's In The Bag!

Turn your study of word origins into a relay game that your students will love! Gather five brown lunch bags. Label each bag with a different team name or number. Then choose 15 words with origins other than English. Write each word inside a paper-bag outline on the chalkboard. On a sheet of paper, write a clue that contains the origin and meaning of each word (see the example). Make five copies of the clue sheet; then cut the clues on each sheet into strips, keeping the original sheet as an answer key. Place one set of 15 different clue strips in each bag.

To play:

1. Divide your class into five teams.
2. Assign each team a different bag; then place the bags where each team can access them easily.
3. Explain that the *etymology* of each word listed on the board is in its bag.
4. Tell each team that its objective is to pull a strip from its bag and write the word from the board that matches the clue on the strip. (Any team may use a dictionary for help.)
5. As quickly as a team matches a clue to its word, have it say, "etymology"; then check that team's groupings for accuracy.
6. If all a team's matches are correct, have its members wait while the other teams finish.
7. If a team's matches are not correct, direct that team to correct them.
8. After all teams have finished, discuss each word in turn.
9. Reward the first team that correctly matched each word to its origin and meaning with a small treat.

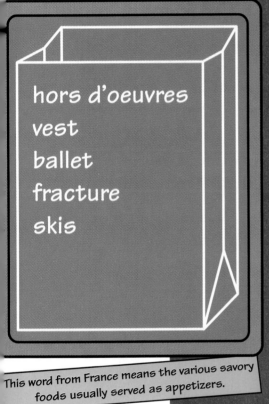

hors d'oeuvres
vest
ballet
fracture
skis

This word from France means the various savory foods usually served as appetizers.

Weave A Word Web

Help your students understand the structure of base words with this web-wise activity. Cut out a large circle from construction paper. Label that circle "base words"; then post it on a large wall or bulletin board. Next cut out ten medium-size circles and a supply of smaller circles—five to ten more than the number of students in your class. Label each medium-size circle with a different base word; then attach each medium-size circle to the larger circle with string or yarn to create a web. Put the smaller circles aside.

Challenge each student to find a different word built from one of the posted base words. Direct her to write that word and its meaning on one of the smaller circles and connect it to the appropriate base-word circle with yarn. Extend this activity by tracing a class supply of a spider outline onto black construction paper. Each time a student identifies ten appropriate words, write her name on the spider with chalk and attach it to the web. Reward each student who achieves "spider status" on the word web with a special treat.

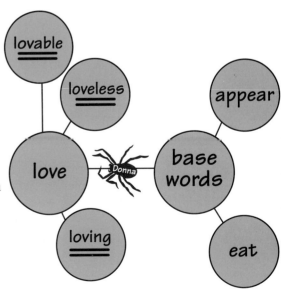

lovable
loveless
appear
love
base words
Donna
loving
eat

READING

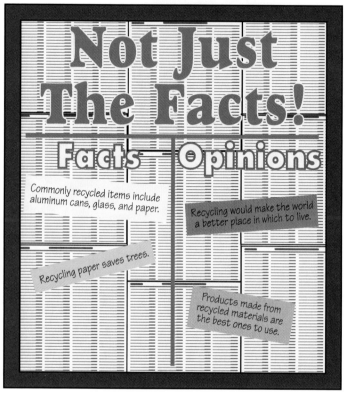

Not Just The Facts!

Give your students the scoop on fact and opinion with this simple newspaper activity. Cover a bulletin board or wall space with sheets of newspaper. Label one side of the board "Facts" and the other side "Opinions." Then find one statement of fact and one statement of opinion in a newspaper article. Write each statement on a different sentence strip. Share the sentences with your students and have them explain the difference between a fact and an opinion. (A *fact* can be proven to be true; an *opinion* is what someone believes to be true.) Place the sentence strips on the appropriate sides of the bulletin board.

Pair your students; then give each pair a section from a newspaper, a marker, and two sentence strips. Direct each pair to search its newspaper section for statements of fact and opinion; then instruct the pair to write an example of each type of statement on a sentence strip. After each pair shares its examples, post them on the appropriate side of the bulletin board.

Creative Cause And Effect

Think of all the different excuses for not having an assignment completed you've ever heard from students. Then follow the steps below to offer your students a chance to give you some truly creative excuses!

1. Explain that a *cause* and an *effect* go together—whenever there is a cause or reason, there is a result or effect.
2. Write the list of sample effects and appropriate connecting words at the right on the chalkboard.
3. Discuss how some connecting words signal a cause, and others signal an effect. For example, "*Because* I looked for my dog after he ran away, I didn't study for my science test" or "My little sister spilled chocolate pudding on my homework last night, *so* I don't have it today."
4. Have student volunteers use the lists to create several cause-and-effect sentences.
5. Afterward give each student an 8 1/2" x 11" sheet of white paper. Challenge her to come up with a clever cause for one of the effects listed on the board.
6. Next have her write a cause-and-effect sentence on her paper, draw an accompanying illustration, and share her resulting—and entertaining—excuse with the class. Afterward, if desired, give each student a copy of "Penelope's Perilous Party!" on page 152 to complete as directed.

Effects

- don't have my homework
- was talking
- forgot to study for a science test
- didn't finish my book report
- don't have a pencil
- got sent to the principal's office
- was running in the hallway
- can't remember my multiplication tables
- missed the bus
- am not sitting In my own seat

Connecting Words For:

Causes: because, since, as, whenever, if
Effects: resulted in, as a result, consequently, for this reason, therefore, so, so that

Get The Idea?

Turn tissue boxes into handy sorting centers for practice with spotting main ideas and supporting details. Attach a pocket labeled with a different main-idea sentence to each side of an empty tissue box. Label a supply of tagboard strips—at least three for each main idea—with a different detail sentence. Store these strips in the center of the box. Place the box at a center along with a self-checking key. Have each student who visits the center pull out the strips, place each strip in the correct pocket, and check for accuracy. For additional practice, duplicate a copy of "I've Got Your Number!" on page 154 for each student to complete.

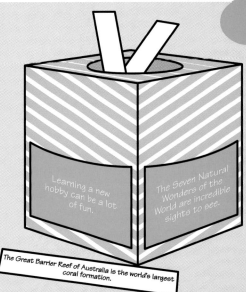

Learning a new hobby can be a lot of fun.

The Seven Natural Wonders of the World are incredible sights to see.

The Great Barrier Reef of Australia is the world's largest coral formation.

Picture-Perfect Inferences

Help your students develop a better understanding of making inferences with the following picture-perfect activity. Cut several pictures from magazines and share them with your class. As you share each picture, ask a question about it such as, "Where is this person going?" Have each student answer the question and list on a sheet of paper the clues in the picture that helped him infer the answer. After showing all the pictures, have each student share his responses. Explain to your students that their responses were similar because of what they inferred from the picture clues and the similarity of their own experiences. Tell students that just as in the pictures, the stories we read contain information that may not always be stated directly. Explain that readers often have to use sentence clues and personal experiences to fully understand what is read. Follow up the activity by duplicating a copy of "Get The Hint?" on page 153 for each student.

Concluding Comics

You'll have your students drawing all sorts of conclusions with this comical activity! Search through newspapers and cut out several comic strips with at least three sequence boxes. White-out the caption in each box. Add a new caption that gives a humorous clue about what is happening in the picture of each box, leaving the last box's caption blank. Do this for each comic strip. Next glue and laminate each comic strip to a different sheet of construction paper. Place these sheets at a center along with a wipe-off marker. Instruct the student to use the clues in the captions of each comic strip to write a concluding caption for the last box.

Extend this activity by having each student choose one of the comic-strip characters for creating his own concluding comic. Post your students' comics around the classroom to tickle a few funny bones!

LITERARY DEVICES

It Figures!

Figure it's time to add a little zip to your students' writings? Explain to students that *figurative language* helps a person communicate a clear and interesting picture with words and is often humorous. Share several forms of figurative language—such as those listed below—with your students, giving an example of each form. (Also see the idioms on page 147.) Then give each student a 4" x 11" sheet of white paper and instruct her to create an original figurative expression. Have the student write her expression in the form of an illustrated newspaper headline. Finally have her share her headline, explain its meaning, and tell which type of figurative language it represents. Post all the headlines on a wall or bulletin board titled "Hilarious Headlines." Extend this activity by challenging each student to write an article detailing *who, what, when, where, why* and/or *how* about a chosen headline.

- **Idiom**—an expression that means something other than the usual meaning of the words
  Example: Since it's raining cats and dogs, you'd better take your umbrella!
- **Simile**—compares two unlike things using *like* or *as*
  Example: My mouth is as dry as a desert.
- **Metaphor**—compares two unlike things directly
  Example: Her heart is an ice cube.
- **Hyperbole**—an exaggerated comparison
  Example: Annie was so hot she melted.

You Don't Say?

Combine a study of animals with the thrilling sensation of sound. Share with your students the different devices that writers use to make their sentences sound more pleasing (see the examples). Next have your students brainstorm a list of unusual animals. Record students' responses on the chalkboard. Then place a five-foot sheet of bulletin-board paper, colorful markers, and various reference materials on a large table. Challenge each student to use the reference materials to find an interesting fact about one of the animals listed. On the bulletin-board paper, have him write a sentence about that animal using one of the devices you shared. If desired, direct each student to draw a colorful illustration to accompany his sentence. After each student has added his sentence to the paper, display the banner; then invite each student, in turn, to share his sensational sentence about an amazing animal with the class.

- **Alliteration**—the repetition of beginning consonant sounds
  Example: The sidewinder snake slithers silently on the sand.
- **Assonance**—the repetition of vowel sounds in words
  Example: Explain how rain makes the pavement dangerous.
- **Consonance**—the repetition of consonant sounds anywhere in words
  Example: Remember to put the baby in the crib.
- **Onomatopoeia**—words whose meanings sound like their pronunciations
  Example: A honeybee buzzes.

Amazing Animals

The sidewinder snake slithers silently on the sand.

A honeybee buzzes.

Ants are organized animals.

A three-toed sloth eats tree leaves.

PUBLIC SPEAKING and RESEARCH

Speechless? Not For Long!

Does the thought of speaking in front of a group have your students tongue-tied? Help each student get over her nervousness by having her share a familiar story of her choice. First discuss the keys to a successful speech: speaking in a loud, clear voice; speaking expressively and with inflection; using complete sentences; and maintaining eye contact with the audience. Also discuss how using props helps clarify and add interest to a speech. Next instruct each student to choose a story to share (see the list below).

Provide each student with an index card and various art supplies. Direct the student to write notes for her speech on a 3" x 5" index card. Also have her prepare a small prop. Suggest that she first practice alone; then assign her to a small group for presenting her speech. Have each group evaluate its members' speeches, in turn, using the criteria described above.

Can't Think Of Anything To Share? Then...

→ Tell a favorite joke.
→ Recite a tongue twister, poem, or limerick.
→ Share a fairy tale.
→ Retell a fable or tall tale.
→ Recount a mystery or ghost story.
→ Tell about a TV show, movie, or sports game.
→ Narrate an important personal event or a favorite family story.

> There once was an old man named Rick,
> Whose favorite pet was a tick.
> When they walked out at night,
> The whole town would take flight
> From that feeble old man named Rick.

AROUND THE WORLD

Put a different spin on using reference books with this hands-on activity. Gently spin a globe. In turn, direct each student to place her index finger on the spinning globe, slowly causing it to stop. When the globe stops, have her name the country at the spot where her finger is pointing and consider that country to be her assigned topic. Afterward give each student a sheet of 9" x 12" light-colored construction paper, markers or colored pencils, and an atlas or encyclopedia. Have each student pretend that she is a geographic researcher who has been given the task of exploring her assigned country for the purpose of creating a travel poster. Direct her to design the poster so that it creatively provides five important facts about her country—such as the region or continent in which the country is located, its latitude and longitude, its capital, its population, and its major landforms and waterways. Have students share their posters; then display them around the room as prompts for journal writing or for writing persuasive and descriptive paragraphs.

If desired, follow up this activity by having students complete the "Where In The World?" reproducible on page 155. Or duplicate "The ABCs Of Report Writing" on page 156 and guide your students through the steps of a full-fledged research project!

Punctuation Rules

Use a period:
- **at the end of a declarative sentence—a sentence that makes a statement**
  I enjoy playing basketball.
- **at the end of an imperative sentence—a sentence that makes a request**
  Please bring me that measuring cup.
- **after a person's initials**
  A. J. Wydell
- **after an abbreviation**
  Mrs. Jones
  Dr. McIntosh

Use a question mark:
- **at the end of an interrogative sentence—a sentence that asks a question**
  What number does Mike Smith wear?

Use an exclamation point:
- **to express strong feeling or emotion**
  Ouch!
  Leave me alone!
  Wow!

Use quotation marks:
- **to show a direct quotation**
  Jennifer said, "I am going to the movies with Carrie."
- **to show the titles of written works—poems, plays, stories, or songs**
  "West Side Story"
  "America the Beautiful"

Use an apostrophe:
- **to show that one or more letters have been left out to form a contraction**
  can't—can not
  won't—will not
  don't—do not
- **to show possession**
  Carolyn's keys are in the car.
  The boys' game was over an hour ago.

Use a hyphen:
- **to divide a word between syllables at the end of a line**
  The automobile sales-
  man is named Mr. Sears.
- **to join parts of some compound words**
  drive-in, father-in-law
- **to write number words from 21 through 99**
  twenty-one

(Continued on the next page)

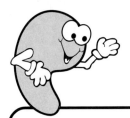

Punctuation Rules

Use a comma:

- **to separate items in a date or address**
  August 22, 1970
  Bardstown, Kentucky 40051

- **after the greeting and closing of a letter**
  Dear Andrew,
  Yours truly,

- **to separate words or phrases in a series**
  Sharon bought eggs, bread, and milk at the store.

- **with quotations to set off the exact words of the speaker from the rest of the sentence**
  Jimmy said, "I want to visit my niece in North Carolina."

- **to separate a noun of direct address from the rest of the sentence**
  Rob, did your team win the hockey game last night?

- **to separate a long clause or phrase from the independent clause following it**
  As I was walking on the beach, I found several conch shells.
  When Jeff bought his new car, he sold his old one.

- **to join two simple sentences into a compound sentence**
  Madeline went to sleep, but Mackenzie stayed up to watch television.

- **to set off an *appositive***
  (a word or phrase that renames the noun or pronoun before it)
  Adrienne, a great gymnast, won first place at the meet.

- **with an *interrupter*** (a word, phrase, or clause that interrupts the main thought of a sentence) Swimming, I feel, is the best exercise.
  In the end, however, Carlin couldn't come to the party.

- **when writing the last name first**
  Lundein, Gregory

Use a colon:

- **after the salutation of a business letter**
  Dear Mr. Metcalf:

- **in writing times**
  3:45

- **before a list or series**
  There were three contestants: Angela, Sarah, and Jackie.

- **after the speaker in a play or dialogue**
  Nicholas: When are we leaving?
  Alex: We leave in about 20 minutes.

Use a semicolon:

- **between the independent clauses of a compound sentence when a conjunction is not used**
  Martin washed the car; John waxed it.
  Beverly and Michael went to Hawaii; they stayed there for two weeks.

Capitalization Rules

To *capitalize* means to begin a word with a capital letter. The following items should always be capitalized:

- **the first word in a sentence**
  <u>W</u>e went to the store yesterday.

- **proper nouns**
  names of people
  <u>B</u>everly <u>C</u>leary

  geographic names
  <u>N</u>ew <u>J</u>ersey
  <u>J</u>upiter
  <u>E</u>urope
  <u>H</u>illside <u>S</u>treet
  <u>M</u>ississippi <u>R</u>iver

  historic events
  <u>S</u>tamp <u>A</u>ct
  <u>C</u>ivil <u>W</u>ar

  names of days or months
  <u>W</u>ednesday
  <u>D</u>ecember

  national and local holidays
  <u>E</u>aster

- **proper adjectives**
  <u>S</u>panish
  <u>A</u>merican

- **the pronoun *I***
  When <u>I</u> heard the news, <u>I</u> shouted for joy.

- **titles and initials**
  <u>C</u>aptain Kirk
  <u>M</u>rs. Krolikowski
  <u>R</u>. <u>J</u>. Hayes

- **words used as names**
  Will you ask <u>D</u>ad if we can go to the movies?
  We saw <u>A</u>unt <u>E</u>llie at the park.

- **first word in the greeting and closing of a letter**
  <u>D</u>ear Julie,
  <u>Y</u>our friend,

- **titles of written works (first word, last word, all main words)**
  <u>S</u>ports <u>I</u>llustrated for <u>K</u>ids
  <u>T</u>he <u>W</u>izard of <u>O</u>z

- **abbreviations**
  P.T.A.
  USA
  Dr.

Idioms

An *idiom* is a phrase which means something different than what each of its words taken one-by-one means. For example, "Hold your horses" does not mean "restrain your horses." Instead, the phrase means "wait, or slow down."

Examples:

My brother is driving me up the wall.

Barry always has a trick up his sleeve.

My friend and I don't always see eye to eye.

Ray has a frog in his throat.

Michelle cried her eyes out during the movie.

My little sister can be a pain in the neck sometimes.

I have a bone to pick with my sister.

My mother said my brother was skating on thin ice.

It is raining cats and dogs outside, so be sure to take an umbrella.

My father asked me to lend him a hand.

Jake almost bit my head off when I asked him to help me do the dishes.

I think John has lost his marbles!

I am going to be in hot water if I don't finish this assignment.

Andrew's advice to him went in one ear and out the other.

You just hit the nail right on the head!

Ben is in the doghouse.

Does this ring a bell with you?

Carrie got cold feet and wouldn't go to the haunted house with us.

I held my tongue even though I disagreed with his opinion.

I was shaking in my boots after I watched that horror show.

Ready Reference

Synonyms

(words that have similar meanings)

afraid–scared	considerate–kind	fix–repair	loud–noisy
alike–same	cry–weep	funny–humorous	many–several
angry–mad	drowsy–sleepy	happy–glad	nice–pleasant
begin–start	enjoys–likes	hard–difficult	odd–strange
buy–purchase	easy–simple	healthy–well	powerful–strong
closed–shut	false–untrue	jump–leap	story–tale
cold–chilly	find–discover	late–tardy	toss–throw
complete–finish			wonderful–great

Antonyms

(words that have opposite meanings)

above–below	crooked–straight	later–sooner	rough–smooth
absent–present	dangerous–safe	loose–tight	save–spend
accept–reject	deep–shallow	narrow–wide	sour–sweet
alike–different	destroy–repair	noisy–quiet	succeed–fail
asleep–awake	generous–selfish	open–closed	tame–wild
begin–finish	guilty–innocent	peace–war	terrible–wonderful
backward–forward	healthy–sick	polite–rude	true–false
believe–doubt			whisper–yell

Homophones (Or Homonyms)

(words that sound alike but are spelled differently and have different meanings)

ant–aunt	fair–fare	mail–male	scene–seen
ate–eight	feat–feet	meat–meet	son–sun
bare–bear	heard–herd	one–won	threw–through
beet–beat	hear–here	pair–pear	to–too–two
blew–blue	hole–whole	plain–plane	wait–weight
capital–capitol	know–no	right–write	weak–week
cent–sent–scent	loan–lone	sail–sale	wear–where
dear–deer			which–witch

148
©1997 The Education Center, Inc. • *The Mailbox® Superbook* • Grade 5 • TEC454

Packing Up Parts Of Speech

Patty Prescott is positively popping with excitement! She's packing her bags and heading to the annual Parts-Of-Speech convention. Help Patty pack her bags by putting each underlined word into the correct parts-of-speech suitcase.

Nouns
(name persons, places, or things)

Verbs
(show action or being)

Adjectives
(describe nouns or pronouns)

Adverbs
(describe verbs)

Pronouns
(take the place of nouns)

1. The <u>mouse</u> <u>swiftly</u> ran under the <u>staircase</u>.

2. Mr. Simon, the <u>librarian</u>, <u>loudly</u> told the students that <u>they</u> were too noisy.

3. <u>We</u> <u>sang</u> a <u>beautiful</u> song as the <u>bus driver</u> drove us to the zoo.

4. My <u>lazy</u> cat just eats, sleeps, and <u>quietly</u> <u>purrs</u> all day long!

5. Even though Samantha thought the race was <u>easy</u>, <u>she</u> <u>fell</u> just a <u>short</u> distance from the finish line.

6. Wow, <u>you</u> <u>ate</u> that piece of pie <u>quickly</u>!

Bonus Box: On the back of this sheet, write a sentence using any three of the underlined words above. Choose each word from a different suitcase. Underline the three words you chose.

Note To Teacher: Use with "Parts-Of-Speech Word Wall" on page 134.

Tune In To Spelling

Write your spelling words on the television screen below. Then read each of the following activities. Choose the number of activities you will complete. After completing each activity, color the box next to that task to indicate that you have finished it.

I will complete _____ activities this week.

1. Find and cut out the letters that spell each spelling word in a newspaper or magazine. Arrange the letters to spell each word; then glue the letters onto a sheet of construction paper.

2. Think of a way to classify the words on your list; then group your words according to that classification.

3. Write the letters that spell each word on index cards, a different letter on each card. Shuffle the cards, then play a game of Word Fish with a friend.

4. Create a different code for each letter of the alphabet. Spell each word in code; then give your list to a friend to solve.

5. Choose five words. Write a different sentence using the letters of each word. For example, *real:* Robin **e**agerly **a**te **l**asagna.

6. Make up a riddle for each word; then give your riddles to a friend to solve. Example: *What has four letters and rhymes with cat?* Answer: *that*

7. Practice spelling your words with your parent.

8. Write each of your words one time each. Estimate the total number of vowels and consonants in all the words on the spelling list. Then count to check the accuracy of your estimate.

9. Choose three different spelling words. Write each word in a way that illustrates its meaning.
Example: FRIGID

10. Write one sentence that contains as many of your spelling words as possible.

11. Have a friend write a list of the words, misspelling ten of them. Identify the misspelled words by circling them; then spell each word correctly.

12. Choose five different spelling words. Write each letter of each word on a different strip of construction paper. Glue the strips together to create a word chain for each word.

13. Spell each word on your list, substituting a blank for each vowel. For example, spell *docile* as d _ c _ l _. Then pair up with a classmate and solve one another's puzzles.

14. Choose five different words. For each word, write as many different rhyming words as possible. For example: *weigh: pray, convey, neigh, obey*

15. Write the letters of each word on a different index card. Shuffle the cards and place them in a paper bag. Pull out one letter at a time. Try to spell one of your words with the letters you pulled from the bag. Continue to play until you spell all of your words.

☆ = **A Star Show!**

☆ = **B Great Show!**

☆ = **C Good Show!**

©1997 The Education Center, Inc. • *The Mailbox® Superbook • Grade 5 • TEC454*

Note To The Teacher: Use with "Tune In To Spelling" on page 137. Before duplicating, program the stars on the sheet with the number of activities a student should complete to earn each grade. Provide each student with scissors, glue, markers or colored pencils, index cards, newspapers or magazines, a paper bag, and construction paper. If desired, have the student store her contract and written work in her "Tune In To Spelling" folder.

Spicy Synonyms!

Herbs such as sage, rosemary, and thyme spice up foods and make them taste better. In a similar way, descriptive words add a spicy flavor to writing! A *thesaurus* is a special book that's full of words and synonyms. Use a thesaurus to help you replace each word in bold print below with three other descriptive synonyms. Write the synonyms for each word in the blanks provided on the spice jars.

1.
We had a **good** day at the zoo.

1._____
2._____
3._____

2.
The weather outside was **nice**.

1._____
2._____
3._____

3.
I often **eat** too much food at a holiday meal.

1._____
2._____
3._____

4.
The **sad** dog slept by the bed.

1._____
2._____
3._____

5.
The circus clown was very **funny**.

1._____
2._____
3._____

6.
The **large** building rose 200 feet into the sky.

1._____
2._____
3._____

7.
The beach was covered with **beautiful** shells.

1._____
2._____
3._____

8.
I **walked** along the path to the park.

1._____
2._____
3._____

Bonus Box: Choose one synonym from three different spice jars. Use each word in a separate sentence. Write your new sentences on the back of this sheet.

Note To Teacher: Use with "Dip Into Synonyms And Antonyms" on page 138.

Name _____

Penelope's Perilous Party!

Poor Penelope—her party was a disaster! She thought she had planned quite precisely, but one thing just led to another! Follow the directions below to help Penelope figure out what caused each disaster.

Directions: Read each cause and effect statement. Match each effect to its cause by writing the appropriate letter in the blank next to that number. Then, on the back of this sheet, use the connecting words at the bottom of this page to write a sentence with *five* of your cause-and-effect matches. (You may need to rearrange, change, or add words to create your sentences.)

Example: Because her brother stuck a pin in the balloon, it popped.

Causes:

____ 1. Four invitations to Penelope's friends got lost in the mail.

____ 2. Penelope's mom said that there were hardly any decorations left at The Party Palace.

____ 3. Penelope's Doberman pinscher got loose and jumped on the table that held the cake.

____ 4. Prudence, Penelope's best friend, said that her stomach felt queasy.

____ 5. Peter put a fake snake in a gift box and gave it to Penelope.

____ 6. Paul and Perry insisted that they saw a UFO flying over the backyard.

____ 7. A freak thunderstorm caused the electricity to go out.

____ 8. Penelope's baby brother, Preston, removed the tags from two identically wrapped gifts.

____ 9. The pizza delivery person had a flat tire and was late.

____ 10. Penelope tripped over her new pair of Rollerblades®.

Effects:

A. Everyone was starving by the time the pepperoni pizza arrived.

B. Penelope's guests couldn't listen to the music recordings they had brought.

C. None of the decorations matched.

D. Prudence had to leave the party early.

E. Penelope crashed to the floor and bruised her patella.

F. Penelope screamed and knocked the punch bowl onto the floor.

G. Penelope didn't know which gift was from whom.

H. Paulette, Pamela, Parker, and Patrick didn't attend the party.

I. Chocolate cake flew from one corner of the room to the other!

J. Everyone left in the middle of Penelope's game and ran outside to look at the sky.

Connecting Words

Causes: because, since, as, whenever, if
Effects: resulted in, as a result, consequently, for this reason, therefore, so, so that

Bonus Box: Recall a humorous event in your life. Create five of your own cause-and-effect sentences to describe what happened.

Note To The Teacher: Use this sheet with "Creative Cause And Effect" on page 140.

Get The Hint?

Authors often don't tell you everything you want to know about a story. Sometimes you have to use sentence clues and your own experiences to figure things out for yourself. Read each of the sentences below. Use the clues that describe each situation to help you answer the question that follows it. Underline the clues; then write your answer on the line provided on each file folder.

1. The students in Mrs. Adams's class are helping her decorate for the upcoming month's holidays. They've put up red heart-shaped cutouts, pictures of Abraham Lincoln and George Washington, and biographical posters of famous African-Americans.
   Question: For which month are the students decorating?

2. Jason was very excited about his new adventure. He quickly put on his goggles and fins, then jumped into the crystal-clear water.
   Question: In what kind of adventure is Jason participating?

3. With her heart thumping, Leslie stepped up to the podium and shuffled the notecards in her hand. The audience quietly waited for her to begin.
   Question: What is Leslie preparing to do?

4. The only sounds in the quiet room were the opening and closing of books, the shuffling of papers, and the occasional cough of an occupant. The rows of shelves were filled with an assortment of books, magazines, and reference materials.
   Question: What type of room is this?

5. John knew he'd have to hide his mother's present. But where would he hide it? His mother would certainly identify the floral fragrance. He couldn't put it in a drawer—it would get crushed; besides that, he needed to keep it in water so it wouldn't wilt.
   Question: What is the present John has for his mother?

6. "I can't believe your parents stuck you with that job again!" Chris said to his friend. "Think of all of the things you have to do—feeding, changing diapers, and reading a bedtime story. Yuck!"
   Question: What job does Chris's friend have to do?

7. The man in the lab coat adjusted the lens of the microscope so he could clearly see the specimens wriggling on the slide. He told his assistant to hold all his calls so he could continue his work.
   Question: What kind of work does this man do?

8. As the young girl rested her head on the cushioned seat, she was offered a drink and a snack. Suddenly there was an abrupt jerking movement and she noticed a flashing message that warned her to fasten her seat belt.
   Question: Where is the young girl?

Bonus Box: Write a paragraph with a question like the ones above to give to a classmate. Be sure to include at least three clues to help your classmate figure out the correct answer.

Note To The Teacher: Use with "Picture-Perfect Inferences" on page 141.   153

I've Got Your Number!

Dan Doolittle is truly a dog lover. You could say it's his business to love dogs because Dan earns his money by dog-sitting. This week Dan's neighbors are on vacation so he is watching their dogs Buster, Mel, Little Bit, Tabitha, and Samantha. Dan is supposed to leave a note describing each dog's behavior for the week, but he's been so busy that he forgot to write a main-idea sentence.

Directions: Help Dan match each main-idea sentence with one of the five paragraphs below. Write the letter of the matching main-idea sentence in the space provided on the dog bowl.

Remember: A main-idea sentence identifies the topic of a paragraph. It ties the detail sentences together with the topic.

Main-Idea Sentences:
A. Buster is basically just a big bully.
B. Mel has been quite mischievous.
C. A little bit lazy is how I'd describe Little Bit.
D. Tabitha is a talkative tattletale.
E. Samantha is supremely snobby.

1 She slept every day until 10:00 A.M. and couldn't manage to clean up her mess after finishing her food. Then one day after delaying our walk because of a three-hour nap, she insisted that she could go only as far as the fire hydrant at the corner of the block.

2 The first thing he did was to hide the *Dandy Dog* shampoo in the dishwasher. Then when I saw that someone had had an accident on the kitchen floor, he pointed his paw at one of the other dogs. Oh, and after I wrote this note, he attempted to tear it up with his teeth.

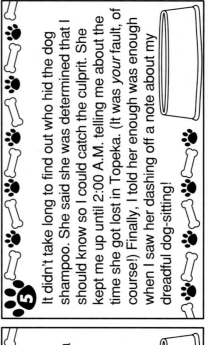

3 Talk about a temper! She practically bit my head off when I told her I couldn't comb her hair! When I told her the *Dandy Dog* shampoo was gone, she demanded I go buy some more. And boy, what a dazzling diamond she has on her dog tag!

4 Fighting the others in order to be first in line for food was his favorite pastime. Then, on a picnic at the park, he terrorized a terrier and took her dog treat. But the last straw was when we went out for a walk. He bit Boo-Boo, your neighbor's dog.

5 It didn't take long to find out who hid the dog shampoo. She said she was determined that I should know so I could catch the culprit. She kept me up until 2:00 A.M. telling me about the time she got lost in Topeka. (It was *your* fault, of course!) Finally, I told her enough was enough when I saw her dashing off a note about my dreadful dog-sitting!

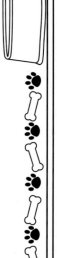

Bonus Box: Do you know a dog with a unique personality? Write a paragraph describing this dog. Be sure to include a topic sentence and three detail sentences that support your main idea.

©1997 The Education Center, Inc. • *The Mailbox® Superbook • Grade 5* • TEC454 • Key p. 317

Note To The Teacher: Use with "Get The Idea?" on page 141.

Name _____

Where In The World?

Directions: Choose a country or state to research. Use reference books—such as an atlas, an encyclopedia, and an almanac—to find information on the topics shown. Then follow the directions below for creating a clue booklet about your country or state.

Step 1: Write your facts on the lines provided.
Step 2: Color and cut out the patterns. Use a hole puncher to make a hole in the top of each pattern. Assemble the patterns with a brad so that the "Where In The World?" pattern is on top.
Step 3: Exchange your booklet with a classmate to see if he or she can determine the name of your country or state. Have that classmate write his or her answer on the back of your booklet.
Step 4: Check your classmate's answer. If it is incorrect, help your classmate find the correct answer.

Location: _____

To the north: _____   To the south: _____

To the east: _____   To the west: _____

Geography and climate: _____

_____

Nearest body of water: _____

Nearest geographic feature: _____

Language(s) spoken: _____

Population: _____

Other features: _____

_____

Bonus Box: On another sheet of paper, write a paragraph briefly explaining why you would or would not like to live in the place described above.

WHERE IN THE WORLD?

Note To The Teacher: Use after "Around The World" on page 143 or as an independent activity. Supply each student with appropriate reference materials, scissors, a hole puncher, crayons, and a brad.

The ABCs Of Report Writing

So—you've been assigned a report, and you're not sure how to begin? Learning the steps of writing a report is as simple as learning your ABCs! Read the information listed beside each block below. Then, as you complete each part of your report, color that block to show that you've completed that step.

Assemble Resources **A**

After you've chosen a topic that interests you, head for the library to gather information about it. Research reference books—such as dictionaries, encyclopedias, almanacs, and atlases—and other nonfiction books on your topic.

Begin Note Taking **B**

Write down questions that you have about your topic. Write each question on a different index card. Then use the resources you gathered to research the answers to your questions. Write your answers, or notes, on each index card using short sentences that are in your own words.

Construct An Outline **C**

Plan your report by making an outline. First write the topic of your report as the title. Think of the topic of each question on your notecards as a main idea on your outline. Decide which main idea you will tell about first and write it next to Roman numeral I. Write your second main idea next to Roman numeral II, and so on. Then, under each main idea, write the answers to your questions as details. Write each detail next to a different capital letter: A, B, C, and so on.

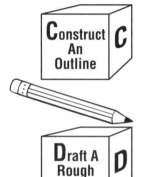

Draft A Rough Copy **D**

Read the first main idea in your outline. Write it as the topic sentence of your first paragraph. Then use the details in your outline to add sentences that give details about that main idea. Start a new paragraph for each new main idea and supporting details.

Edit And Revise **E**

Read your report to yourself and think about how you could improve it. Ask yourself questions such as those shown below. Use editing marks to make changes on your paper.
- Do I have interesting main-idea sentences, and did I indent each new paragraph?
- Do my details tell more about the main-idea sentences?
- Did I use my own words, and are my sentences clear and complete?
- Did I spell my words correctly?
- Did I use punctuation marks correctly?

Finalize Your Paper **F**

Type or neatly write a final copy of your work. Check the copy one last time for correct spelling, capitalization, and punctuation. Place your report in a cover to keep it neat and organized.

Give Others Credit **G**

Make a *bibliography,* or list, of the sources you used to write your report. List your sources alphabetically by the author's last name (or by the title if no author is given). Follow the example that shows an entry's correct order, capitalization, and punctuation. Place the bibliography at the end of your report.

For a book: Author (last name, first name). Title (underlined). City where the book was published: Name of publisher, copyright date. Example: Kroll, Steven. Pony Express! New York: Scholastic Inc., 1996.

Note: Ask your teacher or media specialist for help in writing a bibliography entry for an encyclopedia, a magazine, a film, and a pamphlet.

Hold A Presentation **H**

Remember your audience! Look at your listeners as you share your report. Speak slowly and clearly. Create a visual—such as a poster, graph, or model—to make your presentation more exciting.

Note To The Teacher: Use after "Around The World" on page 143. Or provide each student with a copy to use as a guide whenever an independent research project is assigned.

WRITING

Writing

Introducing The Writing Process

An acrostic is a great way to help your students remember the steps of the writing process. Copy the acrostic in the illustration onto a poster. Then display the poster in your classroom as a visual reference for your students. If desired give your students copies of the reproducibles on pages 174, 175, and 176 to use when they write.

People—Prewrite
Find—First Draft
Reading—Revise
Educational—Edit and Proofread
Fun—Final Copy
and
Interesting—Illustrate

Stop, In The Name Of Writing!

This eye-catching visual should definitely get your students' attention when they write! From white construction paper, cut the letters *S, T, O,* and *P.* Glue the letters in the center of a red octagon-shaped cutout. Next glue the stop sign near the top of a sheet of poster board. Then list the questions below the stop sign as shown.

Does what you've written make sense?
Do you have a topic sentence?
Did you indent each paragraph?
Did you use capital letters where they were needed?
Did you punctuate correctly where needed? Is your
   paper neatly written?
If you answered yes to all these questions, *GO* ahead
   and turn in your writing!

Keeping Up With The Stages

This simple organizational tip will help you quickly and efficiently keep track of your students' writing progress. Cut all but the bottom 4 1/2 inches from six half-gallon cardboard milk cartons; then cover each bottom section with Con-Tact® paper. Label each covered carton bottom with a different stage of the writing process—*Prewrite, First Draft, Revise, Edit and Proofread, Final Copy,* and *Illustrate*—as shown. Give each student in your class one tongue depressor. Have the student write her name on one side of the tongue depressor with a permanent fine-tipped marker. Then provide the student with two movable eyes and an assortment of arts-and-crafts materials with which to decorate the back side of her depressor. Before beginning your writing class, have each student place her depressor in the carton that tells where she is in the writing process. With a glance you will be able to check an individual student's progress without interrupting the whole class!

Creative Story-Map Forms

Instead of relying on a standard story-map form, add a little creativity to your next story-planning session. Draw and label one of the story maps in the illustration on a poster. Ask your students to study the map to see if it seems to have the shape of an animal, a person, or an alien. Poll students to get suggestions for naming the story-map shape; then allow your students to vote to select a name. Record that name on the poster. Then display the poster on a classroom wall for use as a visual reference each time your students plan new stories. If desired, periodically sponsor a contest to create a new story-map shape for the class to use.

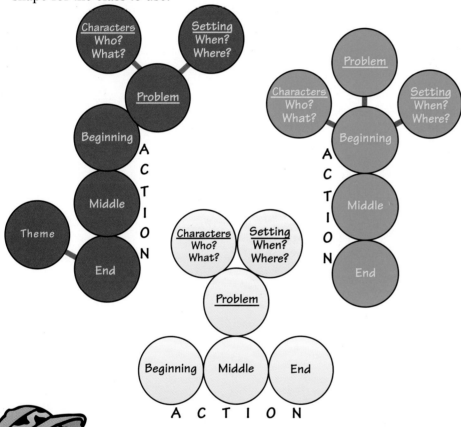

Chair To Share?

Making sure that all your budding authors have opportunities to share their work has never been easier than with this idea! Designate a special chair in your classroom to serve as your "Author's Share Chair." Use a permanent black marker to list each student's name on a dry-erase board. Attach a dry-erase pen to the board; then post the board near the chair. When a student decides to share her writing with the rest of the class, direct her to circle her name on the board. Either at the beginning or end of your scheduled writing time, allow several students whose names are circled to share their writings. After each student shares, make a check beside her name to show that she has shared. When all the names have been checked, erase the board and begin again. What a great way to ensure that everyone has a chance to be heard!

Editing Safari

Students love to point out errors in someone else's work! Direct that energy into positive behavior by inviting all your students to join in strengthening proofreading skills. Duplicate a class supply of the form on page 177. Post one form at a time in a conspicuous place in the classroom. Whenever a student thinks she sights an error, allow her to write the error—along with her proposed correction—in a space on the form. Clarify with the class that only the first student to spot a particular error may post it on the form. As one form fills with entries, respond in writing or one-on-one to each student editor who proposed a correction. Use that opportunity to commend a correctly spotted error or to explain a mistake. If desired give each student editor a bonus point or a small treat for every correct response she made.

Clustering Ideas

Demonstrate the usefulness of organizing ideas for writing with this colorful activity. Explain that *clustering* is a method of organizing ideas before writing. Give each student one sheet of 11" x 14" newsprint and 13 die-cut construction-paper circles—one red, four blue, and eight yellow. Then direct each student to follow the steps below.

1. Write your writing topic on the red circle and glue it to the center of your newsprint.

2. Write four supporting details about your topic, each detail on a different blue circle.

3. Glue each blue circle to the newsprint around the red circle.

4. Draw a line from the red circle to each blue circle.

5. Elaborate on every supporting detail by writing additional information on each of the yellow circles.

6. Glue each yellow circle around its corresponding blue circle, drawing a line from each yellow circle to the blue circle.

7. Refer to the organizer to write a paragraph.

If desired, give each student a copy of page 178 as another aid. Students should see how much easier writing is with a little organization!

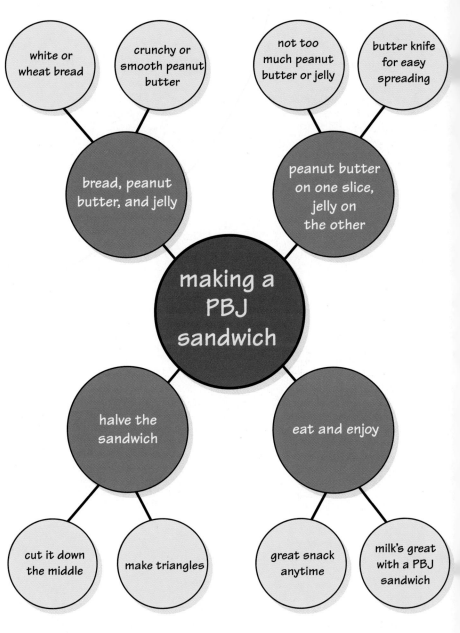

Hitting The High Notes Of Note Taking

Your students should hum the sweet tune of success with this lesson on note taking! Begin by reminding students that successful note taking involves selecting and rewording only the important ideas, not copying all the information available on a topic. Write the "Tips For Note Taking" from page 179 on the board and review them with your students. Next assign each student a nation to research. Give each student a copy of page 179 for guiding his note taking from available resources. Then have each student use his notes to write an informative paragraph about his assigned nation.

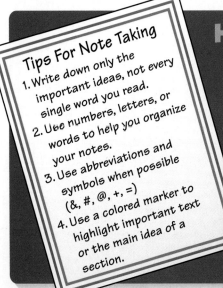

Tips For Note Taking
1. Write down only the important ideas, not every single word you read.
2. Use numbers, letters, or words to help you organize your notes.
3. Use abbreviations and symbols when possible (&, #, @, +, =)
4. Use a colored marker to highlight important text or the main idea of a section.

Writing Summaries

More Than A Book Review

When writing a book review, a student shares her understanding of and opinion about a book. Take book reviews to another level in your classroom by having each student write a review, giving it a special focus such as suspense, humor, adventure, or math. Direct the student to reveal the review's focus in her first paragraph. Then instruct her to highlight three of her book's suspenseful events, discussing each event in a different paragraph. In the closing paragraph, have her issue a suspense-filled invitation to others to read her book. You're sure to get a book review that tells more than the usual *What is this book about? What is the theme or message of this book?* and *What do I like about this book?* After all the reviews have been completed, classify and file them in subject-organized notebooks in your room library. Then allow your students to consult the notebooks to decide which books to read next!

Getting The Point

Zero in on the main idea of a selection with an activity dedicated to writing one-sentence summaries. In advance cut interesting, one-paragraph stories or informational articles from old workbooks, magazines, or newspapers. Mount each paragraph on a different sheet of colored paper, one for each pair of students. Distribute a different paragraph to each pair with directions to read the paragraph, glean its main idea, and then write a one-sentence summary of it. Have each pair share responsibility for reading aloud its paragraph and one-sentence summary. As each summarizing sentence is shared, write it on the board and challenge the other students to recall details from the paragraph that support that main idea. As a class discuss whether the sentence needs to be revised. Afterward give that pair an index card on which to write its revised sentence, including a large exclamation point somewhere on the card. Staple each index card to its corresponding paragraph for display on a bulletin board titled "We Get The Point."

> A man was given a pair of ceremonial moccasins made by the Nez Percé Indians.
>
> **!**

Say It In A Nutshell

Approach the writing of summaries through comic strips. Have each student bring in a favorite comic strip cut from a local newspaper. Direct her to trace the strip's main character onto a sheet of duplicating paper. Next have her summarize the strip's content—from that character's point of view—inside a large speech bubble above the character's head. After she colors the character and tapes the comic strip to the bottom edge of the paper, allow each student to share both her comic strip and summary with the class. If desired repeat this activity using popular songs from cassette tapes or CDs that you have approved.

Writing Biographies

Build A Better Biography

This fun-filled lesson is just what you need to teach your students how to write a biography! Begin by explaining the definition of *biography*—a story a writer tells about another person's life. Then ask students to list ways in which a writer can find out about another person's life. Help your students conclude that interviewing a person is one method of gathering material or information for a biography. Direct each child to select an adult relative to interview. Then provide each student with a copy of page 180. If desired have each student add to the bottom of his interview sheet additional interview questions that he would like to ask the person. After each student has conducted his interview, have him use the information he gathered to write a biography of his interviewee and share it with the class.

This Is Your Life!

Want to add a little drama to the writing of biographies? Extend the activity at the left by challenging your students to write and present skits about the lives of the people they've interviewed (or about whom they've read). Within the text of the skit, direct each student to reveal information about the outstanding events from that person's life. Then schedule time for each student to practice and perform his work in a "This Is Your Life" presentation.

Autobiography Bonanza

Add some excitement to a lesson about how to write an autobiography by using photographs and an interesting twist on maps. Explain that an *autobiography* is a story a writer tells about his or her own life. Ask each of your students to bring in photographs or colored drawings of important events in his life. Give each student a 12" x 18" sheet of paper on which to draw a meandering path. Next direct each student to glue and label the pictures along the path to create a sequential and pictorial map of his life, beginning at birth and continuing to the present. Then have the student use his life map as the basis for writing a narrative of his life. After all the students have completed their writings, display the life maps and autobiographies on a bulletin board or wall space titled "It's A Wonderful Life!"

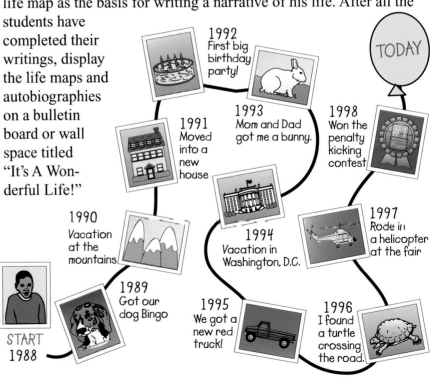

1992 First big birthday party!

1993 Mom and Dad got me a bunny.

1991 Moved into a new house

1998 Won the penalty kicking contest

TODAY

1990 Vacation at the mountains

1994 Vacation in Washington, D.C.

1997 Rode in a helicopter at the fair

1989 Got our dog Bingo

1995 We got a new red truck!

1996 I found a turtle crossing the road.

START 1988

Personified-Letter Exchanges

Bring the letters of the alphabet to life for a friendly-letter-writing activity. First write the letters of the alphabet on index cards, a different card for each letter and student. Repeat this procedure with slips of paper; then fold the slips of paper and place them in a container. Give each student one index card. Then instruct a student to draw from the container one slip with a letter on it that is different from the one on her index card. Have each student pretend that she is the letter on her index card. Then direct her to write a friendly letter with lots of questions to the alphabet letter written on her slip of paper. For example, if a student with the letter *F* on her index card draws a slip with an *S*, she writes "Dear S" and then could ask how letter *S* feels about being one of the most-used letters in the alphabet. Afterward have her deliver the question-filled letter to the student holding the *S* index card so that student can write a response. In turn, explain that she, too, should receive a friendly letter to which she can respond.

Dear S,

Handling Requests And Complaints By Mail

Transform a real-life situation into an ideal opportunity to teach a lesson on writing business letters. Think of a recent personal experience about which you could register a complaint. For example, share that your french fries were greasy and undercooked the last two times you visited your favorite fast-food restaurant. Suggest that, on your behalf, each student write a business letter registering a complaint to the manager of that restaurant. Remind each student to state specifically what was wrong, why it was a problem, and how it should be corrected. Then look for other real-life situations for incorporating the writing of business letters. For example, if a student has an upcoming report, suggest that he write to an organization or to a particular individual requesting helpful information. What better way to answer the much-asked question, "Why do I have to know how to do this?" than through real-life situations?

Book-Related Mail

Set up a post office in your classroom that's just for sharing about books. Assign an existing cubbyhole to each student for use as a mail bin. Or create mail bins by gluing and stacking as many clean Pringles® cans as needed in rows of five. Near the mail bins, post a laminated chart that lists the names of your students. Each week have every student write the title of the book she's currently reading next to her name with a wipe-off marker. If any student sees that a classmate is reading a book she has read, direct her to write a friendly and conversational letter to that student expressing her personal thoughts about the book. Explain that each student will be expected to respond to all letters she receives.

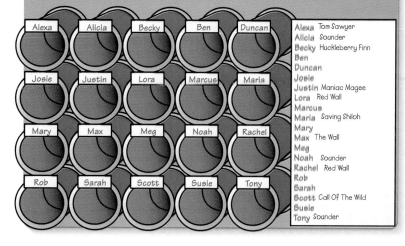

Alexa	Alicia	Becky	Ben	Duncan
Josie	Justin	Lora	Marcus	Maria
Mary	Max	Meg	Noah	Rachel
Rob	Sarah	Scott	Susie	Tony

Alexa	Tom Sawyer
Alicia	Sounder
Becky	Huckleberry Finn
Ben	
Duncan	
Josie	
Justin	Maniac Magee
Lora	Red Wall
Marcus	
Maria	Saving Shiloh
Mary	
Max	The Wall
Meg	
Noah	Sounder
Rachel	Red Wall
Rob	
Sarah	
Scott	Call Of The Wild
Susie	
Tony	Sounder

Writing Narratives And Comparisons

Creative Comparisons

Give your next comparative-writing lesson a new angle—or shape! Challenge each student to create a new design for the most common graphic organizer—the Venn diagram—by overlapping two triangles, squares, or trapezoids. Give each student one sheet each of white and black construction paper, scissors, and glue; then direct students to follow these steps:

1. Cut the shapes for your organizer from white construction paper.

2. Overlap the shapes, and then glue them to a sheet of black construction paper.

3. Draw in the lines for the section that overlaps.

4. Use the organizer for comparing two similar subjects (see the illustration).

5. Refer to the organizer to write a paragraph telling how the two subjects are alike.

6. Staple the paragraph to the bottom edge of the black paper.

Display your students' work on a bulletin board titled "Comparisons Of A Different Shape!"

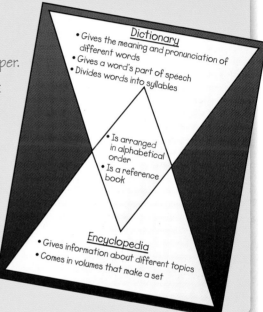

Dictionary
• Gives the meaning and pronunciation of different words
• Gives a word's part of speech
• Divides words into syllables

• Is arranged in alphabetical order
• Is a reference book

Encyclopedia
• Gives information about different topics
• Comes in volumes that make a set

Thoroughly Modern Fairy Tales

To practice narrative writing, challenge each of your students to modernize a fairy tale. Give each student a copy of page 181. Next have each student choose a favorite fairy tale on which to base a story written in first or third person. Explain that the tale to be written should have a plot similar to its original but contain a present-day setting and feature characters dressed in current fashions and using modern conveniences. For example, a child could have Cinderella arriving at the ball in a limousine and wearing a gown designed by a popular designer. Cinderella could dance until midnight to the sounds of a popular rock band and leave behind a satin evening shoe. As a follow-up, have each student transform her story into a picture book to share with a younger class or student.

Dare To Compare

Motivate your students to write comparatively by having them analyze story characters. Pair your students; then give each student a copy of page 182. Direct each partner to complete his reproducible about a different character. Afterward instruct the pair to compare the information on their sheets to find out what their two characters have in common. Then have the partners work together to write a paragraph that tells how the two characters are alike.

Writing To Describe

Writing Warm-Up

Begin your next writers workshop with this challenging exercise aimed at fine-tuning each student's descriptive-writing ability. Explain that each student will be writing a how-to, or *expository,* paragraph about a specific experience. Have the student select a topic from the list at the right. After each child has selected his topic, explain that he cannot use certain words in his paragraph. For example, if a student chooses to write a paragraph about making a banana split, do not allow him to use the words *banana, ice cream,* and *spoon* so that he has to describe those items in a different way. Inform each student of the words he cannot use; then challenge him to write his paragraph.

Topic	Words Not To Use
brushing teeth	toothpaste, water, toothbrush, bathroom
making a bowl of cereal	milk, pour, spoon, cereal, bowl
riding a bike	pedal, brake, seat, bike
making a banana split	banana, ice cream, spoon

Descriptive Duos

Fine-tuning descriptive writing requires lots of practice. Take a different approach by having your students describe a picture in two different ways for two entirely different purposes. First enlist your students' help with cutting out and mounting interesting pictures from old magazines onto sheets of construction paper. Then have each child choose a different picture, such as a dog curled up asleep, from the collection. Direct him to first write a paragraph describing his subject in a positive way (the dog as a beloved pet) and another paragraph that portrays his subject in a negative way (same dog as the culprit who just killed a chipmunk). Finally, have each student make WANTED posters for the subjects of his two paragraphs. Direct him to copy his two paragraphs side by side on the bottom half of a 9" x 12" sheet of white construction paper, leaving space at the top half to illustrate the dog described in each paragraph. Display your students' work on a bulletin board titled "Descriptive Duos."

Writing To Explain

Treasure-Hunt Adventures

Allow each of your students to practice how-to writing by sending a classmate on a treasure hunt through a favorite book! First have each student read a book from your class or school library. As the student reads, instruct him to create a list of treasure-hunt clues—plus a key—that will direct another classmate to find different words, phrases, sentences, or paragraphs "buried" in that book. Then challenge him to write the clues as directions for a classmate to follow in his search. Store the self-directing hunts along with their self-checking keys at a center next to your room library.

Treasure Hunt For <u>The Cay</u>

Treasure Hunt For <u>The Cay</u> Key

A Rendezvous For Two

Use maps to have some fun with how-to writing. Pair your students; then give each pair a local city or county map. Have each partner choose a different starting location on the map; then direct the pair to select a meeting place on the map. Next have each partner write a set of directions that explains how he will get to this meeting place from his starting location. Remind each student to begin his paragraph with a topic sentence that states his destination and to then use words and phrases that clearly and logically point out the most direct route to follow. For example: *Go south on Main Street. Turn east on Maple Avenue.* After writing, direct the partners to read each other's directions, testing them for accuracy. Then use the reproducible activity on page 183 as a great follow-up.

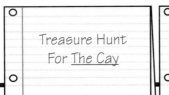

The Art Of Deciphering

Clarify your students' understanding of graphic organizers by having each student write a paragraph that explains a particular organizer. First have your students scour magazines and newspapers for examples of charts; pictographs; and circle, line, bar, and stem-and-leaf graphs. Direct your students to cut out and mount each graphic organizer they find on a different sheet of construction paper. Next distribute a different organizer to each student, directing her to write a paragraph explaining how to read that chart or graph and understand the information it provides. For example, a student explaining the steps of long division in a flow chart should first state the chart's purpose and then its flow according to the direction of the arrows. Display your students' paragraphs with the charts and graphs they explain on a bulletin board titled "Clearing The Air About Charts And Graphs."

Favorite Fruits At Hudson Elementary

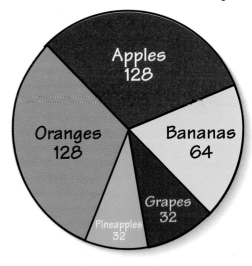

Apples 128
Bananas 64
Oranges 128
Grapes 32
Pineapples 32

Writing To Persuade

You Talked Me Into It!

Television commercials constantly influence viewers with persuasive tactics. Utilize some of this *medium's* methods by having *your* students transform persuasive paragraphs into television commercials of their own. Assign each student a topic that can be argued from either a *for* or *against* position, such as "A Woman Should Be Elected President." Have each student choose a stance and state it in the topic sentence of his paragraph. Explain that he should then support his position with three detail sentences that give reasons, facts, and/or examples. After editing, give each student one sheet of 9" x 12" white construction paper. Instruct each student to draw a large-screen television on his paper. Afterward direct him to copy his paragraph onto the screen, then color and cut out the screen. Display your students' screens on a bulletin board titled "Talk Me Into It!"

Convince A Fourth Grader

As an end-of-the-year project, challenge each of your current students to write a picture book that will persuade an upcoming class member to be successful in fifth grade. Direct each student to fill the pages of his book with illustrated advice and examples that an upcoming fifth grader could appreciate. For example, suggest that one page be devoted to giving advice about getting along with the teacher, one be about developing good study habits, and another be about consequences! Suggest that the student title his book "How To Be A Successful Fifth Grader." During the last week of school, have him present his book to a current fourth grader as a gift.

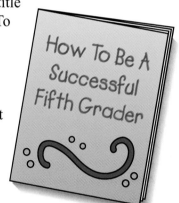

Win Me Over

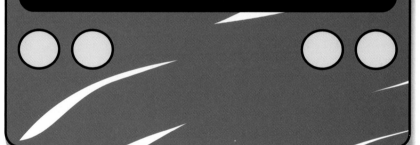

Turn your classroom into a persuasive writers' forum. As a class brainstorm topics that can be argued from a *pro* and *con* standpoint. Write your students' suggestions on the board as sentences. For example: *"Teenagers should have a 10:00 P.M. curfew on weekdays."* Afterward pair your students; then have each pair choose one of the topics from the board and decide which partner will be *for* the subject and which partner will be *against* it. Direct each partner to write a persuasive paragraph that gives at least three reasons, facts, or examples to support his view and share them with the class. After hearing each argument, have the class think about the issues raised by each position and vote to determine the winning position.

Writing Poetry

Color Poems

What color is a good day? To answer this question, challenge your students to write couplets that connect colors and emotions. First read aloud *My Many Colored Days* by Dr. Seuss (Random House, Inc.; 1996). Then ask your students to consider the question, "If emotions had color, what color would each emotion be?" To help students make specific responses, distribute colorful markers, pencils, or crayons that have unusual names—such as *watermelon* and *marigold*—written on them. Next give each student a copy of the reproducible on page 184 to complete as directed. As he completes the sheet, suggest that he use interesting color names and model his couplet after those in Dr. Seuss's book. If desired, have each student choose one of his couplets to copy onto an appropriately colored, irregular shape of paper. Then display the shapes over black background paper on a bulletin board titled "Our Many Colored Days."

"My Many COLORED Days"

Some days are yellow
Some days are blue

On different days I'm different too
You'd be surprised how many ways I

CHANGE on different days
colored

[ ]

On royal purple days,
I feel smart and clever

All Aboard The "Qua-train"

Get your students on board the poetry-writing train with this activity on quatrains. Write the following quatrain on the board:

> I get up for school at eight.
> Never once have I been late.
> By nine o'clock I'm at the bus stop
> Or riding to school with my dear pop.

Point out to students that the first two lines rhyme, as do the second two lines. Explain that it is also acceptable to have the first and third lines and the second and fourth lines of a quatrain rhyme. Pair your students; then have each pair write its own poem—featuring at least two quatrains—about a typical day at school. After your students have finished writing, have each pair present its poem orally. Then compile all the poems in a binder for your classroom library.

Crazy About Couplets

This unique approach to poetry will have your students going crazy over couplets! Provide each student with a magazine, glue, and scissors. Direct each student to cut out any ten words from her magazine. Explain that each word will become part of a different *couplet*—a two-line verse form that expresses one thought and often rhymes. Write the two couplets below on the board and discuss them with your students. Then direct each student to write ten couplets, gluing a cut-out word at the end of one line in each couplet as shown. Remind your students that the two lines of a couplet should express one thought and usually rhyme. Invite your students to share their couplets with the class; then post them on a bulletin board titled "Crazy About Couplets."

> I rode the Ferris wheel at the fair,
> While the whipping wind blew my hair.
>
> The leaves fell slowly from the tree,
> Having reached the end of a long journey.

> Last week I learned to skate
> I was proud because it really felt
> **GREAT!**

Lighthearted Limerick Lesson

Your students could howl over this humorous exercise in writing limericks. Begin by explaining the standard limerick-rhyming pattern to your students: lines one, two, and five rhyme and have three stressed syllables; and lines three and four rhyme and have two stressed syllables. Next share the following limerick with your students:

> There once was a man named Thad
> Who went along with every new fad.
> He got a tattoo;
> Then dyed his hair blue.
> The final result was quite sad.

After sharing the limerick, direct each student to write his name at the top of a sheet of paper. Then have the student write the first line of a limerick about any subject. Next ask each student to pass his paper to the student on his right. Instruct each student to then write a second line for the limerick he receives. Continue in this manner until all five lines of the limerick have been written. Then have the last student return the paper to its original owner. Conclude by having each student share his resulting limerick.

Jake Willet

There once was a girl named Kay
Who went outside to play every day.
But she tripped on a log
And kissed a tree frog.
Now "ribbit" is all she can say!

Inventing Some Poetry

Introduce the concept of invented poetry to your students with this lighthearted activity. First share the example of alphabet poetry in the illustration. Next explain that an alphabet poem uses a section of the alphabet as the outline for a humorous list poem. Then challenge each student to choose any section of the alphabet and create her own list poem.

All
Boys
Consume
Delicious
Eggplant
For
Good
Health!

Editing Symbols

Writers use special marks called *editing symbols* to help them edit and revise their work. Editing symbols are used to show what changes a writer wants to make in his or her writing.

Symbol	Meaning	Example
⬭	Correct spelling	animl
ℓ	Delete or remove.	dogg
◡	Close the gap.	f i sh
∧	Add a letter or word.	lives in tree a
#	Make a space.	flies/south
⌐⌐	Reverse the order of a letter, a word, or words.	plants eats
⟨,⟩	Insert a comma.	the crab an arthropod
⊙	Insert end punctuation.	Cats purr
⌄	Insert an apostrophe.	a deers antlers
⌄⌄ ⌄⌄	Insert quotation marks.	She said, Look at the pig.
≡	Make the letter a capital.	birds eat seeds.
/	Make the letter lowercase.	a Snowshoe hare
¶	Start a new paragraph.	¶Some dogs have tails.

Different Types Of Paragraph

A **descriptive** paragraph describes the way a person, a place, a thing, or an idea looks, sounds, smells, tastes, or feels. For example:

You can tell a lot about Boomer just by looking at his face. The first thing you notice about him is the way he cocks his head to one side. With warm, brown eyes peeking through layers of coarse, gray-white fur that covers his body and tail, he usually looks disheveled. His pale-pink tongue usually hangs from the left side of his mouth. His ears are alertly perked, giving the impression that he's ready, willing, and able to spring into action at a second's notice. Despite his short legs, he's a contented mongrel from head to tail.

A **persuasive** paragraph expresses an opinion supported by facts and examples to get the reader to agree with the writer's position. For example:

Anyone being greeted by Boomer should wear old clothes. He loves to jump up and place his paws at your waist when he greets you. He did this after running to greet my friend last week. Our yard was still wet from a rain shower, and my friend went home with dirty pawprints on his clothes! Last Saturday, Boomer knocked over the oil can I was using to oil my bike. Mom had planned to attend a wedding and was walking toward the car when Boomer decided to tell her good-bye. You can guess the rest!

A **narrative** paragraph tells a story by providing the details of an experience. For example:

Giving my dog a bath is a weekly chore I dread. Last week was the worst experience yet. Boomer got into the tub willingly and let me work the shampoo into his coat; but when I started to rinse him, he bolted. Because he was so soapy, trying to catch him was like trying to hold on to a greased pig. Before I finally corralled him, he had left a slippery trail throughout the house, upsetting every piece of furniture in his path! What a nightmare! Not only did I have to finish giving Boomer his bath, but I also had to straighten up his disastrous mess to appease my mom!

An **expository** paragraph gives information about a topic by explaining an idea, giving directions, or showing how to do something. For example:

When taking Boomer for a walk, stick to a regular routine. First make certain that he is on a leash and that no one else is walking his dog in the same area. Boomer loves to socialize, and if another dog's in sight, he'll pull you in that direction instead of where you want to go. Go around the block in a clockwise direction, stopping at Mrs. Geddy's house last. She gives Boomer treats, and if you go there first, you'll have a difficult time getting him to complete his walk!

Journal Topics

September

September is Self-Improvement Month. This month celebrates the importance of lifelong learning and self-improvement. Name something about yourself that you'd like to improve, and then list the steps you will take to do this.

Apples abound this month! How many dishes can you think of that are made with apples? List them.

National Pet Memorial Day falls annually on the second Sunday in September. Write a description of a pet you have now, one you have had in the past, or one that you would like to have in the future. Include a message that recognizes the pet's best qualities.

The summer has come to an end and it's time for heading back to school. If you were commissioned to design "the ultimate" school, what would your school be like?

The planet Neptune was first discovered on September 23, 1846. Pretend that a unique species lives on the planet. Describe the physical characteristics of these creatures, and then tell what a day in their life is like.

October

National Dessert Month is held each year in October. Describe the best dessert imaginable.

Create a new monster for Halloween. Describe what the monster looks like; then tell what it would do on Halloween night.

Peace, Friendship And Good Will Week falls annually the last seven days in October. Its purpose is to establish good human relations throughout the world. Write a letter to the people of the world telling them five ways they can make the world a friendlier place to live.

October celebrates Get Organized Week. Think of the most unorganized person you know. Describe what this person can do to get himself or herself organized.

Germany, once a divided country, was reunited on October 3, 1990. How would you feel if the United States were a divided nation? How do you think your life would be different if this happened?

November

National Authors' Day is observed on November 1. Write a letter to your favorite author telling what you like about his or her books. Give the author some suggestions on what he or she could write about in an upcoming book.

November 3 is the birthday of John Montague, the Earl of Sandwich. What did he invent? The sandwich, of course! Write a recipe for a new and unusual sandwich.

Mickey Mouse first appeared in a cartoon on November 18, 1928. Draw a cartoon featuring a new kind of mouse.

Hunting is a very popular sport this time of year. Write a paragraph telling why you are for or against this sport.

Write about your favorite family Thanksgiving Day tradition.

The Christmas shopping season traditionally begins on the Friday after Thanksgiving. If you could get the *perfect* gift for everyone in your family, what gift would you get each member, and why?

December

Many people celebrate the holiday season by decorating a freshly cut tree. Imagine you are a tree that is just about to be cut down. Write a dialogue between yourself and a tree cutter.

Emily Dickinson is considered to be one of America's greatest poets. Most of her poems—published after her death in 1886—were found written on such things as scraps of paper and the backs of envelopes. Write your own poem on an unusual material in honor of her birthday (December 10, 1830).

Underdog Day falls annually on the third Friday in December. Name a book character that you think is an *underdog,* or someone predicted to lose. Tell why you think this character is an underdog.

Winter begins in December with the coming of the *winter solstice,* the shortest day of the year. Curling up in front of a fire with a good book, steam from a cup of hot cocoa—what are some of the things that remind you of winter?

December 31 is New Year's Eve. Before setting goals for the New Year, list all the things you have accomplished this past year.

Journal Topics (continued)

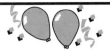

January

If you could have one wish for the New Year, what would it be?

Z Day on January 1 honors people whose names begin with the letter *Z* and are usually thought of as last. Describe what your day would be like if everything suddenly started going in reverse order.

January 11 is International Thank You Day. Write a letter to yourself expressing thanks for something you did for someone else.

Civil rights leader, minister, and Nobel Peace Prize winner Dr. Martin Luther King, Jr., was born on January 15, 1929. Explain what the word *prejudice* means to you; then decide if you think you are or are not prejudiced. Write your response.

Begin the New Year with some innovative thinking! Describe an innovative way of doing an ordinary activity, or a new invention you'd like to create.

February

Responsible Pet Owner Month is celebrated in February. Write a broadcast for a local radio station reminding pet owners how to care for their pets.

Need an excuse to just do nothing all day long? Since Nothing Day is celebrated in February, here's your chance! Describe a day in which you had nothing to do except what you wanted.

Many animals have a difficult time finding adequate food and shelter during the cold winter months. Write about the kind of animal you'd like to be during the wintertime. What would you do to survive?

February 16 is Heart 2 Heart Day. Write a heart-to-heart conversation that you'd like to have with your parent.

The Chinese celebrate their New Year during the month of February. If you could go back to the old year and change one thing, what would it be?

March

People magazine was launched on March 4, 1974. Imagine yourself on the cover of the magazine 20 years from now. Why would you be chosen as the magazine's Person Of The Year?

Theodor Seuss Geisel, better known as *Dr. Seuss,* was born on March 2, 1904. Write the title of your favorite Dr. Seuss book, and then tell why it is your favorite.

Write about what life would be like if the color green were made illegal.

On March 18, 1995, Michael Jordan announced he was returning to professional basketball after resigning 17 months earlier. Is there something you quit that you wished you hadn't? Explain.

List the things about spring that make you feel happy.

April

April Fools' Day is observed on April 1. Who in your family has the best sense of humor? Describe something funny this person said or did.

Eggs are a popular food this month. Name a food that you absolutely hate. Describe the taste, texture, appearance, and smell of the food.

Earth Day was first celebrated on April 22, 1970, with the slogan "Give Earth A Chance." Its purpose was to bring attention to our need to care for the earth. Think of a slogan for this year's Earth Day; then tell how you would promote the day.

National Library Week is celebrated in April. If you could ask anyone in the world to read a book to you, whom would you ask? What book would you read together, and why would you choose that book?

In 1910, President William Howard Taft began a new sports tradition by throwing out the first baseball of the season. If you could be a star at any sport, which one would it be, and why?

May

America's premier Thoroughbred horse race, the Kentucky Derby, first began on May 17, 1875. Describe an animal that you consider to be truly beautiful.

National Teacher Day falls annually on the Tuesday of the first full week in May. List all the duties your teacher has to perform within a year. Then pay tribute to your teacher through a kind word or action.

Limericks, funny five-lined poems, were made popular by a man named Edward Lear. Limericks follow a specific rhyming pattern: the first, second, and fifth lines rhyme; and the third and fourth lines rhyme. In honor of Lear's May 12 birthday, write a limerick of your own.

Memorial Day (the last Monday in May) pays tribute to those who have died, especially those who have died in battle. Do you think America should get involved in wars with other countries? Why or why not?

With the end of May approaching, summer is in the forecast! Plan a summer vacation for yourself and your best friend.

"Write" On Target!

Writing is a *process*—a series of steps followed to get a specific result. When you write, the writing process points you in the right direction, supplying you with the tools you need to reach your goal—a good piece of writing. As you complete each part of the writing process listed below, write the date on the line next to it. When you are finished, staple this checklist to the top of your final copy.

Writing Process Steps

Final Draft
Proofreading
Editing
First Draft
Prewriting

Step 1: Prewriting

_____ I brainstormed a list of possible topics and then decided on one topic.

_____ I identified my audience. My audience is _____.

_____ I identified my purpose. My purpose is _____.

_____ I clustered my ideas using a graphic organizer.

Step 2: First Draft

_____ I wrote my first draft.

_____ I read over my first draft and made necessary changes.

Step 3: Editing

_____ I had a classmate edit my first draft.

_____ I reviewed my classmate's suggestions and made necessary changes to my writing.

Step 4: Proofreading

_____ I read my writing carefully to check for errors in spelling, capitalization, punctuation, grammar, and form.

Step 5: Final Draft

_____ I completed my final copy.

Note To The Teacher: Give a copy of this checklist to each student whenever he begins a new writing assignment.

Peer-Editing Checklist
As you read over your classmate's writing, complete the following checklist.

Author _____ Peer Editor _____

Title Of Work _____

Composition	YES	NO
Does the paper have a main idea?	____	____
Does the author stick to the topic?	____	____
Does the author write in complete sentences?	____	____
Does the author provide details to support the main idea?	____	____
Does the paper have a concluding sentence?	____	____

Style		
Does the author use a variety of sentence types?	____	____
Does the writing sound like the author?	____	____
Can you tell how the author feels from his/her writing?	____	____
Does the paper contain colorful and rich vocabulary?	____	____

Mechanics		
Does the author indent before beginning each new paragraph?	____	____
Does each sentence begin with a capital letter?	____	____
Are the names of specific people, places, and things (proper nouns) capitalized?	____	____
Does each sentence end with a punctuation mark?	____	____
Is dialogue correctly punctuated with quotation marks?	____	____
Does the author use commas to separate items in a series?	____	____
Does the author use apostrophes to show ownership or contractions?	____	____

Usage		
Does the author make the correct word choices (*here* or *hear, there* or *their)?*	____	____
Do the subjects and verbs in each sentence agree *(The dog was...* not *The dog were...)?*	____	____

What did you like best about this paper? _____

_____

What suggestions for improvement would you make to the author? _____

_____

©1997 The Education Center, Inc. • *The Mailbox® Superbook • Grade 5 • TEC454*

Note To The Teacher: Give each student a copy of this peer-editing checklist to attach to his writing. Then have another student use the checklist to provide feedback to the author.

Ready, Set, Evaluate!

Evaluating your own writing is one way to help yourself become a better writer. After completing your next writing assignment, fill out this checklist. Then attach the checklist to your completed assignment.

Title: _____

Date written: _____

Purpose: _____

Audience: _____

Type of writing: _____

One thing I did well was _____

_____

_____

The thing I like best about this piece is _____

_____

_____

One thing I had difficulty with while writing this piece was _____

_____

_____

One thing I would change about this piece if I were to write it over would be _____

_____

_____

Note To The Teacher: Give one copy of this form to each student whenever you want the student to evaluate his or her own writing.

Editing Safari

While reading your way through the jungle of written work in the classroom each day, be on the lookout for errors in spelling, punctuation, and wording. Report any sightings of mistakes on this form. Fill out the chart completely. Remember: Only the first hunter to sight a specific error may report it!

Hunter's Name	Location Of Error	The Error	How To Correct The Error

Note To The Teacher: Use this form with "Editing Safari" on page 159. Duplicate a class supply of the form to have on hand; then post one form at a time for students' use.

Name____ *Writing: organizing a paragraph*

Piecing It All Together

Directions: Fill in the puzzle pieces below to help you organize your writing.

Topic Sentence

____

____

Supporting Detail

____

Supporting Detail

____

Supporting Detail

____

Concluding Sentence

____

____

____

____

Note To The Teacher: Use this sheet with "Clustering Ideas" on page 160 or anytime a student has a paragraph-writing assignment.

A Noteworthy Place

Directions: Take notes about your assigned country on the lines below.

Tips For Note Taking
1. Write down only the important ideas, not every single word you read.
2. Use numbers, letters, or words to help you organize your notes.
3. Use abbreviations and symbols when possible (&, #, @, +, =).
4. Use a colored marker to highlight important text or the main idea of a section.

USA   GREECE

Country: _____

A. Government
   1. _____
   2. _____
   3. _____

B. People/Way Of Life *(population, language spoken, living conditions)*
   1. _____
   2. _____
   3. _____

C. Geography *(area, landforms, location)*
   1. _____
   2. _____
   3. _____

D. Climate *(weather)*
   1. _____
   2. _____
   3. _____

E. Economy *(natural resources, agriculture, manufacturing)*
   1. _____
   2. _____
   3. _____

F. Other Important Information
   1. _____
   2. _____
   3. _____

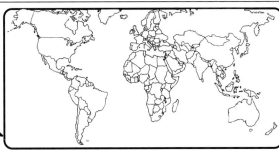

ZAIRE   BRAZIL

Note To The Teacher: Use this sheet with "Hitting The High Notes Of Note Taking" on page 160.

In Search Of Biographical Information

A *biography* is a story a writer tells about another person's life. One way to gather information for a biography is to conduct an interview with that person (or with people who knew the person well). Use the interview questions below to find out information about your subject. Use the blank lines at the bottom of this sheet to list any additional questions you want to ask. Then write a biography about your subject using the information you collect.

What is your full name? _____

When were you born? _____

Where were you born? _____

Do you have any brothers or sisters? If so, what are their names? _____

_____

What is your earliest memory? _____

_____

Where did you attend school? _____

What was your school like? _____

What are your hobbies? _____

What do you consider to be your greatest accomplishment in life so far? _____

_____

Other Questions:

_____

_____

_____

_____

_____

_____

I've A Story To Weave

Directions: Use the questions below to plan a story that includes all the important details of *who,* *what, when, where,* and *how.* For some questions, you can write a ✓ in a box to show your answer.

_____
Title Of Story

What kind of story will you write?
☐ A short story
☐ A tall tale
☐ A fable
☐ A humorous tale
☐ Other:_____
_____

When does the story happen? Name the year, the season, or the time of day.
_____
_____
_____

Where does the story take place?
_____
_____
_____

Who are the characters in your story?
_____
_____
_____
_____

What is the hero's (or heroine's) main goal?
☐ Rescue someone ☐ Win a race, prize, or contest
☐ Find a treasure ☐ Return safely from a trip
☐ Solve a mystery ☐ Achieve fame
☐ Escape danger ☐ Invent something
☐ Other:_____

Who or what gets in the hero's way?
_____
_____
_____

What problems does the hero have to solve to reach his goal?
_____
_____
_____

What happens to the hero and the other main characters at the climax?
_____
_____
_____

What is the theme of your story? (What lesson or moral does it teach?)
_____
_____
_____

Note To The Teacher: Use this sheet with "Thoroughly Modern Fairy Tales" on page 164.

Character planning and analysis

To Be Or Not To Be!

Directions: Fill in the guide below to help you create or analyze a story character. You can give some answers by checking the appropriate boxes.

Title of story _____

Name of character _____

Basic facts

Age: _____ ☐ Male ☐ Female

Job or grade in school: _____

Talents: _____

Hobbies: _____

Likes (food, music, etc.): _____

Dislikes: _____

Pets: _____

How does the character look?

Height: _____

Weight: _____

Hair color and length: _____

Eye Color: _____

Clothes: _____

Other: _____

How does the character move?

☐ Quickly ☐ Slowly
☐ Gracefully ☐ Clumsily
☐ Proudly ☐ With a swagger

Character's role in the story

☐ Hero/Heroine ☐ Villain

☐ Other: _____

What is the character like?

☐ Friendly ☐ Unfriendly ☐ Happy
☐ Sad ☐ Mean ☐ Shy
☐ Brave ☐ Scared ☐ Serious
☐ Smart ☐ Not smart ☐ Happy-go-lucky
☐ Silly ☐ Neat ☐ Sloppy
☐ Other: _____

How does the character talk?

Tone of voice: ☐ Loud ☐ Average ☐ Soft
Speed of speech: ☐ Fast ☐ Average ☐ Slow
Pitch of voice: ☐ High ☐ Medium ☐ Deep
Type of words used: ☐ Big words ☐ Simple words
Other: _____

What problem is the character trying to solve in the story?

_____

A simile or metaphor that best describes this character: _____

Note To The Teacher: Use this reproducible with "Dare To Compare" on page 164 or whenever a student has a story-writing assignment.

Meet Me!

Good directions give all the steps in the correct order. Use the map below as a guide to help you practice writing the directions for Parts A and B.

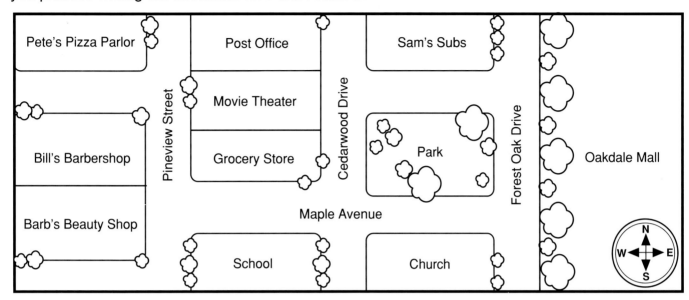

A. Study the map to find out how you could travel from Pete's Pizza Parlor to meet two friends at the mall. With a pencil, trace the path you would take. Then write a paragraph explaining this path on the lines provided. Use time-order words such as *first, next, then,* and *finally* to show the order of your steps.

_____

_____

_____

_____

_____

_____

B. Pretend that you and your friends are going to a movie after leaving the mall. On the lines provided, write numbered steps that tell how to get from the mall to the movie theater.

_____

_____

_____

_____

_____

_____

> **Bonus Box:** After the movie, pretend that you have to run an errand. Select a location on the map and write directions on the back of this sheet telling how to get to this place from the movie theater.

Note To The Teacher: Use this reproducible with "A Rendezvous For Two" on page 166. Duplicate one copy for each student.

How Many Colors Do You Feel?

If your feelings had color, which colors would they be? Make the ovals below into faces that show the moods you sometimes experience. Label the ovals. Then use markers or crayons to color each face the color you think goes with that feeling. Next to each face, write a rhyming *couplet* that describes that color of day for you. A couplet is a two-line poem that rhymes, like the ones below.

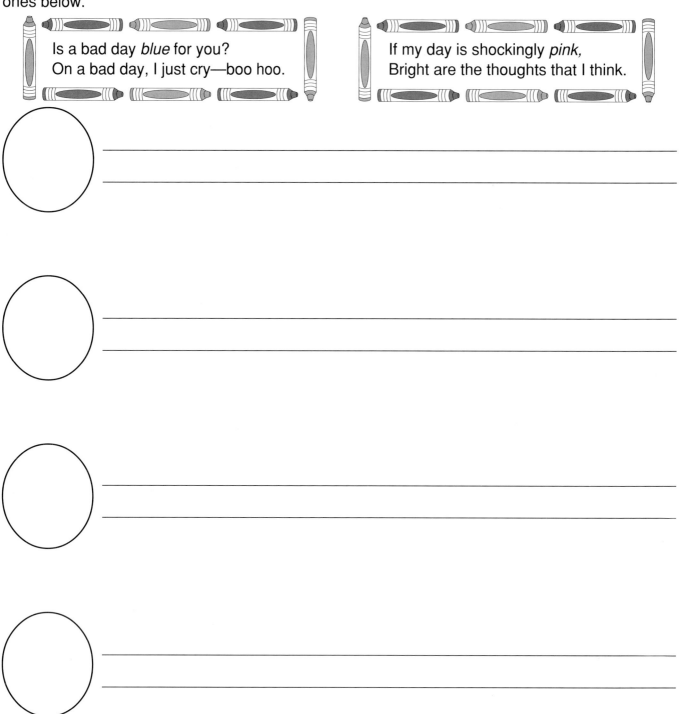

Is a bad day *blue* for you?
On a bad day, I just cry—boo hoo.

If my day is shockingly *pink,*
Bright are the thoughts that I think.

Bonus Box: Just how many colors *do* you feel during the day? Use the back of this sheet to draw faces and write couplets for *all* the different colors a day can be for you.

Note To The Teacher: Use this sheet with "Color Poems" on page 168. Duplicate one copy of the sheet for each student. Also supply each student with colored markers or crayons.

LITERATURE

Ideas For Any Book

A Picture Is Worth 1,000 Words!

An appealing way for students to show their understanding of a novel is to have them rewrite and simplify the story into a picture book. Discuss with your students the importance of selecting key events and sequencing them in correct time order. Then give each student one large poster-size sheet of white construction paper, a ruler, and crayons or markers. Instruct the student to use the ruler to divide her sheet of construction paper into eight equal sections and number them as shown. Direct each student to design a title page in section 1. Tell her to illustrate each event and write a brief description of it in each of the following seven sections. Then direct each student to fold her sheet lengthwise, creating four sections on each side. Next instruct the student to fold the paper accordion-style as shown.

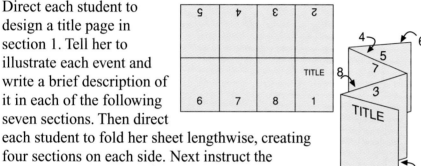

Making Predictions

Making predictions is a great critical-thinking exercise to incorporate with literature. Duplicate and distribute one copy of page 196 to each student; then select a picture book of your choice. Show your students the cover illustration and read the title. Have students make predictions about the story's plot by completing page 196 as directed. Have student volunteers share their predictions with the rest of the class; then read the picture book to your students. Your students will enjoy learning whether they accurately predicted the plot. The "Make Your Prediction" form is also great to use with students when beginning a new chapter of a novel.

✔ Check Out The Polls

To find out the types of literature your students like to read the most, take a poll. Write the following literature genres on the chalkboard: Sports, Adventure, Mystery, Horror, Realistic Fiction, and Science Fiction/Fantasy. Then instruct each student to write her favorite genre on a scrap of paper. Collect the papers and compile all the information into a bar graph similar to the one shown. Next poll your students by asking the following question: "Is reading cool?" Display the results in a circle graph similar to the one shown below.

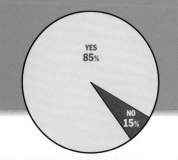

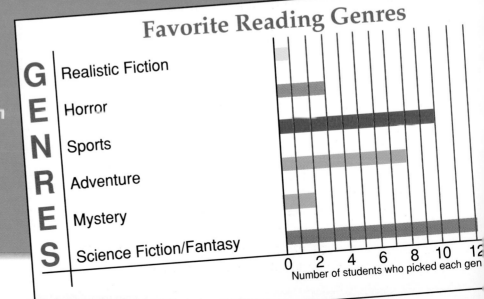

Favorite Reading Genres

MAP IT OUT

Keeping up with the story line of a current novel can be challenging, especially if it jumps from past to present and from one setting to another. Use a bulletin-board display to help students keep track of events. Cover a bulletin board with paper; then use yellow construction paper to make three cards labeled *Beginning*, *Climax*, and *Conclusion* as shown in the illustration. Add illustrations of characters or settings to the board. Post six or more sheets of white construction paper (or one sheet for each major event) on the board as shown. Then connect the sheets with yarn or string. For each major event, have a student write a brief summary on the appropriate blank sheet of construction paper. Refer to the story map often while reading the novel to help your students keep track of the time and place.

N7814C

Event 1

Event 2

Event 3

Event 4

Event 5

Event 6

CLIMAX

Event 7

Event 8

Mapping Out Hatchet

BEGINNING

CONCLUSION

Parallel Plots

Often a novel will have more than one plot. *Mrs. Frisby And The Rats Of NIMH* by Robert C. O'Brien (Scholastic Inc., 1971) is a perfect example of a novel that contains parallel plots. One plot deals with Mrs. Frisby (a mouse) and her family. The second plot deals with a colony of intelligent rats that have escaped from the National Institute of Mental Health. Each plot has a separate story line, but eventually the two plots become intertwined. Parallel plots make for an interesting read; however, the reader can sometimes confuse one plot with another plot. To help avoid this problem, have your students keep a timeline of events for each plot. Duplicate a class supply of page 197 and distribute one copy to each student. Instruct each student to briefly describe the major event for each plot as it occurs in the novel. (If the plot includes more than six events, distribute a second copy of page 197 to each student.) This exercise will help students clearly visualize the order of events for each plot.

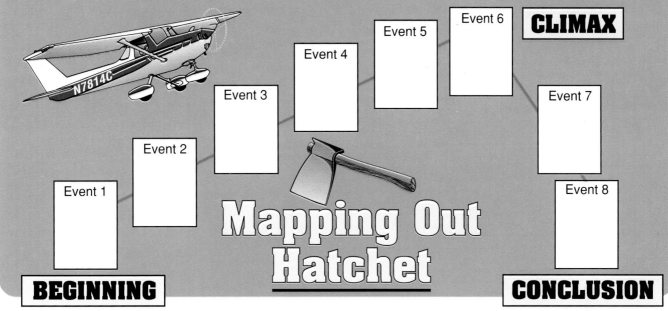

Mrs. Frisby And The Rats Of NIMH

Plot #1
The Rats

Escape from NIMH

Build underground city

Climax

Plot #2
Mrs. Frisby

Timothy's sickness

Goes to see Mr. Ages

Climax

The 50 States Book Race

Motivate your students to read by challenging each student to read 50 books, each set in a different U.S. state. Encourage students to read a variety of novels and picture books. Create a large chart containing the state abbreviations across the top and each student's name down the left-hand side. Place a sticker in the appropriate state column as each student finishes reading a book. Duplicate a supply of "The 50 States Book Race" on page 199. Place a hanging-file box near the chart that contains a folder for each student. Instruct each student to fill out one sheet for each book he reads and then file it in his folder. Periodically pull a completed sheet from each student's file and hold a brief conference to discuss the book. Award the first student to read one book from each state a special prize, such as a gift certificate. Give every student who reads 50 books a copy of "The 50 States Book Race Award" on page 199 and a treat—such as candy, a bookmark, or a free book.

Student	AL	AK	AZ	AR	CA	CO	CT	DE	FL
Sue			☺	☺	☺				
Peggy	☺	☺							
Chris	☺			☺	☺				
Irv					☺	☺			
Joe			☺		☺		☺	☺	
	☺								
			☺						☺
		··					··		

Picture Perfect

Have your students create a portrait gallery of the characters in the novel you are currently reading. Divide your students into small groups—one group for each main character in the novel. Enlarge and duplicate one copy of the "Character Frame" on page 198 for each group. Instruct each group to complete the character frame for its assigned character. Tell each group to describe its character's personality traits and physical traits. Then have each group list the other characters who are involved in its character's life, briefly describe its character's involvement in the plot, and illustrate its character in the center square of its reproducible. Direct each group to present its work to the rest of the class; then create a portrait gallery by posting each "Character Frame" on a wall or bulletin board in the classroom.

Word Web

Gleaning an unfamiliar word's meaning from its context is an important skill for intermediate students to develop. Help your students strengthen this skill by enlarging and duplicating a supply of the "Word Web" reproducible on page 198. Keep this reproducible handy for times when students encounter unfamiliar words that are important to a story line. Select one student to write the unfamiliar word in the center of the reproducible. Have another student record the sentence from the novel in which the word appears. Direct two students to use a dictionary and a thesaurus to find and record a dictionary definition and a synonym for the word. Next call on a student to write a sentence relating the word to a personal experience. To keep track of the unfamiliar words your class encounters, cover a bulletin board with black paper. Then draw a large spiderweb on the board using white chalk. Each time a "Word Web" is completed, post it on the spiderweb. Periodically refer to the board to reinforce the new vocabulary.

Picture-Book Activities

Have You Read Any Great Math Lately?

Integrate math and literature with Jon Scieszka's *Math Curse* (Viking Children's Books, 1995). This picture book deals with a girl's fear of math. Her teacher, Mrs. Fibonacci, tells the class that almost everything is a math problem. Soon everything the girl thinks about becomes a math problem. She begins to think that Mrs. Fibonacci has put a math curse on her. By the end of the book, the girl overcomes her fear and is ready to tackle any math problem. The book is packed with critical-thinking problems and humor. One such problem deals with the number of M&M's® it takes to equal the length of the Mississippi River. Have your students solve a similar math problem. Divide your students into small groups; then assign each group a different object—such as the door, a window, or the chalkboard. Instruct each group to estimate the number of M&M's® it will take to measure the length of its item. Then give each group a centimeter ruler for measuring the actual length of its assigned item. Have each group compare the results and present its findings to the rest of the class. Conclude the activity by passing out individual packages of M&M's®.

The Lowdown On Canines

Looking for a great way to integrate science into your reading program? Introduce your next unit on animals by reading *How Dogs Really Work!* by Alan Snow (Little, Brown And Company; 1993). Snow does a wonderful job of combining fact, fiction, and humor. The book humorously covers such topics as the brain, the central nervous system, the sense of smell, communication, movement, and general care and maintenance. After reading this book to your class, ask each student to create a poster titled "How I Really Work!" Have students humorously explain how they eat, talk, move, hear, smell, or see, using *How Dogs Really Work!* as a model. Instruct each student to include an illustration and explanation for each action featured on his poster. Have each student share his completed poster with the rest of the class. Then display the posters around the classroom.

They Called It Macaroni?

Almost everyone is familiar with the tune of "Yankee Doodle," but how many of your students know the history behind the song? *Yankee Doodle: A Revolutionary Tail* by Gary Chalk (Dorling Kindersley, Inc.; 1993) gives the history behind the tune as told by a cartoon mouse. The reader learns about causes of the Revolutionary War as well as important information such as the origins of the American flag. After reading the book to your class, distribute one large sheet of white construction paper and markers to each student. Have the class brainstorm a list of symbols that represent freedom—such as a dove and the Statue of Liberty. Then instruct each student to design his own flag that represents freedom and unity. Have each student share his flag with the rest of the class and explain the meaning of each symbol used. Display the flags around the classroom or in a hallway for everyone to enjoy.

BOOK-REPORT IDEAS

Cross-Stitch Samplers

Most books have a moral, a message, or a lesson. Have each student use a cross-stitch sampler as a medium for expressing the lesson of his novel. Give each student two 8 1/2" x 11" sheets of 1/4-inch graph paper and a variety of colored pencils. Instruct each student to think of a phrase that expresses the moral of his story. Then have him write that phrase on one sheet of graph paper, using a regular pencil and placing Xs in the boxes to spell the letters of each word or phrase. After he writes the phrase, have the student draw various symbols related to the book around the phrase. Once the rough draft is complete, have the student use colored pencils to create the same design on his other sheet of graph paper. After each student has completed his sampler, have him present it to the class and explain the meaning of his phrase and its connection to the novel.

Photo Cubes

For an easy art-project book report, have each student construct a photo cube displaying various aspects of his book. Have each student bring in a cube-shaped tissue box. Provide each student with colored construction paper, scissors, glue, and markers. Instruct the student to cover each side of his cube with a different-colored sheet of paper. Tell each student to use five sides of his box to illustrate important characters, the setting, the plot, major events, and the novel's conclusion. On the sixth side, instruct each student to write the title and author of his book. Have each student present his cube to the class, describing each side in detail to his classmates. Then display the cubes for others to enjoy.

STORY HATS

Have your students make fashion statements by presenting story-hat book reports! Give each student a 14" x 23" sheet of newsprint and crayons. Have each student follow the directions below to create his hat.

Directions:

1. Fold a 14" x 23" sheet of newsprint in half as shown.
2. Place the fold at the top; then fold down the top corners so that they meet in the center as shown.
3. At the lower edge, fold up the top flap twice as shown.
4. Flip the hat and repeat Step 3.
5. Section off the hat's brim into frames for illustrating the sequence of events of your book's plot.
6. Use the two sides at the top of your hat for writing the book's title and author, and a summary of your favorite part.

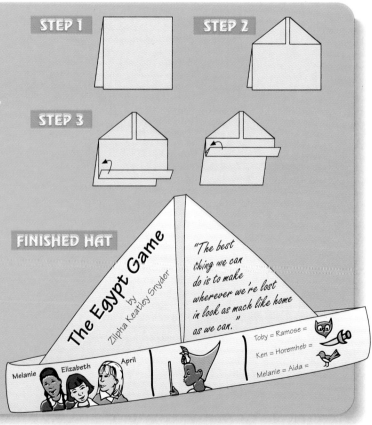

STEP 1   STEP 2

STEP 3

FINISHED HAT

What's In That Purse Or Wallet?

Items in a person's purse or wallet can reveal a lot about that person's personality. Brainstorm with your students a list of items that may be found—such as a driver's license or ID card, photos of friends and family, cash, shopping or to-do lists, membership cards, car keys, pens, medicine, food, and notes or letters. Instruct each student to collect at least five items that would be found in the purse or wallet of the main character of his novel. Tell the student to put his items in a real purse or wallet, or make one out of construction paper or cloth. Have each student present his character's wallet or purse to the class and explain the significance of each item.

Good To The Last Drop!

Recycle those two- or three-pound coffee cans piling up in the teachers' lounge or at home by having your students create two-way book-report peek cans with them. Send a letter home about a month before beginning this activity asking parents to send in empty coffee cans of the appropriate size. Collect enough cans so that each student has one can. Then give each student a can, a supply of colored construction paper, markers, tagboard, clear tape, scissors, and these directions:

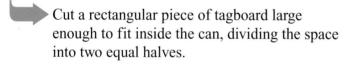 Cut a rectangular piece of tagboard large enough to fit inside the can, dividing the space into two equal halves.

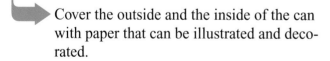 Cover the outside and the inside of the can with paper that can be illustrated and decorated.

➤ Think of two events from your novel to illustrate on the outside of the can.

➤ Create a different 3-D action scene in each half of the can's interior. For example, show two different settings from the novel—such as a day scene and a night scene, or an inside and an outside scene.

Have each student present his peek can to the class; then display each can in the class for all to enjoy.

Filmstrip Book Reports

Change those obsolete filmstrips into new ways for your students to present their book reports! Fill a bucket with one part bleach and one part water. Wearing rubber gloves, submerge the old filmstrips in the solution. Let them soak overnight; then rinse the filmstrips with water and allow them to air-dry. Cut the blank filmstrips so that each student gets a strip of ten frames. Give each student a supply of soft, waxy, colored pencils. *(Water-based markers are too transparent and they smear. Permanent markers leave no room for error.)* Duplicate one copy of page 200 for each student. Instruct each student to use this reproducible as a planning sheet for his filmstrip. Inform students that each scene should be simple and uncrowded. Tell each student that he also needs to write a brief script or narration for each scene. Suggest that students tape-record their scripts, adding interesting sound effects.

The Pentagon Spy
Franklin W. Dixon

Joshua Korba–Auctioneer

"This book receives two thumbs-up!"

Credits: Created by Troy Eason

Better Than A Book Report!
Creative Ways To Share About The Book You Just Read

Directions: When you finish reading a novel, choose a project from the list below to complete. When your project is finished, place a check in the box next to it.

_____ Write a newspaper with stories describing events that happened in the novel you read. Include articles that describe interesting details about one of the book's main characters or its setting.

_____ Create a time capsule for the main characters in your story. In the time capsule, include important items from the story that help tell what happened in the book. Present your time capsule to the class and explain why each item it includes is important.

_____ Design a set of finger puppets to represent the main characters in your favorite scene in the story. Act out the scene for your classmates using the puppets.

_____ Select a scene from the novel to act out. Rewrite the scene in script form. Ask classmates to act out the roles of characters in the scene. Practice the scene; then perform it for your classmates.

_____ Design a travel brochure that advertises the setting of the story as a tourist spot. Fold an 8 1/2" x 11" sheet of white paper into thirds. Fill the brochure with information on sites and activities of interest, dining and lodging establishments, and any information that would help tourists.

_____ Design a poster to advertise your book to other readers. Use lots of colorful adjectives to capture the reader's interest. Be sure to include the story basics—such as the title, the author's name, the illustrator's name, and a short summary of the book—on the poster.

_____ Construct a diorama that shows an important scene from the story. Make the diorama three-dimensional with the help of various arts-and-crafts materials.

_____ Write a short commercial advertising the book. Then record it on an audiocassette tape. At the beginning of the tape, be sure to give your name, the book's title, and the author; then record your commercial.

_____ Find 15 new vocabulary words introduced in the novel. Create a glossary in which you define each word and draw an illustration to go with the definition.

_____ Create a mobile featuring cutouts and pictures that show the major events of the novel. Be sure to arrange the hanging shapes in the order they happened in the story.

_____ Design a coat of arms to represent the main character of the story. Decorate the coat of arms with symbols that represent the character's personality. On the back of the coat of arms, write a paragraph that gives your reasons for including each item.

_____ Write an acrostic poem to represent the main character of your story. To do this write the letters in the character's name vertically on a sheet of paper. Then, after each letter, write an adjective describing the character that begins with that letter.

_____ Dress as your favorite character from the book. Present a short summary of the book to your classmates. See if they can determine your identity based on your costume and speech.

_____ Pretend you are a news reporter interviewing the main character from the story. Write a list of questions and the responses you think the interviewee would give.

_____ Design a creative book jacket for the story. Be sure to make your design appealing so that it interests readers. Include the title, the author's name, the illustrator's name, a short summary of the novel, and illustrations on the book jacket.

_____ Create a collage to represent one of the characters in the story. Cut pictures and words from magazines. Glue them to paper to create a collage that describes the character.

_____ Write a sequel to the story. Use the information you learned about the characters as you read the book.

_____ Decorate a paper bag with scenes from the book. Write the title, the author's name, and a brief summary on the bag. Then place three items relating to the story inside the bag. Present the bag to your class and explain the items it contains.

_____ Cover a square box with paper. On one side of the box, write the title and author of the book you read. Record the five Ws—_who, what, when, where,_ and _why_—on the other sides.

_____ Design a "Wanted!" poster featuring one of the characters in the story. Be sure to mention the character's name, a description, and what he or she is wanted for; then draw the character on the poster.

_____ Design a bookmark that advertises the novel. Write the title, the author's name, and a summary of the story on the bookmark. Also add an illustration of an important scene from the book.

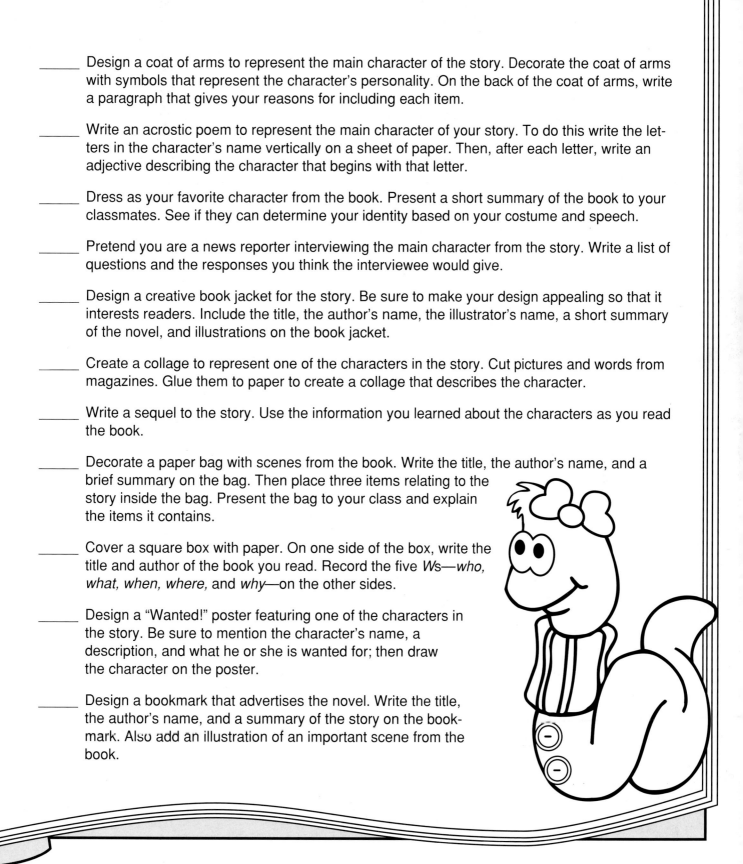

John Newbery
Award Winners
1970–1997

1997—*The View From Saturday* by E. L. Konigsburg

1996—*The Midwife's Apprentice* by Karen Cushman

1995—*Walk Two Moons* by Sharon Creech

1994—*The Giver* by Lois Lowry

1993—*Missing May* by Cynthia Rylant

1992—*Shiloh* by Phyllis Reynolds Naylor

1991—*Maniac Magee* by Jerry Spinelli

1990—*Number The Stars* by Lois Lowry

1989—*Joyful Noise* by Paul Fleischman

1988—*Lincoln: A Photobiography* by Russell Freedman

1987—*The Whipping Boy* by Sid Fleischman

1986—*Sarah, Plain And Tall* by Patricia MacLachlan

1985—*The Hero And The Crown* by Robin McKinley

1984—*Dear Mr. Henshaw* by Beverly Cleary

1983—*Dicey's Song* by Cynthia Voight

1982—*A Visit To William Blake's Inn* by Nancy Willard

1981—*Jacob Have I Loved* by Katherine Paterson

1980—*A Gathering Of Days* by Joan W. Blos

1979—*The Westing Game* by Ellen Raskin

1978—*Bridge To Terabithia* by Katherine Paterson

1977—*Roll Of Thunder, Hear My Cry* by Mildred D. Taylor

1976—*The Grey King* by Susan Cooper

1975—*M. C. Higgins, The Great* by Virginia Hamilton

1974—*The Slave Dancer* by Paula Fox

1973—*Julie Of The Wolves* by Jean Craighead George

1972—*Mrs. Frisby And The Rats Of NIMH* by Robert C. O'Brien

1971—*Summer Of The Swans* by Betsy Byars

1970—*Sounder* by William H. Armstrong

Suggested Read-Alouds

- *Jumanji* by Chris Van Allsburg
- *Falling Up* by Shel Silverstein
- *Something Big Has Been Here* by Jack Prelutsky
- *The Best School Year Ever* by Barbara Robinson
- *The Incredible Journey* by Sheila Burnford
- *The Indian In The Cupboard* by Lynne Reid Banks
- *Mrs. Frisby And The Rats Of NIMH* by Robert C. O'Brien
- *Sounder* by William H. Armstrong
- *The BFG* by Roald Dahl

- *An Occasional Cow* by Polly Horvath
- *From The Mixed-Up Files Of Mrs. Basil E. Frankweiler* by E. L. Konigsburg
- *Island Of The Blue Dolphins* by Scott O'Dell
- *Hatchet* by Gary Paulsen
- *Bridge To Terabithia* by Katherine Paterson
- *The Castle In The Attic* by Elizabeth Winthrop
- *The Boggart* by Susan Cooper
- *Shiloh* by Phyllis Reynolds Naylor
- *Bull Run* by Paul Fleischman
- *Poppy* by Avi
- *The War With Grandpa* by Robert K. Smith

The 50 States Book Race

Student's Name: _____

Title Of Book: _____

Author's Name: _____

State Setting: _____

_____

_____

Main Characters: _____

_____

_____

_____

_____

Brief Summary: _____

_____

_____

_____

_____

_____

_____

Critique: _____

_____

_____

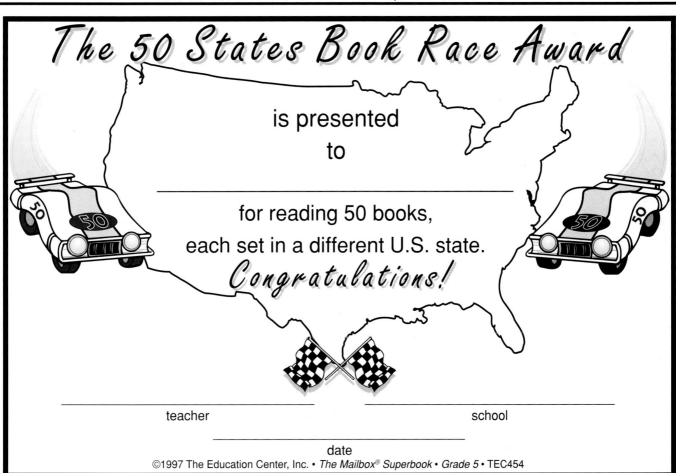

The 50 States Book Race Award

is presented

to

_____

for reading 50 books,
each set in a different U.S. state.

Congratulations!

_____   _____
teacher   school

_____
date

Note To The Teacher: Use both reproducibles above with "The 50 States Book Race" on page 188.

Name ____ *Planning a filmstrip*

Lights, Camera, Action!

Directions: Planning and storyboarding are important parts of preparing a filmstrip presentation. *Storyboarding* is sketching out each scene before you actually begin working on the final product. Use a pencil to sketch out a basic scene for each frame below. Write a rough draft of the script for each scene in the space provided at the right of each frame.

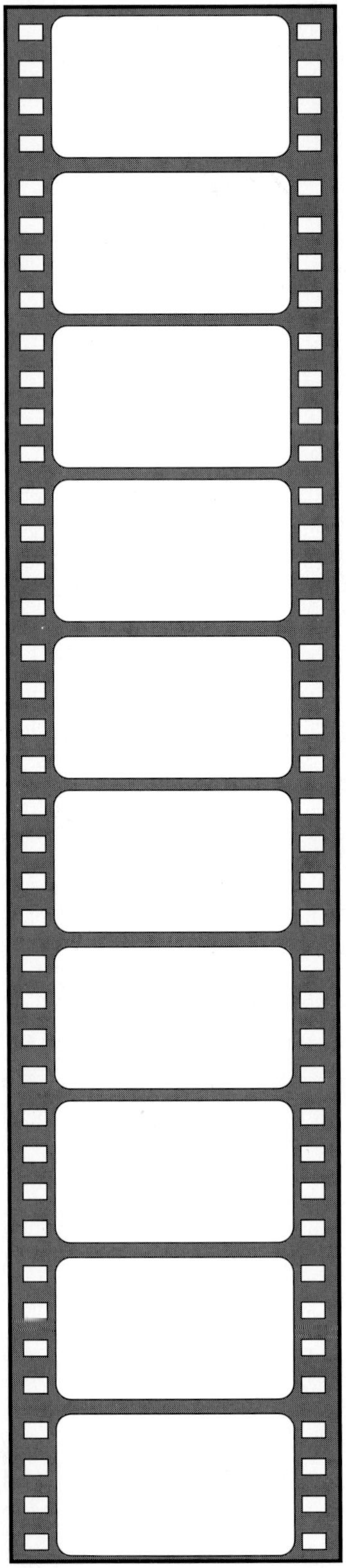

Frame 1: ____________________
(Title) ____________________
(Author)

Frame 2: ____________________
(Characters) ____________________

Frame 3: ____________________
(Setting) ____________________

Frame 4: ____________________
(Event 1) ____________________
____

Frame 5: ____________________
(Event 2) ____________________
____

Frame 6: ____________________
(Event 3) ____________________
____

Frame 7: ____________________
(Climax) ____________________
____

Frame 8: ____________________
(Resolution) ____________________
____

Frame 9: ____________________
(Critique) ____________________
____

Frame 10: ____________________
(Credits) ____________________
____

 Note To The Teacher: Use this reproducible with “Filmstrip Book Reports” on page 191.

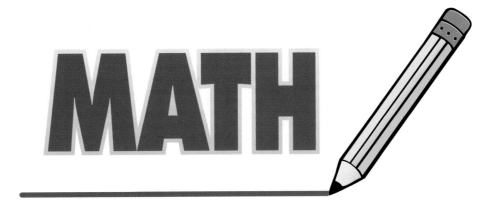

PLACE VALUE

Spinning And Rounding

Round and round she goes...where she stops, nobody knows! Reinforce your students' rounding skills with this whole-class game. Create a spinner on a blank overhead transparency as shown in the illustration. Project the spinner on your overhead projector; then select one student to spin the spinner for the entire game. Show the selected student how to use a paper clip and a pencil to spin the spinner. Next divide your class into groups of two or three students. Direct each group to copy a place-value chart to the hundred millions place onto a sheet of loose-leaf paper and have another sheet handy for recording answers.

To play the game:
1. Call out a large number—such as 234,670,823.
2. Instruct each group to write that number correctly in its place-value chart.
3. Have the selected student spin the spinner.
4. Give the groups one minute to round the number to the place value shown on the spinner and write an answer on the second sheet of paper. For example, if the spinner pointed to "Hundred Thousands," each group would round 234,670,823 to 234,700,000 and record it on paper.
5. After one minute call, "Pencils down." Visit each group to check its answer, giving each group one point for a correct answer.
6. Continue calling numbers for a desired number of rounds. Declare the team with the most points at the end of the game the winner.

For additional practice with rounding, see the reproducible activity "Sparky's Spectacular Sale" on page 220.

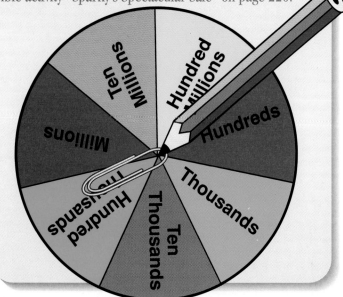

Putting Numbers In Their Places

Square off with numbers and give your students lots of practice in writing, comparing, and adding large numbers with this whole-class place-value game. To prepare for the game, use a black marker to label three sets of ten index cards with the digits 0–9. Shuffle the cards and place them facedown in a pile. Pair your students; then give each pair a sheet of centimeter graph paper and a colored pencil or crayon. Instruct each pair to use its colored pencil to outline a 2 cm x 9 cm rectangular box on the graph paper (see the illustration). Explain that the box will be used as a frame for an addition problem. Further explain that you will call out different numbers one at a time for the pairs to write inside the boxes. Share that the object of the game is to get the largest sum.

To play the game:
1. Draw one card from the pile and announce its number.
2. Direct each pair of students to write that number inside any one of the nine boxes in the first row.
3. Draw and call out a total of nine numbers for the first row and nine numbers for the second row.
4. Instruct each pair to add together the two numbers it built to find the sum.
5. Have one member of each pair record its sum on the chalkboard.
6. As a class, compare the numbers and determine the largest number.
7. Check the accuracy of the computation that resulted in that number. If it's correct, give each of the students in that pair a small treat.
8. Play another round by reshuffling the cards and having each pair outline another box on its graph paper.

To vary the game, ask for the smallest sum or change the operation from addition to subtraction.

1 CENTIMETER GRAPH PAPER

```
    4 7 9 0 4 2 3 2 5
    9 5 0 1 2 7 5 8 1
  1,4 2 9 1 6 9 9 0 6


    8   4   6     1
```

Round-The-Room Review

Time will be a factor in this fun whole-class game for reviewing addition and subtraction! Choose the skill(s) on which you want the game to focus—such as addition and subtraction to the hundred millions place, or subtraction with or without zeros. Distribute one index card to each student in your class. Direct each student to write one addition or subtraction problem that uses that skill on her card. Collect the cards and sequentially number each one in the upper left-hand corner.

To play:

1. Have each student number a sheet of notebook paper equal to the number of index cards.
2. Distribute one numbered index card to each student.
3. Tell each student that she will have one minute to solve the problem on the card and record her answer next to the corresponding number on her paper.
4. After one minute say, "Pass"; then have each student pass her card to the next student.
5. Continue play until each student has solved every card's problem. Check the answers together.

5

$$5,350,032$$
$$+1,237,895$$

6

$$4,678,013$$
$$-2,946,804$$

How Do Your Interests Rate?

Earn top ratings for this group activity on finding averages! Divide your class into groups of four students. Name one of the topics listed at the right. Instruct each group member to rate that topic on a scale from one to ten with ten being the best. Then have each group compute the average of its four ratings. For example, if one group's ratings were 3, 4, 3, and 5, then that group's average rating would be 3.75. Continue the activity by naming a new topic and having each group rate it, then compute the average rating. After playing a few rounds, require that each group estimate the average rating before actually computing it.

Topics To Rate:

- books written by Gary Paulsen
- watching a baseball game
- pizza with mushrooms
- chocolate ice cream
- school on Saturday
- Christmas
- math class
- dance music
- chewing gum
- art class
- recess

pizza with mushrooms

$$\begin{array}{r} 3 \\ 4 \\ 3 \\ +\ 5 \\ \hline 15 \end{array}$$

$$4\overline{)15}$$

Tic-Tac-Toe Math

$$5\overline{)555} \qquad 2\overline{)23} \qquad 2\overline{)24}$$

$$3\overline{)393} \qquad 8\overline{)56} \qquad 7\overline{)497}$$

$$4\overline{)848} \qquad 2\overline{)17} \qquad 2\overline{)633}$$

Add some zest to reviewing basic computation with this version of tic-tac-toe. Divide your class into pairs; then give each pair a calculator. Draw a tic-tac-toe board on the chalkboard and write a different math problem in each square. Instruct each pair to copy the board onto a sheet of loose-leaf paper. To play, direct Player One to choose a square and solve the problem written in that square. Have Player Two check the computation on the calculator. If the answer is correct, instruct Player One to place an *x* in that square. If incorrect, then allow Player Two to place an *o* in that square and take his turn choosing a square and working a problem. Declare the first player to get three *x*'s or *o*'s in a row the winner. To play another round, write different problems in the tic-tac-toe board on the chalkboard.

SPINNING FOR MULTIPLES

Put a new spin on reviewing multiples! Invite five student volunteers to come to the chalkboard and stand facing the class. Write a different digit from 1 to 10 on the board above each volunteer's head. Instruct the remaining students, one at a time, to call out a two-digit number. Direct each student at the board to spin in place one time when a number is called that is a multiple of the number written above his head. If he does not spin or spins at the wrong time, have that child sit down and select another to take his place. Everyone will want in on the action!

TAG-TEAM DIVISION

Take the confusion out of remembering the steps of long division with this class game. Familiarize your students with the four main steps of the process—*divide, multiply, subtract,* and *bring down;* then divide your class into groups of four. Instruct each group to form a straight line facing the chalkboard. Explain that each group will work the same problem. Also explain that each step of the division process will be worked by a different member of the group. For example, in the problem $6897 \div 5$, the first person will divide 6 by 5, the second person will multiply 1 by 5, the third person will subtract, the fourth person will bring down the next number, and the fifth person will start dividing again. Give the first group to work the problem correctly one point; then call out a new problem and continue in the same manner. After playing several rounds, declare the group with the most points the winner.

$$
\begin{array}{r}
26\ r2 \\
20\overline{)522} \\
\underline{40} \\
122 \\
\underline{120} \\
2
\end{array}
$$

QUICK TIP: FOR STUDENTS WHO HAVE DIFFICULTY REMEMBERING THE STEPS OF DIVISION, USE THE FOLLOWING MNEMONIC DEVICE: DAD (DIVIDE), MOTHER (MULTIPLY), SISTER (SUBTRACT), AND BROTHER (BRING DOWN)

VISIONS OF FRACTIONS

Your students will be *seeing* fractions with this Geoboard activity! Make an overhead transparency of dot paper and display it on an overhead projector. Distribute one Geoboard, several copies of dot paper, and a supply of rubber bands to each student. Instruct each student to divide her Geoboard in half in as many different ways as possible, recording each method on dot paper. Invite a few students to come to the overhead and share one of their designs with the class. Continue the lesson by having each student discover how to divide a Geoboard into fourths and then eighths. Finally challenge each student to divide her Geoboard so that it simultaneously shows the fractions *one-half, one-fourth,* and *two-eighths.* Have her list several equivalent fractions or equations that can be shown on a Geoboard. For example, a student could write *1/4 = 2/8* and *1/2 = 2/4 = 4/8,* or *1/4 + 1/4 = 1/2* and *1/4 + 2/8 + 1/2 = 1.* Follow up this activity by giving each student a copy of "Fraction Quilt" on page 221 to complete as directed.

Note: Since this is an exploration activity designed to get students to see and think about fractions, it will probably take several class periods to complete.

FRACTION STATIONS

Show students how much fun learning about fractions can be with this class activity. Set up each of the stations listed below; then give each student a chart similar to the one shown. Send an equal number of students to each station. Instruct each student to complete the activity at that station, recording the results on his chart. Give a signal to have students move to the next station. Students will enjoy the activities so much, they'll hardly be aware that they're practicing fractions!

- **Trash-Can Slam:** Student stands ten feet from an empty trash can and attempts to throw 20 pieces of balled-up paper, one at a time, into the can.

- **Golf:** Student uses a wrapping-paper tube or a plastic bat to putt a plastic golf ball into a coffee can taped to the floor six feet away. (six attempts)

- **Milk-Carton Toss:** Student attempts to toss a small rubber ball into one of several empty (and completely opened) pint-sized milk cartons positioned side by side in a shoebox eight feet away. (eight attempts)

- **Bowling:** Student rolls a tennis ball and attempts to knock down ten capped liter-size plastic soda bottles half-full of water positioned in a bowling-pin formation 15 feet away.

- **Ring Toss:** Student attempts to toss a plastic lid with the center removed over one leg of a chair turned upside down ten feet away. (seven attempts)

Station	Total Attempts	Successful Attempts	Fraction
Trash-Can Slam	20	12	3/5
Golf	6	3	1/2
Milk-Carton Toss	8	6	3/4
Bowling	4	2	1/2
Ring Toss	9	7	7/9

RECIPES FOR SUCCESS

Your favorite recipe could be the winning recipe for helping your students master fractions! Target a specific skill by choosing from the recipe activities below.

- **Simplifying fractions:** Change the specified amount of every ingredient in a favorite recipe to an equivalent fraction. For example, change 1/4 cup sugar to 5/20 cup sugar. Distribute a copy of the revised recipe to each student; then have him rename the fractions in the ingredient list in simplest form.

- **Adding fractions:** Distribute a copy of any two recipes with similar ingredients to each student. Instruct her to compile a shopping list after calculating how much of each ingredient will be needed to make both recipes. For example, if one recipe calls for 3/4 cup sugar and the other calls for 1/3 cup sugar, then a total of 1 1/12 cups of sugar would be needed for both recipes.

- **Subtracting fractions:** Give each student a copy of the same recipe. On the board list the recipe's ingredients. Next to each ingredient, write an amount greater than what the recipe requires. Explain that the quantities on the board represent how much of each ingredient is on hand. Then have each student determine how much of each ingredient on the board

would be left after preparing the recipe he was given. For practice in solving multistepped problems, direct each student to find out how much of each ingredient would remain after doubling the recipe.

- **Multiplying fractions:** Distribute a copy of the same recipe to each student. Have her double, triple, or quadruple the recipe by multiplying the quantity of its ingredients by *2, 3,* or *4.*

- **Dividing fractions:** Revise the ingredients of one or more recipes for snack foods by multiplying the measurements by any whole number. For example, if a recipe calls for 3/4 cup flour, multiply 3/4 by 3 to get 2 1/4 cups flour and so on. Then have each student reduce the measurements on his copy of the revised recipe to reflect the amount needed for 1/3 of the recipe *(2 1/4 ÷ 3 = 3/4).* As an extra incentive, ask parents to send in the necessary ingredients so that each group can prepare that recipe using the reduced quantities. You can bet that your students will make sure their calculations are correct!

SORTING IT ALL OUT

Is this fraction closer to 1, 1/2, or 0? Let your students decide by mentally calculating the answer! Divide your class into groups of three or four students. For each group, program a set of 15–20 index cards, each labeled with a fraction less than 1—such as *3/8, 1/6,* or *5/7.* Instruct each group to sort its fraction cards into three groups: *closest to 1, closest to 1/2,* or *closest to 0.* Direct each group to discuss and then write about the method it used to sort the cards. Then call on each group to explain how it completed the task.

PAPER TOSS

What does a balled-up piece of paper have to do with fractions? Nothing—but it sure makes this two- to four-player center game fun! Using self-stick labels and a marker, label the inner bottom of six coffee cans with a different mixed number. Cover any rough edges on the rim of each can with masking tape. Create two answer keys, one showing all possible sums for adding together any two mixed numbers, and another showing the sum of each mixed number plus 1/2. Store the answer key in a file folder near the center game.

To play:

1. Arrange the cans in a bowling-pin formation on the floor; then place a length of masking tape about ten feet from the cans.
2. Have each player in turn stand behind the masking-tape line and toss two balled-up pieces of paper, one at a time, into the cans.
3. Instruct each player to find and record the sum of the two mixed numbers inside the cans where his paper wads landed.
4. If one of the paper wads misses a can and hits the floor, have that player record the fraction *1/2* as the number for that toss.
5. If both paper wads miss a can, have that player lose his turn.
6. Continue in this manner until each player tosses two paper wads five times each.
7. Have each student check his answers by the answer key; then declare the player with the most correct answers the winner.

Vary the game by affixing new labels with different mixed fractions inside each can, or by changing the operation from addition to multiplication or division. To follow up, give each student a copy of "It's Off To Camp We Go!" on page 222 to complete as directed.

FROM FRACTIONS TO PERCENTS

Give your students practice in changing fractions to percents and vice versa with this variation of tic-tac-toe. On the chalkboard write the 14 fractions listed below. Have each student draw a game grid on paper. Next instruct each student to choose any nine of the fractions on the board, writing each fraction in a different square on his grid. After each child has created his board, call out an equivalent percent (for example, 20%) from the list below. Write that percent on another area of the chalkboard. Instruct each student to change that percent to a fraction on a sheet of paper. Have every student who correctly changed the percent to its matching fraction (for example, 1/5) write an *X* in the section of his tic-tac-toe board containing that fraction. Continue calling out different equivalent percents until a student gets three *X*s in a row on his board and calls out, "Tic-tac-toe!" Have that student read his fractions and their equivalent percents back to you. If he's correct, declare him the winner and instruct your students to create new boards for another round of play.

Vary the game by having students fill their tic-tac-toe boards with percents; then call out fractions during the game. Instruct each student to convert the called fraction into a percent and mark his board if he has a match.

Percents

20%	16%
30%	50%
25%	60%
75%	65%
40%	70%
15%	35%
80%	45%

$\frac{1}{5}$	$\frac{10}{25}$	$\frac{1}{2}$	$\frac{7}{20}$
$\frac{3}{10}$	$\frac{3}{20}$	$\frac{3}{5}$	$\frac{9}{20}$
$\frac{1}{4}$	$\frac{4}{5}$	$\frac{13}{20}$	
$\frac{3}{4}$	$\frac{4}{25}$	$\frac{7}{10}$	

$\frac{4}{25}$	$\frac{4}{5}$	$\frac{9}{20}$
$\frac{1}{5}$	$\frac{1}{2}$	$\frac{3}{4}$
$\frac{7}{10}$	$\frac{3}{10}$	$\frac{3}{5}$

DECIMALS

DUELING DECIMAL CARDS

Boost students' confidence in reading and writing decimals with this simple game. Give each student four index cards and a pair of scissors for cutting each index card into thirds. Direct her to label one card with a decimal point and ten cards with the numbers 0–9. Have her discard the 12th card. Call out a number that can be built using any combination of the 11 cards—such as *3,405.78* or *103.56*. Challenge each student to arrange her cards on her desktop to form the called number. Circulate to assess students' work. Write the correct standard form on the chalkboard; then have each student check her answer, giving herself one point for each correct answer.

Vary the game by calling out several numerals and a decimal point in a specific order and having students form the number and then write it in word form. To check, write the correct word form on the chalkboard and have the student give herself one point for each correct answer.

CREATE A NUMBER

Help your students write and order decimals with this challenging activity! Pair your students; then write a decimal point and three different digits—such as *4, 6,* and *8*—on the chalkboard. Challenge each pair to write all 24 possible numbers that can be formed from those three digits and the decimal point. Explain that each digit should be used only once in each number and that no number should be repeated. After writing all 24 possible numbers, challenge each pair to list the numbers in greatest to least order. Vary this activity by changing or adding to the digits that are used or by removing the decimal to compare just whole numbers. Extend this activity by giving each student a copy of "We Build Numbers!" on page 223 to complete as directed.

864.	6.84
846.	6.48
684.	4.86
648.	4.68
486.	.864
468.	.846
86.4	.684
84.6	.648
68.4	.486
64.8	.468
48.6	
46.8	
8.64	
8.46	

PUTTING DECIMALS TO USE

Give your students practice in problem solving as well as ordering and computing decimals with this activity. Collect an assortment of sales flyers and newspapers. Pair your students; then give each pair several of the collected papers, a sheet of construction paper, a glue stick, scissors, and the directions below.

1. Scour the newspapers and flyers for 15 numbers that have decimals.

2. Cut out and paste the numbers on construction paper in least to greatest order.

3. Use the cut-out numbers to make up five word problems dealing with addition, subtraction, or multiplication. Make a separate key for the problems.

4. Staple the problems and key to the construction paper and give it to your teacher.

During the next math class, pair your students as before. Redistribute the problems, making sure that no pair gets its own problems. Direct each pair to solve the problems and check its answers by the corresponding key. If desired, extend the lesson by solving money problems. Simply give each student a copy of "Costly Conversations" on page 224 to complete as directed.

GEOMETRY

THAT'S NOT A RECTANGLE!

Introduce the area of irregular figures to your students with graph paper and scissors. First make an overhead transparency of a sheet of centimeter graph paper; then display the transparency on an overhead projector and follow the steps below.

1. Select a student to use an overhead marker to draw a 5 x 7 rectangle on the transparency.
2. Review how to find the area of a rectangle (l x w = area). Calculate the area of the drawn rectangle; then check the answer by counting each square unit inside the rectangle.
3. Select another student to draw a 2 x 2 square on the transparency.
4. Compute the area of the square; then check by counting the squares.
5. Cut out the figures drawn on the transparency; then arrange them on the overhead so that they form an irregular figure (see the illustration).
6. Challenge each student to determine the area of this new figure. Guide students to conclude that the area of this new figure can be found by adding the area of the original rectangle to the area of the original square.
7. Trace the new figure on a blank transparency, dividing the figure to show its two original figures.
8. Demonstrate how to find the area of the two different figures, then add their areas together to determine the total area of the new figure.

After demonstrating a few more examples, provide more practice with this new skill by distributing a copy of "One Step At A Time!" on page 225 to each student. For a great review of different geometric figures, also see "Puzzling Polygons" on page 226.

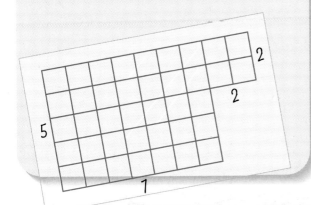

PROTRACTOR PICTURES

Pull out the protractors for this symmetrical activity! Give each student a sheet of white drawing paper, a ruler, and a protractor. Instruct him to fold his paper, dividing it in half vertically. Next have him use his ruler to trace the fold line. Also have him use his protractor to create a design with ten line segments on the left half of the paper. Explain that each line segment must start on the dividing line but can extend through an existing line segment, resulting in multiple line segments as shown. After making the design, direct each student to exchange papers with a partner. Have each student pretend that the dividing line on the paper is a mirror; then have him use his protractor to duplicate the design he sees on the left half of the paper onto the right half. Inform the student that he must measure each line segment's length and each angle's degrees so that what he draws becomes an exact mirror image of the original. Instruct each student to return the vertically symmetric design to its original owner; then allow students to use colored pencils or crayons to decorate their designs. Display the designs on a bulletin board titled "It's Symmetrical!"

QUICK REFERENCE

For an alphabetical list of common geometric terms, see page 216.

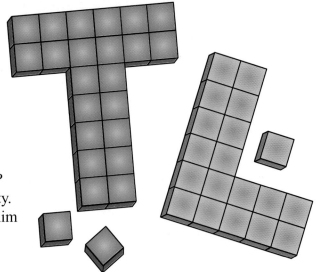

ALPHABET AREA

Need an easy activity for reinforcing area and perimeter? Give each student a pile of color tiles. Call out a letter of the alphabet and instruct each student to create that letter with his tiles. Require that each part of the letter be two tiles wide as shown. Have the student calculate both the perimeter and the area of that letter. Continue calling letters—*L, T, H, F, E,* and *P* are the easiest—until students feel comfortable with the activity. Then challenge each student to use the manipulatives to help him find the perimeter and area of each letter in his first name.

figure 1

HANDS—ON CUBES

Give your students a two-day experience in spatial awareness with this challenging, hands-on geometry activity. Duplicate several sheets of one-inch graph paper for each pair of students. Next make two overhead transparencies of the graph paper. Bring in an empty box; then follow the steps below to guide your students in creating three-dimensional figures.

figure 2

1. Demonstrate how the box can be cut so that it lies flat. Inform your students that the flattened figure is called a *net*.
2. Display one of the transparencies you made earlier and draw the net of a cube (see fig. 1) on it.
3. Draw the same net on a sheet of one-inch graph paper and cut it out.
4. Show students how to fold the net to create a cube.
5. Pair your students; then give several sheets of graph paper and scissors to each pair.
6. Challenge each pair to draw ten other nets that will fold into cubes.
7. Direct each pair to cut out each net and test it.
8. Have each pair draw the nets that did fold into cubes on an uncut sheet of graph paper.
9. Invite each pair in turn to come to the overhead and draw one of its nets on the remaining transparency (see fig. 2). As each pair shares, instruct the other pairs to record any nets they did not discover on their graph paper.
10. Have the pairs store their nets until the next math class.

During the next math lesson, direct each pair to write the letters *n, e, t,* and *s* in appropriate blocks on each net so that when the net is cut and folded into a cube, the word *nets* can be read horizontally, and the top and bottom blocks are blank. Suggest that each pair mentally fold a cube before writing any letters on it. Require that all four letters be recorded on a net before cutting it out. If desired, allow no erasing! This is a difficult— but fun—visualization that gets easier after the first few attempts.

COORDINATE CODES

Transform your students into expert decoding sleuths with this point-plotting activity for partners. Give each student one copy of a large labeled quadrant. Have each student plot all the letters of the alphabet on his quadrant. Then instruct one student to write a message to his partner using the coordinates he plotted. Direct the partner to use the coordinates to decipher the coded message. As a variation, allow students to use the quadrants for practicing their spelling and vocabulary words.

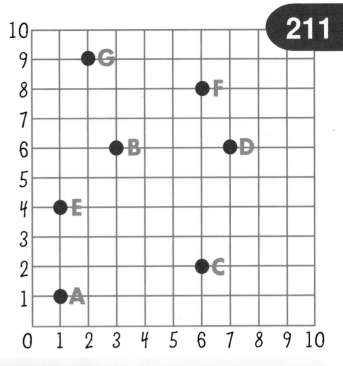

DISCOVERING PI

Is the formula for finding the circumference of a circle just a bunch of numbers and symbols to your students? Collect a variety of objects with circular tops or bases, such as drinking cups, coffee mugs, round glue sticks, lids from bottles or jars, and a roll of tape. Then follow the steps below to help your students understand the *meaning* of those numbers and symbols.

1. Review the definitions of circumference (the distance around a circle) and diameter (a line segment that passes through the center of a circle and has both endpoints on the circle).
2. Pair your students; then give each pair a 12-inch ruler, a calculator, a length of string (long enough to measure the circumference of the largest object in your collection), and five circular items.
3. Demonstrate how to use the string and ruler to measure the circumference and diameter of one of the objects.
4. Instruct each pair to measure and record the circumference and diameter of its five items on a sheet of loose-leaf paper.
5. On the chalkboard, draw a chart (see the illustration) to record your students' findings.
6. Allow each pair to record one or two of its measurements on the class chart.
7. Direct each pair to use its calculator to divide the circumference of each object it recorded on the board by its diameter.

Object	Circumference	Diameter	C ÷ D =
mug	7 in.	1.8 in.	3.89 in.
plant pot	15 in.	4.25 in.	3.53 in.
cup	6.75 in.	2.25 in.	3 in.

8. Instruct the pairs to study the chart and comment on any patterns that they see. Guide the pairs to conclude that each quotient is approximately 3.
9. Explain that the relationship between the circumference of a circle and its diameter can be expressed by using pi—or π—which is equivalent to 3.14. Point out that the recorded measurements are not exact because of the method of measurement.
10. Introduce the formula for finding the circumference of a circle—circumference = pi x diameter, or $C = \pi \times d$. Also introduce the formula for finding the diameter of a circle—diameter = circumference ÷ pi, or $d = C \div \pi$.

Remembering these formulas should now be much easier for your students!

A HANDY REFERENCE OF COMMON MATH FORMULAS IS ON PAGE 217.

MEASUREMENT

REAL-LIFE MEASUREMENT

Get down to the nitty-gritty of hands-on measurement with this at-home assignment. Make a list of tasks similar to those below for your students to complete at home with their parents. During the next class, compare students' measurements and make class graphs displaying the information where appropriate.

1. List ten things in your house that are about one centimeter long.
2. List ten things in your house that are about one meter long.
3. Use three different units to measure your mom's or dad's height.
4. Calculate the areas of the biggest and smallest rooms in your house.
5. Name five places that you and your family would like to visit; then calculate the distance of each place from your hometown.

FOLLOW MY RULES

See how adept your students are at using rulers and following directions with this partner game. Provide each student with a ruler and two sheets of drawing paper. Instruct him to use one sheet of paper and his ruler to create a design consisting of ten line segments. Tell him that each successive line segment he draws must be perpendicular to the previous one (see the illustration). Have each student place his second sheet of paper over the top of his design and trace the exact starting point of his design with a pencil. Then follow the steps below.

1. Pair your students.
2. Have one student give his partner the sheet labeled with the starting point of his design.
3. Direct that same student to give step-by-step oral directions to his partner on how to duplicate his design. For example, he could say, "Start at the labeled point and draw a 4-inch line segment heading east. From that point, draw a 5 1/4-inch line segment heading north."
4. Have the student continue giving directions in this manner until the design is complete.
5. Direct each pair to place one design on top of the other to see if they match. If not, have the pairs determine how to make the attempt more accurate.
6. Instruct each pair to repeat the process using the other partner's design.

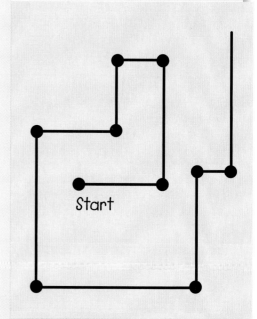

Start

To create a design using a metric ruler, give each student a smaller sheet of drawing paper.

FOR ADDITIONAL MEASUREMENT ACTIVITIES, SEE "A 'GRAM-TASTIC' RACE" ON PAGE 227, A REPRODUCIBLE GAME FOR COMPARING UNITS OF WEIGHT, AND "BLACKOUT!" ON PAGE 228, A FUN REPRODUCIBLE ON FINDING ELAPSED TIME.

GRAPHING GRADES

Make graphs come alive by having each student keep track of her own grades. Select one subject area, such as spelling, and have each student record her test grades in her notebook for one grading period. At the end of that period, instruct each student to design a line, stem-and-leaf, or bar graph displaying her test results. Then have the student determine the mean, median, and mode of her test scores. Students will be practicing data collection, and you'll have a great work sample to show at parent conferences.

TIMELY PIE GRAPHS

Data collection comes to life with this activity. Have each student select a family member to be the subject of his study. Explain that each student should chart the time his subject spends each day for five consecutive days on activities such as sleeping, eating, working, doing homework or housework, etc. After all the data has been collected, instruct the student to find the average daily time spent on each activity. Explain that each average should be rounded to the nearest hour and that the times may have to be adjusted to equal 24 hours. Next direct the student to display his data as a colored pie graph. Finally have him analyze the graph to answer questions such as "Which activity occupies most of the subject's time? The least?"

MEAN, MEDIAN, & MODE

Use your students' interests to introduce mean, median, and mode. Divide your class into groups of five or six students; then give each group one copy of one-inch graph paper and scissors. Have each group member, in turn, add the name of his favorite food to the graph paper, writing one letter in each block. Instruct the group to count the total number of letters in each word on its paper, write the total for each word on an extra square of graph paper, and then cut apart the squares. Next tell the group to arrange its cut-out words in least to greatest order by number of letters per word, positioning each numbered square next to a word with that number of letters. Finally guide each group through the instructions below for finding the *mean*, or average; the *median*, or middle number; and the *mode*, the number that occurs most often.

Mean: Find the average (mean) word length by arranging the words in order by length from shortest to longest, aligning the letters as shown. Rearrange the letters until all the words have the same number of letters. If there is a remainder, demonstrate how to round it or show it as a decimal.

Median: Find the middle number (median) by arranging the numbered squares in order from least to greatest, then counting to the middle. If there are two middle numbers, add the two numbers together, then divide by 2.

Mode: Plot the numbers on a line plot. The number that occurs most frequently is the mode.

4	C	A	K	E			
5	P	I	Z	Z	A		
5	F	R	I	E	S		
7	C	H	I	C	K	E	N
9	S	P	A	G	H	E	T	T	I

PATTERNS

MULTIPLICATION AND DIVISION PATTERNS

Point out patterns in multiplication and division by showing students a shortcut for multiplying or dividing multiples of ten. Write the sets of equations (not the explanations) shown below on the chalkboard. Have students search for a pattern in each set of equations. Then explain how to use patterns with the zeros to make multiplying and dividing multiples of ten easier.

$8 \times 3 = 24$
$8 \times 30 = 240$ (Multiplying by multiple of 10 = add 1 zero to product)
$8 \times 300 = 2,400$ (Multiplying by multiple of 100 = add 2 zeros to product)
$8 \times 3,000 = 24,000$ (Multiplying by multiple of 1,000 = add 3 zeros to product)

$5 \times 6 = 30$
$50 \times 6 = 300$ (Multiplying by multiple of 10 = add 1 zero to product)
$500 \times 6 = 3,000$ (Multiplying by multiple of 100 = add 2 zeros to product)
$5,000 \times 6 = 30,000$ (Multiplying by multiple of 1,000 = add 3 zeros to product)

$24 \div 3 = 8$
$240 \div 3 = 80$ (Dividing a multiple of 10 = 1 zero in quotient)
$2,400 \div 3 = 800$ (Dividing a multiple of 100 = 2 zeros in quotient)
$24,000 \div 3 = 8,000$ (Dividing a multiple of 1,000 = 3 zeros in quotient)

HUNDREDS-BOARD PATTERNS

Help your students see that patterns are all around—even in multiplication and division! Give each pair one hundreds board and a handful of beans or other hundreds-board markers. Explain that you will call out directions for them to follow on their hundreds boards. Also explain that if they follow your directions correctly, a pattern should appear on their boards. Instruct each pair to cover all numbers whose digits add together to equal 9. For example, a student could cover the digits 1 and 8 in the number 18 because they add together to make 9 ($1 + 8 = 9$). Then ask each pair if they can find anything else in common with the covered numbers. Guide students to recognize that they are all multiples of nine (9, 18, 27, 36, 45, 54, 63, 72, 81). Next direct the pair to cover, in turn, the multiples of 3, 4, 5, 6, 7, 8, and 10. Have the pairs discuss the patterns each set of multiples makes before clearing their boards.

HUNDREDS BOARD

1	2	3	4	5	6	7	8	9	10
11	12	13	14	15	16	17	18	19	20
21	22	23	24	25	26	27	28	29	30
31	32	33	34	35	36	37	38	39	40
41	42	43	44	45	46	47	48	49	50
51	52	53	54	55	56	57	58	59	60
61	62	63	64	65	66	67	68	69	70
71	72	73	74	75	76	77	78	79	80
81	82	83	84	85	86	87	88	89	90
91	92	93	94	95	96	97	98	99	100

CALCULATORS

CHATTY CALCULATORS

Let your students discover just how much calculators can talk by having them create talking word problems! Demonstrate how certain numbers on the calculator look like letters when the calculator is turned upside down. Then copy the chart in the illustration onto the chalkboard. Have each student form a word—such as *goggles*—using only the eight letters on the board. Explain that a letter may be used more than once. Give each student a calculator and an index card. Have the student use the chart on the chalkboard to translate his word into digits. For example, *goggles = 6066735*. Next instruct him to enter those same digits into the calculator backwards as *5376606*. Then have him turn his calculator upside down to read the word *goggles*. Use the steps below to create a sample word problem for the word *goggles*.

1. Divide the number you reversed (5,376,606) by 6; then subtract 890,000 to get 6,101.
2. Write an equation showing exactly what you did. For example: 5,376,606 ÷ 6 = 896,101 – 890,000 = 6,101.
3. Reverse the operations of your equation to create a problem; then write it on an index card. For example: 6,101 + 890,000 x 6 = ?
4. Check the answer to your problem. Does the answer reveal a word when the calculator is turned upside down?
5. Add a clue to your problem so that it reads like a question, such as "What might you wear when you go swimming?"

Then have each student write a problem on his index card for the word he formed earlier. Collect the index cards; then, during the next class, read aloud each problem on the cards one at a time, challenging your students to solve each one.

CALCULATOR COMPETITION

Surprise your students by handing them calculators to complete their next math assignment! Duplicate a class set of addition, subtraction, multiplication, and division problems taken from a sixth- or seventh-grade math text. Distribute one copy of the problems to each student. Then give the class a predetermined amount of time—about ten seconds for each problem on the sheet—to complete as many problems as possible. Remind each student to enter the numbers in the calculator carefully and accurately to avoid getting incorrect answers. Reward the student who gets the most correct answers with a small treat.

What might you wear when you go <u>swimming</u>?

6,101 ÷ 890,000 x 6 = _____

o = 0
i = 1
e = 3
h = 4
s = 5
g = 6
l = 7
b = 8

SEE A HANDY LIST OF COMMON PROBLEM-SOLVING STRATEGIES ON PAGES 218 AND 219. TO PRACTICE THOSE STRATEGIES, CHECK OUT THE GREAT REPRODUCIBLE ACTIVITIES ON PAGES 229 AND 230.

Geometrically Speaking

angle—a figure formed by two rays with a common endpoint (vertex)

circle—a closed plane figure in which all the points on its boundary are an equal distance from the figure's center point

cone—a space figure with one circular base and one vertex

congruent—having the same size and shape

cube—a space figure with six congruent, square faces

cylinder—a space figure with two congruent, circular bases and no vertices

diameter—a line segment that passes through the point at the center of a circle and has both endpoints on the boundary of the circle

edge—a line segment formed where two faces of a space figure intersect

face—a flat surface of a space figure

hexagon—a six-sided polygon

intersecting lines—lines that cross at one point

line—a collection of points along a straight path that goes on and on in both directions and has no endpoints

line segment—a part of a line having two endpoints

parallel lines—lines in the same plane that do not intersect

parallelogram—a quadrilateral whose opposite sides are parallel and equal

pentagon—a five-sided polygon

perpendicular lines—intersecting lines that form right angles at their intersection

plane—an infinite set of points on a flat surface extending endlessly in all directions

point—an exact location in space

polygon—a closed plane figure formed by three or more line segments

prism—a space figure with two parallel, congruent bases; a prism is named by the shape of its bases

pyramid—a space figure with four triangular faces and one polygon-shaped base

quadrilateral—a four-sided polygon

radius—a line segment with one endpoint at the center point of a circle and the other endpoint at any point on the boundary of the circle

ray—a part of a line extending from one endpoint in one direction indefinitely

rectangle—a parallelogram with four right angles

rhombus—a parallelogram with four equal sides

space figure—a figure whose points lie in more than one plane

sphere—a space figure formed by a set of points all at an equal distance from the center point

square—a rectangle with four equal sides

triangle—a three-sided polygon

vertex—a common endpoint of two rays forming an angle, two line segments forming sides of a polygon, or two line segments forming the edges of a space figure

Math Formulas

Perimeter

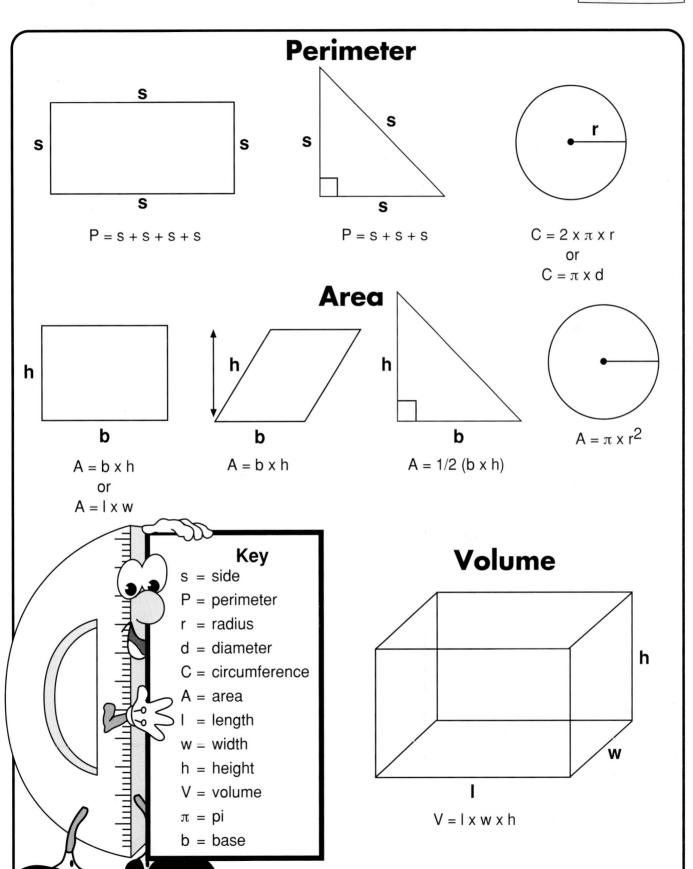

$P = s + s + s + s$

$P = s + s + s$

$C = 2 \times \pi \times r$
or
$C = \pi \times d$

Area

$A = b \times h$
or
$A = l \times w$

$A = b \times h$

$A = 1/2 \, (b \times h)$

$A = \pi \times r^2$

Key

s = side
P = perimeter
r = radius
d = diameter
C = circumference
A = area
l = length
w = width
h = height
V = volume
π = pi
b = base

Volume

$V = l \times w \times h$

Problem-Solving Strategies

Act It Out

To help you see a problem clearly, act it out or use manipulatives to help.

Example:
In a card game, Rob sits across from Meg, Drew is at Meg's right, and Kate complains that Rob's right elbow bumps her left arm. How are the friends arranged?

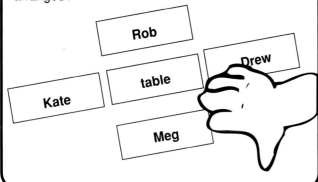

Draw A Picture Or Diagram

Use a picture or a diagram to help you solve a problem.

Example:
Kendra and Max live the same distance from the bridge. Kendra is upstream and Max is downstream. They live 1,258 feet apart. How far does each one live from the bridge?

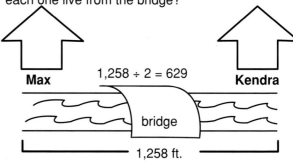

They each live 629 feet from the bridge.

Use Logic

When several facts must work together to make a solution, use thinking skills to help you solve the problem.

Example:
A numeral has three digits. The first digit is an odd number. The last digit is two more than the first. Multiplying its digits gives a product of 70. What is the number?

1. The first digit can be 1, 3, 5, or 7. It cannot be 9.
2. The last digit can be 3, 5, 7, or 9. It cannot be 1 or an even number.
3. The second digit can be any numeral between 0 and 9.
4. Which three possible numerals will give a product of 70?

$5 \times 2 \times 7 = 70$. The answer is 527.

Guess And Check

Take a guess at a problem's answer and check it. If you're not correct, adjust your guess and try again.

Example:
The product of two numerals is 115. What are the two numerals?
Since 115 has a 5 in the ones place, you know it is a multiple of 5.

Guess: $5 \times 20 = 100$ *(The answer is too small.)*

Guess again: $5 \times 23 = 115$ *(Yes!)*
The numerals are 5 and 23.

Find A Pattern

Decide how you get from one numeral to the next numeral in a pattern. Then see if this rule works for the rest of the pattern.

Example:
Degas is making a picture. He places one tile in the first row, four tiles in the second row, and seven tiles in the third row. How many tiles will be in the sixth row?

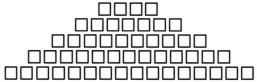

The pattern is *add three.*
The sixth row will have 16 tiles.

Problem-Solving Strategies

Make A List

Make an organized list when you need to show all the possible solutions.

Example:
How many different outfits could you make if you bought one red shirt, one blue tank top, one pair of tan pants, and one pair of gray shorts?

red shirt, tan pants
red shirt, gray shorts
blue tank top, tan pants
blue tank top, gray shorts

You could make four different outfits!

Work Backward

Read the problem. Identify the operations used. Then use *inverse* operations to work backward to the problem's beginning.

Example:
Bill returned from shopping with $3.00. He had spent $9.25 for snacks and $12.75 for comic books. How much money did he have before he went shopping?

Amount Bill had left:	Amount spent on snacks:	Amount spent on comic books:	He started with $25.00!
$3.00 +	$9.25 +	$12.75 =	

$3.00 + $9.25 + $12.75 = $25.00

Simplify

To help you understand a problem, decide on a way to make the numbers simpler.

Example:
At 7:00 A.M. on Friday, Carinda finds this note from her mom: "Your aunt will be here in exactly 1,500 minutes." On what day and at what time will Carinda's aunt arrive?

60 minutes = 1 hour
24 hours = 1 day
1,500 minutes ÷ 60 minutes = 25 hours
25 hours = 1 day and 1 hour.
Carinda's aunt will arrive at 8:00 A.M. on Saturday.

Brainstorm

Think of a new, creative way to look at a problem.

Example:
How do five and nine more make two?
If it's 5 o'clock and you move the hour hand ahead 9 hours, it will become 2 o'clock!

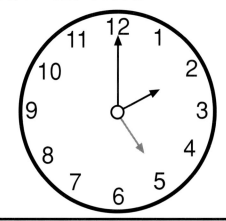

Make A Table, Chart, Or Graph

Use a table, chart, or graph when you need to keep track of data and see how it changes.

Example:
Bruce is 4 years old and Matt is 13 years old. When will Matt be twice as old as Bruce?

	years					
Bruce	4	5	6	7	8	9
Matt	13	14	15	16	17	18

Matt will be twice as old as Bruce in 5 years!

Name _____ *Mixed numbers: addition and subtraction*

It's Off To Camp We Go!

Attention, campers: it's math time! Use the map of Camp Bushytail to help you solve each of the ten problems below. Show all your work on the back of this sheet; then write the correct answers on the lines provided.

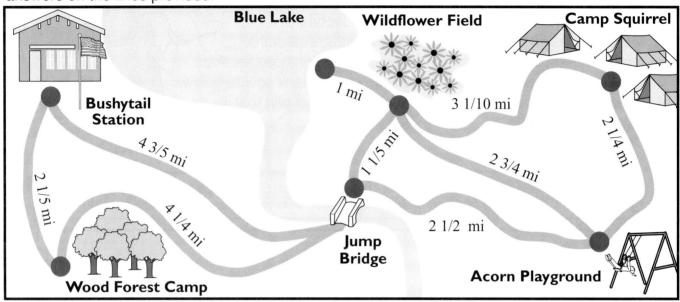

1. On Monday morning the campers hiked from Camp Squirrel to Acorn Playground, then to Wildflower Field. How far did the campers hike that morning? _____

2. While at Wildflower Field on Monday afternoon, the campers decided to hike across Jump Bridge to Bushytail Station. How far was this hike? _____

3. How much farther was the campers' afternoon hike than their morning hike? _____

4. On Monday evening the campers decided it was too late to hike all the way back to Camp Squirrel, so they decided to hike the 2 1/5 miles to Wood Forest Camp and spend the night. How many total miles did the campers hike on Monday? _____

5. Tuesday morning the campers loaded up their gear and hiked from Wood Forest Camp to Jump Bridge, then to Wildflower Field, and then to Camp Squirrel. How far did the campers hike that day? _____

6. On Wednesday camper group A decided to hike from Camp Squirrel to Jump Bridge. How many miles long is the shortest route that the campers can take? _____

7. Camper group B hiked from Camp Squirrel to Acorn Playground, then to Jump Bridge. Which group hiked farther on Wednesday? _____

8. How many miles is it to hike from Bushytail Station to Wood Forest Camp to Jump Bridge, then back to Bushytail Station? _____

9. How many miles is the shortest hike from Camp Squirrel to Jump Bridge, then to Wood Forest Camp? _____

10. If some campers want to hike about 10 miles, which route should they take? Write your answer on the back of this sheet.

> **Bonus Box:** On the back of this sheet, write a word problem that can be solved by using the information from the map above. Exchange papers with another student and solve each other's problems.

©1997 The Education Center, Inc. • *The Mailbox® Superbook • Grade 5* • TEC454 • Key p. 317

We Build Numbers!

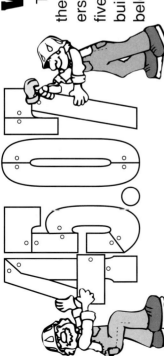

The construction workers at the We Build Numbers shop are having a little trouble with their latest orders. The shop received orders to construct ten new numbers, but the build-ers are having trouble understanding just which numbers the customers want. Cut out the five cards at the bottom of this sheet; then, using all five cards, (each card only once), build a four-digit decimal number that matches each of the ten customer orders listed below. Write each four-digit decimal number in the blanks provided.

1. Greater than 750 _ _ _ _ _ _ _ _

2. Between 540 and 570 _ _ _ _ _ _ _ _

3. Less than 5 _ _ _ _ _ _ _ _

4. Between 70 and 70.5 _ _ _ _ _ _ _ _

5. Between 0 and 0.5 _ _ _ _ _ _ _ _

6. Between 5 and 5.1 _ _ _ _ _ _ _ _

7. Less than 5.7 and greater than 4.5 _ _ _ _ _ _ _ _

8. As close to 40 as possible _ _ _ _ _ _ _ _

9. Between 0 and 0.47 _ _ _ _ _ _ _ _

10. As close to 0 as possible _ _ _ _ _ _ _ _

Bonus Box: Use the digits on your cards to write three more customer orders on the back of this sheet. Then give your sheet to a friend and have him/her build a number that matches each order.

0	4	5	7	•

©1997 The Education Center, Inc. • *The Mailbox® Superbook* • *Grade 5* • TEC454 • Key p. 317

Note To The Teacher: Use with "Create A Number" on page 208.

Costly Conversations

Chatty Charly is always on the phone. She talks to her friends all over the world, including those in Paris, France, and Brussels, Belgium. Use the rates in the chart below to help Charly figure the cost of her phone calls for this month. Show your work on the back of this sheet, then write your answers on the lines provided.

Country Called	Cost Of First Minute	Cost Of Each Additional Minute
Spain	$1.13	$.62
Belgium	$1.56	$.69
Denmark	$1.75	$.98
Ireland	$.98	$.60
Sweden	$1.15	$.65
France	$1.47	$.66

If I talk to Pierre in France for three minutes, it will cost $1.47 for the first minute and $1.32 for the next two minutes. That's a total of $2.79.

1. France for 8 minutes

   Cost = _____

2. Spain for 4 minutes

   Cost = _____

3. Ireland for 11 minutes

   Cost = _____

4. Belgium for 6 minutes

   Cost = _____

5. Denmark for 14 minutes

   Cost = _____

6. Sweden for 7 minutes

   Cost = _____

7. Spain for 22 minutes

   Cost = _____

8. France for 9 minutes

   Cost = _____

9. What is the total cost of Charly's phone bill this month?

   Total cost = _____

10. Which country is the cheapest for a five-minute call? _____

    The most expensive? _____

Bonus Box: On the back of this sheet, write two word problems that can be solved using the table above. Then challenge a friend to solve the problems.

©1997 The Education Center, Inc. • *The Mailbox® Superbook* • *Grade 5* • TEC454 • Key p. 317

224 **Note To The Teacher:** Use with "Putting Decimals To Use" on page 208.

Name _____

ONE STEP AT A TIME!

These problems will be a cinch if you solve them one step at a time! To find the area of each polygon below, first divide the polygon into two rectangles. Next find the area of each rectangle. Then add the measurements of the two rectangles together to find the total area of the irregular polygon. The first one has been started for you.

①

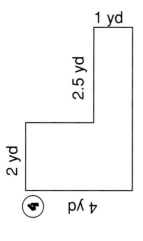

3 cm
4 cm
2 cm
2 cm

A
B

Area of A = __12__ sq. cm
Area of B = _____ sq. cm
Total Area = _____ sq. cm

②

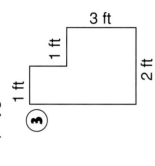

2 cm
1 cm
2 cm
11 cm

Area of A = _____ sq. cm
Area of B = _____ sq. cm
Total Area = _____ sq. cm

③

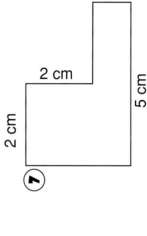

1 ft
1 ft
3 ft
2 ft

Area of A = _____ sq. ft.
Area of B = _____ sq. ft.
Total Area = _____ sq. ft.

④

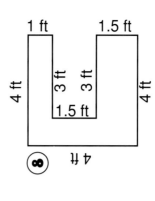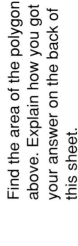

2 yd
2.5 yd
1 yd
4 yd

Area of A = _____ sq. yd.
Area of B = _____ sq. yd.
Total Area = _____ sq. yd.

⑤

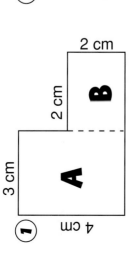

15 mm
25 mm
20 mm
30 mm

Area of A = _____ sq. mm
Area of B = _____ sq. mm
Total Area = _____ sq. mm

⑥

1 cm
1.5 cm
1.5 cm
5 cm

Area of A = _____ sq. cm
Area of B = _____ sq. cm
Total Area = _____ sq. cm

⑦

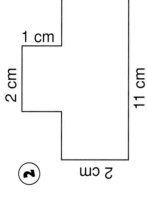

2 cm
1 cm
2 cm
5 cm

Area of A = _____ sq. cm
Area of B = _____ sq. cm
Total Area = _____ sq. cm

⑧

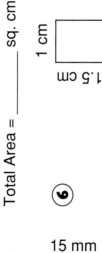

4 ft
1 ft
1.5 ft
1.5 ft
3 ft
3 ft
4 ft
4 ft

Area of A = _____ sq. cm
Area of B = _____ sq. cm
Total Area = _____ sq. cm

Find the area of the polygon above. Explain how you got your answer on the back of this sheet.

Bonus Box: Suppose you wanted to cover each of the eight polygons above with colored paper. If the paper costs $.25 per square unit, how much will it cost to cover each polygon?

Note To The Teacher: Use with "That's Not A Rectangle!" on page 209.

Puzzling Polygons

What's so puzzling about this puzzle? Well, since it's already put together, it's your job to take it apart! The puzzle contains 19 polygons all fitted together. Label each polygon in the puzzle with the letter listed in front of its name below. (The number in parentheses after some of the names tells how many polygons of that type are in the puzzle.)

After you have labeled each polygon, cut the puzzle pieces apart along the bold lines. Arrange the polygon pieces on a sheet of construction paper to create a design; then paste each piece in place. For a final touch, color and title your design.

A square
B rectangle
C parallelogram (2)
D rhombus
E trapezoid

F pentagon (2)
G quadrilateral (2)
H hexagon
I octagon
J decagon

K equilateral triangle
L right triangle (3)
M isosceles triangle
N scalene triangle

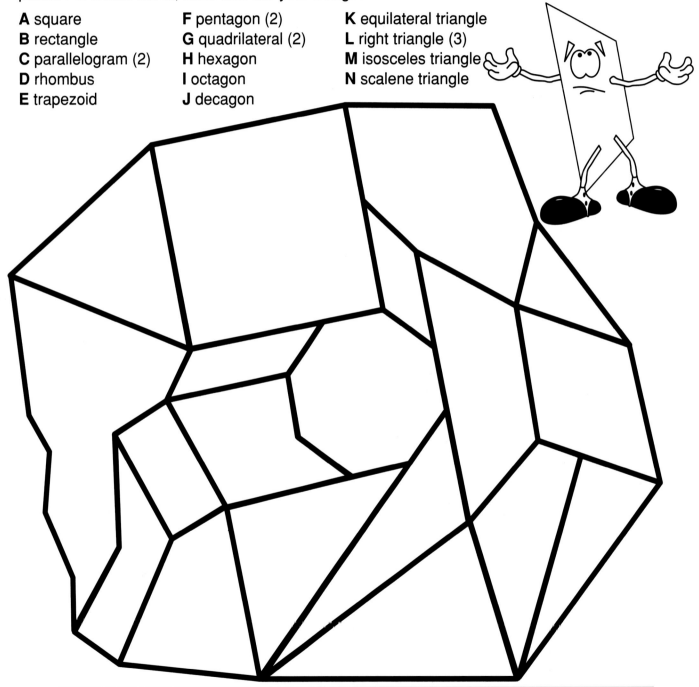

Bonus Box: On the back of your design, write three clues that identify one of the figures listed above. Challenge a friend to read the clues and identify the correct figure.

Note To The Teacher: Use with "That's Not A Rectangle!" on page 209. Duplicate one copy for each student.
226 Also provide each student with a sheet of construction paper, crayons, and a glue stick.

A "Gram-tastic" Race

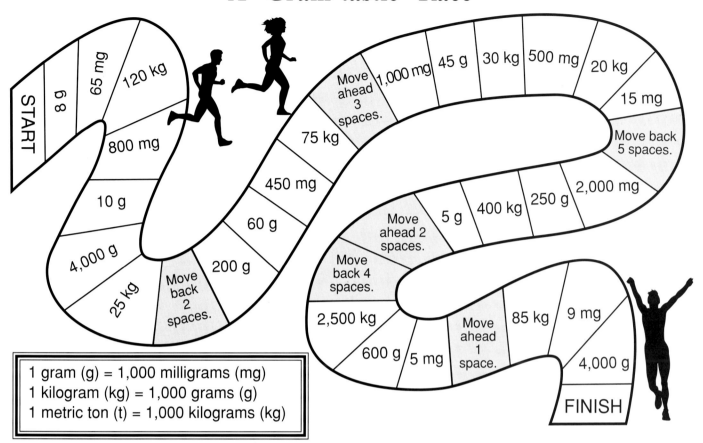

START
8 g
65 mg
120 kg
800 mg
10 g
4,000 g
25 kg
Move back 2 spaces.
200 g
60 g
450 mg
75 kg
Move ahead 3 spaces.
1,000 mg
45 g
30 kg
500 mg
20 kg
15 mg
Move back 5 spaces.
2,000 mg
250 g
400 kg
5 g
Move ahead 2 spaces.
Move back 4 spaces.
2,500 kg
600 g
5 mg
Move ahead 1 space.
85 kg
9 mg
4,000 g
FINISH

1 gram (g) = 1,000 milligrams (mg)		
1 kilogram (kg) = 1,000 grams (g)		
1 metric ton (t) = 1,000 kilograms (kg)		

1 g	500 mg	20 kg
225 g	2,000 kg	1 t
8 mg	5,000 g	6 kg
89 g	12 kg	70 mg

Directions:

Cut out the spinner below; then cut apart the cards on the left and place them facedown in a pile. Spin (see the illustration) to determine who goes first and how many spaces to move your game piece ahead. Draw a card. Compare the weight on the card to the weight on the space with your game piece. Tell which weight is larger (see the table). If you are correct, spin again. If you are incorrect or if the weights are equivalent, do not move your game piece. To win, be the first to arrive at Finish.

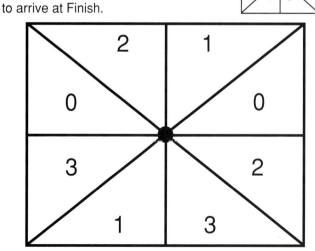

2   1
0   0
3   2
1   3

Note To The Teacher: Provide one copy of this sheet, a paper clip, scissors, a pencil, and two game pieces for each pair of students.

Name _____

Blackout!

Mr. Zapper works at the local power plant. A storm wiped out power to each city listed below at some point during the night. Use the times listed to help Mr. Zapper figure out how long each city was without power. Write your answers on the lines provided.

1. Jobville had no power from 1:12 A.M. to 3:12 A.M. _____

2. Salt River was affected from 1:33 A.M. to 4:43 A.M. _____

3. Twoburg lost power from 10:00 P.M. to 1:20 A.M. _____

4. Parks City was without power from 2:00 A.M. to 3:15 A.M. _____

5. Eynon had no power from 11:30 P.M. to 5:08 A.M. _____

6. Bloomsburg was affected from 12:45 A.M. to 3:00 A.M. _____

7. Lillington lost power from 1:50 A.M. to 2:45 A.M. _____

8. Apex had no power from 4:35 A.M. to 6:15 A.M. _____

When the residents of the cities awoke, they had to reset their clocks. Pretend that the power went off in your house. Use the information below to set your clock with the correct time. Write your answers on the lines provided.

Reset Clock To

9. The power went off at 3:00 P.M. and stayed off for 2 1/2 hours. _____

10. The power went off at 5:15 A.M. and stayed off for 1 hour and 45 minutes. _____

11. The power went off at 10:40 P.M. and stayed off for 45 minutes. _____

12. The power went off at 8:25 A.M. and stayed off for 4 hours and 15 minutes. _____

13. The power went off at 7:30 P.M. and stayed off for 3 hours and 10 minutes. _____

Bonus Box: On the back of this sheet, write a paragraph telling about a time when the power went off at your house. Tell how it affected you and your family.

Organization, Please!

Sometimes the answer to a problem may have many parts. An organized list helps problem solvers organize their thinking about a problem. The list can also help make sure that no choices are left out or repeated. Solve each problem below using the make-an-organized-list strategy. Show your work on the back of this sheet or on loose-leaf paper.

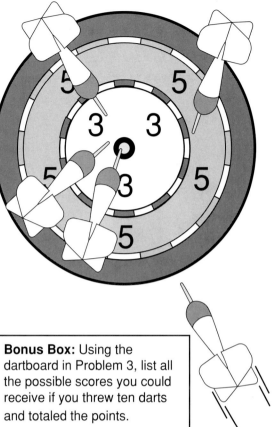

1. Margo wants to buy a $.50 soft drink from a vending machine that only takes exact change. If the machine takes quarters, dimes, and nickels, how many different combinations of coins can she use to buy her drink?

2. Write the year that you were born. List all the possible four-digit numbers that you can make using those four digits.

3. Look at the dart board. List all the possible scores that you could receive if you threw five darts and totaled the points.

Bonus Box: Using the dartboard in Problem 3, list all the possible scores you could receive if you threw ten darts and totaled the points.

Check This Out!

Some problems can be solved by using the guess-and-check strategy. If your first guess is correct, the problem is solved. If not, you must try other possible solutions and recheck. Solve each problem below using the guess-and-check strategy. Show your work on the back of this sheet or on loose-leaf paper.

1. Vince won 40 marbles in a five-day period. Each day he won three more than the day before. How many marbles did he win each day?

2. The sum of the numbers on two basketball jerseys is 56. The product of the two numbers is 735. What are the two numbers?

3. Place the digits 2, 6, 8, and 5 in the boxes below so that when the problem is multiplied, it produces the largest possible product.

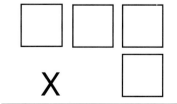

Bonus Box: How would you place the digits in Problem 3 in the same boxes to produce the smallest possible product?

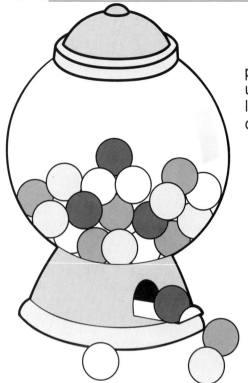

Picture This!

Sometimes it's helpful to use an available picture or draw a picture when trying to solve a problem. The picture helps you understand and use the data in the problem. Solve each problem below using the draw-a-picture strategy. Show your work on the back of this sheet or on loose-leaf paper.

1. Four jars contain a total of 150 gumballs. The third and fourth jars contain a combined total of 80 gumballs. The second and third jars contain a combined total of 90 gumballs. If the third jar contains 65 gumballs, how many gumballs are in the first jar?

2. Ed is older than Antawn. Antawn is younger than Shammond. Shammond is younger than Ed. Jerry is older than Ed. Which person is the oldest?

3. Courtney got on the elevator. She went down four floors, up three floors, and then down five floors. If she ended up on the fourth floor, at what floor did Courtney get on the elevator?

Bonus Box: Write your own problem modeled after one of the problems above. Challenge a partner to find the solution.

Reverse Your Thinking

Sometimes thinking backward will actually put you ahead! Solve each problem below using the working-backward strategy. Show your work on the back of this sheet or on loose-leaf paper.

1. Jenna spent $13.50 of the money she had been saving in her piggy bank at the baseball game. She spent four times that amount the next day on a new radio for her bedroom. She has only $41.25 left. How much did Jenna originally have in her piggy bank?

2. The number of students in Joshua's three-year-old school tripled for the start of the second school year. At the beginning of the third year, 25 new students joined. Joshua's school now has 412 students. How many students were enrolled in Joshua's school during the first year it was open?

3. The game starts at 8:00 P.M. and it takes Cory 20 minutes to walk there from home. Before he leaves, Cory needs to eat dinner, get dressed, and do his homework all of which will take a total of 65 minutes. At what time must Cory get started on his tasks in order to arrive at the game at exactly 8:00?

Bonus Box: For problem number 3, at what time will Cory arrive home if the game lasts 1 hour and 45 minutes?

SOCIAL STUDIES

Map Makers

Familiarize your students with the Western Hemisphere by having them create topographical maps. Enlarge and duplicate a map of the Western Hemisphere onto sheets of 11" x 17" paper. Provide each student with the materials listed below; then guide him through the steps for making a map.

Materials: enlarged Western Hemisphere map, 1 piece of 18" x 24" cardboard, social-studies book or atlas with a topographical map of the Western Hemisphere, half of the no-cook modeling-dough recipe on page 100 of this book (omit the food coloring), different colors of tempera paint, paintbrushes, scissors, glue stick

Steps:
1. Cut out the enlarged map and glue it to the center of the cardboard.
2. Completely cover the map with modeling dough.
3. Look in a social-studies book or atlas to find mountains, valleys, and other landforms; then form the features by pinching the dough with your fingers.
4. Allow your map to dry overnight.
5. Paint your map to show the different elevations on the map.
6. Add a color key to your map.

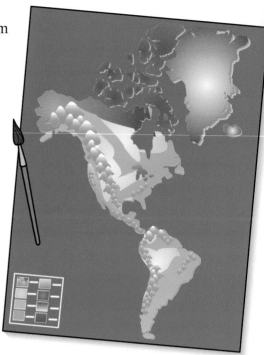

Room-Size Grids

Clear out the desks to make room for map grids! Use yarn to create a large grid on the classroom floor. Secure each length of yarn at both ends and in the center with tape. Label the grid's axes with index cards as shown; then choose an idea from below.

- Place construction-paper symbols representing buildings or parks on the map; then have your students name the location of each symbol.

- "Hide" an imaginary treasure in one of the squares; then have your students find the treasure's location by asking questions such as, "Is it north of A6?" and "Is it south of D3?" Provide construction-paper circles to mark eliminated squares.

- Label the sides of the grid "North," "South," "East," and "West" with index cards. Call out a location; then have a student mark that location by standing in and naming that square. Continue in the same manner by directing that student to call out another location, such as, "Stand in the square that is two blocks west of my square."

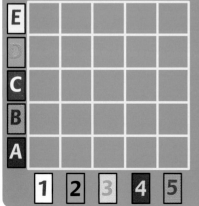

Imagination "State-tion"

Put each student's map-making skills to practice by having her create a map of a new state! Share typical symbols found on a state map. Discuss the information each symbol conveys; then give each student a short length of bulletin-board paper, a copy of the top half of page 248, and colored pencils or crayons.

Instruct each student to complete the reproducible as directed to design her map. Display the completed maps around the classroom.

Landforms In Booklet Form

Take the confusion out of learning about landforms with this booklet activity. Give each student seven sheets of 8 1/2" x 11" drawing paper; then have him cut each sheet in half horizontally. Challenge each student to use his social-studies book and other references to create a booklet page for each of the landforms listed below. Instruct him to include the name of the landform, a definition, an illustration, and an example on each page of the booklet. After each page has been completed, give each student a sheet of 8 1/2" x 11" construction paper. Have the student design a cover for his booklet. Then instruct him to alphabetize the pages of his booklet according to the names of the landforms. Have him assemble his book by placing the cover on top of the alphabetized pages and stapling it along the left side of the cover. What a great reference for students to use throughout their geographic studies!

Volcano
a crack in the earth's crust from which molten rock erupts.

Mauna Loa is a volcano in Hawaii.

Landforms
coast
island
isthmus
canyon
mountain
basin
cape
plateau
valley
volcano
mesa
peninsula
plain

A Hodgepodge Of Map-Skills Practice

Add variety to your map-skills practice by choosing from the following list of creative ideas:

1 On a map of North America, mark the location of the home cities of all the major-league baseball teams. Do the same for professional football, basketball, and/or hockey teams.

2 Using the weather map from a local newspaper, find the ten cities with the highest and lowest temperatures in the United States for that day. Find each of these cities on a U.S. map.

3 Using an atlas or encyclopedia, find the highest mountain on each continent. Mark each mountain's location on a world map (see page 243).

4 Using a local newspaper, find articles that deal with stories around your state. Mark the origin of each story on a state map.

5 On an appropriate map, mark the birthplaces of ten famous people.

6 On a local map, mark the location of each student's residence.

7 List ten of your favorite movies and their settings. Mark the city or country of each movie setting on an appropriate map.

Greensboro
High Point
Asheville
Charlotte
Raleigh
Wilmington

U.S. Regions

Division Decisions

The United States can be divided geographically in several different ways depending upon which textbook series is used. The activities on this page and page 236 can be used regardless of which regional division you use. At the right is a suggested method for dividing the United States into different regions.

Suggested Regions

New England States: ME, NH, VT, MA, CT, RI
Middle Atlantic States: NY, PA, NJ, MD, DE
Southeast States: KY, WV, VA, NC, TN, SC, AR, LA, MS, AL, GA, FL
Great Lakes States: MN, WI, MI, IL, IN, OH
Southwest States: AZ, NM, TX, OK
Plains States: ND, SD, NE, IA, KS, MO
Mountain States: MT, ID, WY, CO, NV, UT
Pacific States: WA, OR, CA, HI, AK

Portrait Of A Region

Looking for a unique activity for motivating students to learn about regions? Form poetry will do the trick! Duplicate one copy of page 245 for each student and distribute them. Read aloud the sample poem about Pennsylvania that is written at the top of the reproducible. Then assign each child a different state from the region you are currently studying. Instruct him to use his social-studies textbook to find the facts he needs to write a poem on the form provided. Explain that the poem should tell its reader about that assigned state. Further explain that each blank line can be filled with either a word or a phrase, but that no words should be omitted from the original form. After each poem has been written, give each student one sheet of drawing paper. Direct him to draw as large an outline of his assigned state as possible on his drawing paper. Then instruct him to copy his poem in the center of the state-outline shape, add illustrations to the poem, and then cut out the outline map that he drew. Post all of your students' poems on a bulletin board titled "Portrait Of A Region."

Torn-Paper Mosaics

Introduce the regions of the United States by having your students create torn-paper mosaics. Duplicate an outline map of the United States for each student in your class on light-colored construction paper. Give each student one of the U.S. maps, glue, and half sheets of 8 1/2" x 11" construction paper in eight different colors. Instruct the student to tear each sheet of construction paper into small pieces, making a different pile for each color. On the chalkboard, write the names of the regions of the United States. Assign a different construction-paper color to each region. Direct the student to cover each region of her map with the corresponding colored pieces of torn paper. Have the student title her map and create a key; then have students refer to these colorful maps throughout your regional study of the United States.

U.S. Regions

Destination: U.S. Regions

Can an imaginary trip actually help your students learn about the regions of the United States? It can with this activity! Duplicate one copy of page 246 for each student and distribute them. Then assign each student a different region of the United States. Have her imagine that she is planning a trip to her assigned region. Then instruct her to fill in each of the patterns on her reproducible as follows:

 Think about the climate of your region. On the lines of the suitcase, briefly describe from head to toe what you could be wearing on a trip to your assigned region.

 On the shopping bag, name three souvenirs you could bring back from this region.

 On each lens of the sunglasses, name a different tourist attraction that you could visit.

 On the lines of the plate, describe a typical regional meal that you could eat while on your trip.

 On the lines of the paw print, name three animals that you could see while visiting this region.

Without revealing her assigned region, invite each student to share the information written on her patterns while her classmates guess which region is being described. What a great way to learn about the characteristics of each U.S. region!

Tourist Attractions

1. Marine World Africa USA in Vallejo, CA

2. Grand Coulee Dam near Spokane, WA

Spinning For Trivia

Is your class ready for some regional trivia? Challenge each student to refer to different resource materials and write four trivia questions about your current region of study. Explain that each trivia question should be accompanied by an answer *and* an interesting fact related to that answer (see the illustration). After all the trivia questions have been written, give each student an 8 1/2" x 8 1/2" square of drawing paper. Guide the student to fold his paper as shown, writing a different trivia question on the outside of each triangular flap. Instruct him to lift each flap in turn and write the answer to the question plus one related, interesting fact on the flap. Instruct the student to write his name and the region's name on the inside square. Mount each trivia square on a bulletin board titled "Spinning For Trivia" by inserting a pushpin through the center of the square, enabling it to rotate. Invite your students to the board to rotate the squares—one triangle at a time—to learn more about your current region of study.

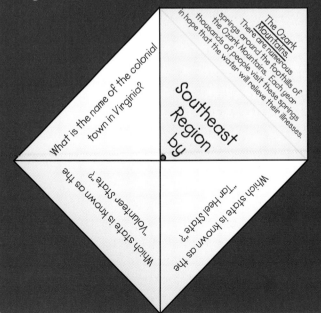

What is the name of the colonial town in Virginia?

The Ozark Mountains There are numerous springs around the Ozark Mountains. Each year thousands of people visit these springs in hope that the water will relieve their illnesses.

Southeast Region by

Which state is known as the "Volunteer State"?

Which state is known as the "Tar Heel State"?

The Western Hemisphere

Pillow Maps

Need a map project for studying any area of the Western Hemisphere? Divide your class into small groups. Assign each group a different area of the Western Hemisphere—the United States, South America, Canada, Mexico, Central America, or the Caribbean. Gather an opaque projector or an overhead projector for students' use. Then give each group a 2' x 2' sheet of white paper, a ruler, colored pencils or crayons, a 2' x 2' piece of white fabric, paintbrushes, bottles of different-colored fabric paint, and these directions:

1. Draw a two-inch frame around the outside of the paper.
2. Inside the frame, draw a map of your assigned area. Include land regions, the national capital, natural resources, and something that represents that area's geography.
3. Use an opaque projector or an overhead projector and a pencil to trace the outline of your map onto the center of your fabric.
4. Paint the map with fabric paints. Allow the paint to dry overnight.
5. Add any remaining details to the map. Again allow the paint to dry overnight.

Enlist a parent volunteer to help with assembling the pillows. Then place the completed pillows in a reading corner for your students to enjoy all year!

State The Location

Review Canada's geography and relative location with this whole-class game. Duplicate one copy of page 247. Laminate the sheet if desired; then cut out the cards, shuffle them, and place them facedown in a pile. Divide your class into groups of two or three students; then give each child a map of Canada. Have one group at a time draw a card and—without looking at a map—write five statements on the board that give the location of the place on the card (see the illustration). Give the group two points for each correct statement. If the group cannot write five statements, allow a map to be used for help; then give the group one point for any additional statements. Meanwhile direct the other students to use their maps to check each statement's accuracy. Declare the team with the most points at the end of the game the winner.

Vary the game by programming cards with information about Mexico, South America, or the United States.

> Edmonton is in Alberta.
>
> Edmonton is in one of the Prairie provinces.
>
> Edmonton is south of the Northwest Territories.
>
> Edmonton lies on the North Saskatchewan River.
>
> Edmonton is west of Regina.

Write All About It!

Your students will make more than headlines with this research activity! While studying the geography of any country, challenge your students to create informative newspapers. Pair your students; then assign each pair a different region—such as the Brazilian Highlands—within the country currently being studied. Give each pair two sheets of drawing paper, the front page of a newspaper, colored pencils, and a copy of the bottom half of page 248 to complete as directed. Display the completed news pages on a bulletin board titled "Extra! Extra! Read All About It!"

Myths And Legends

Native American literature is rich in colorful legends that explain the world and nature. Read aloud some tales that explain natural phenomena, such as why it thunders or why we have seasons (see the list below). Explain that even though these natural happenings can be explained scientifically, the myths help us learn about Native American beliefs and cultures.

After reading several stories, give each pair of students a different topic: *seasons, constellations, thunder, earthquakes, volcanoes,* and so on. Have each pair collaborate to write a myth or legend that explains its topic in a manner similar to the Native American tales they have read. Also have the pair research and summarize the scientific facts about its topic. Next direct each pair to glue its story and facts to a sheet of poster board and label and illustrate it like the one shown. After adding illustrations, invite each pair to contribute its work to a bulletin board titled "Native American Legends: Fact Or Fiction?"

Earthmaker's Tales: North American Indian Stories About Earth Happenings by Gretchen W. Mayo (Walker Publishing Company, Inc.; 1989)

Thirteen Moons On Turtle's Back: A Native American Year Of Moons retold by Joseph Bruchac & Jonathan London (The Putnam Publishing Group, 1992)

The Woman Who Fell From The Sky: The Iroquois Story Of Creation retold by John Bierhorst (William Morrow And Company, Inc.; 1993)

How The Stars Fell Into The Sky: A Navajo Legend by Jerrie Oughton (Houghton Mifflin Company, 1996)

Native Americans Flip Book

Areas all across our nation have a history that is linked to Native Americans. Make the study of these Native Americans a part of your study of the United States. Gather four sheets of 18" x 24" white construction paper for each student. Have students follow the simple directions below to make flip books to help them remember six of the major regions, or culture areas, in which Native Americans lived long ago. Over a predetermined amount of time, direct each student to research at least one tribe from each of the six culture areas. Have the student fill each flap with illustrations and captions related to that region. Post these questions for students to answer as they research:

- Where did the tribe live?
- How was the tribe organized and governed?
- What type of clothing did the people of this tribe wear?
- What types of food did they eat?
- What types of shelter did they use?
- What made this tribe different from other Native American groups?
- Where is this tribe today?

Then have each student flip the pages of his book as he shares his findings with the class.

1. Stack the four sheets of paper as shown (fig. 1).
2. Fold over the top half to form eight layers (fig. 2).
3. Staple the book at each side near the top of the fold.
4. Write "Native American Culture Areas" on the top flap, your name on the second flap, and the names of the six major regions on the remaining flaps as shown (fig. 3).

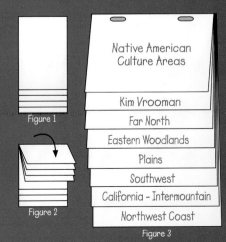

Figure 1

Figure 2

Native American Culture Areas

Kim Vrooman

Far North

Eastern Woodlands

Plains

Southwest

California - Intermountain

Northwest Coast

Figure 3

Exploring The New World

Launch your students on a colonial expedition they won't soon forget with this fun group activity. Divide your class into cooperative groups; then assign each group a different original colony on which to report. Explain that each group will act as a team of surveyors who should find out as much as possible about its colony and report its observations to the king. Expect each group to research the following topics about its colony: physical features, natural resources, and climate. After each group completes its research, have it present its findings to the royal court—the rest of the class. Have the class discuss whether or not colonization in each area should be recommended. On the board make a two-columned chart presenting reasons for and against the colonization of each area.

What In The World?

Here's an activity that will expose your students to the blending of cultures that occurred when the Old World adventurers discovered the New World. Share with students the foods and plants listed below that were introduced in Europe after explorers brought these items back from the New World. Have each student select one item from the list to research; then have him design a poster advertising that item's attributes and possible uses to his fellow countrymen in the Old World. After each student explains his poster to the class, post it for others to see.

Potatoes From The New World!
On Sale For A Limited Time At The Liverpool Docks
Great in soup, stew, baked or roasted!
Try The Latest Edible Treat Straight From The New World!

Items From The New World: corn, potatoes, tomatoes, peppers, chocolate, vanilla, tobacco, beans, pumpkins, avocados, peanuts, pecans, cashews, pineapples, blueberries, sunflowers, petunias, black-eyed Susans, dahlias, marigolds, wild rice

Colonial Craftsmanship

Investigate the craftsmanship of colonial Americans by having your class research the jobs of various skilled artisans whose work was vital to colonial survival. Direct each student to select a trade from the list below that is of particular interest to her. Have the student research that trade and determine which skills a person would need to be successful at that trade. Instruct the student to use the information she gathers to develop a "Help Wanted" advertisement for a colonial newspaper. Remind each student to include in the ad specific job requirements, salary, and benefits as well as whom to contact for more information about the advertised position. (For a map activity about the 13 colonies, see page 249.)

Help Wanted: Wheelwright

Location: Jamestown, Virginia
Job Description: job requires knowledge of the making and repairing of wheels and wheeled vehicles
Salary: commensurate with experience
Benefits: free wheels and meals

Job List:

tailor, wheelwright, miller, blacksmith, silversmith, joiner, cooper, tanner, printer, clockmaker, cabinetmaker, pewterer, whitesmith, hatter, fuller, glassblower, cordwainer, cobbler, gunsmith

The Path To Revolution

Use this informative cause-and-effect activity to familiarize your students with the events that paved America's path to revolution. Begin by recording each of the events below at the top of a different stone-shaped cutout. In chronological order, discuss with your class each event (the cause) and how colonists reacted to it (the effect). Then record the effect of each event on the bottom portion of its stone. Attach the stones in chronological order to your classroom wall to create a visual reminder of the events that caused the American Revolution.

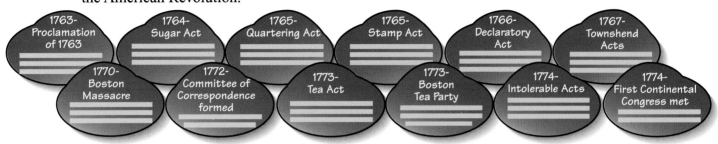

A Revolutionary Idea

The exciting characters in this activity are sure to spark your students' interest in the Revolutionary War! Provide each student with a copy of the hat pattern on page 250. Write the list of famous American Revolutionary figures below on poster board. Then direct each student to select one person from the list to research, finding out the individual's date and place of birth, plus information about his education, his role in the Revolution, his accomplishments, and the date of his death. Instruct each student to record his findings on the hat pattern; then have him color and cut out the hat. Display the cutout hats on a bulletin board titled "Famous Figures Of The American Revolution."

Abigail Adams
John Adams
Samuel Adams
Benedict Arnold
Crispus Attucks
Margaret Corbin
Charles Cornwallis
Benjamin Franklin
Horatio Gates
George III
Nathanael Greene
Nathan Hale
John Hancock
Mary "Molly Pitcher" Hays
Patrick Henry
John Jay
Thomas Jefferson
John Paul Jones
Marquis de Lafayette
Francis Marion
William Moultrie
Thomas Paine
Paul Revere
Betsy Ross
Baron von Steuben
George Washington

Firsthand Information

What better way to learn about people in other time periods than from firsthand information? Historical records, diaries, letters, and government documents not only offer important facts, but they also tell a story of what life was once like. With the help of your school's media specialist, find history books that contain examples of primary sources. Explain to your students that primary sources consist of historical records, diaries, letters, and government documents; then share the examples you collected. Inform your students that they will be using primary sources and what they know about a specific time period to write several journal entries on aged paper to make them look authentic. Allow your students to help prepare the aged paper by soaking sheets of 8 1/2" x 11" duplicating paper in tea and allowing the paper to dry. Explain that each journal entry should be written as if it were penned by a person living during that era with specific details about daily life—including references to appropriate dress, education, religion, politics, and transportation. After each student recopies his journal entries onto the aged paper, have him compile the entries into a booklet. Post the completed student journals for others to read.

April 19, 1775

Today marked the beginning of the war between the colonists and Great Britain. We can no longer be oppressed by the tyrant King George. Hence, we must defend out rights and gain our freedom from his control. If war be the only way to accomplish this goal, then we must go forth no matter what the cost.

Westward Ho!

Hitch up the wagon and prepare your students to explore the American westward movement with this fun simulation! Explain to your students that settlers moving westward were limited in the amount of supplies they could bring with them. Share that a *prairie schooner,* or covered wagon, was only about 4 feet wide and 10–12 feet long. Model these dimensions by cutting two 4-foot lengths and two 12-foot lengths of yarn and arranging them on the floor in a 4' x 12' rectangle. Then have several student volunteers sit within the wagon's outline. Afterward direct each student to list items—such as flour, sugar, and extra wagon wheels—that she would bring along with her on her trip, given the space limitations. Discuss whether or not the items would fit inside the wagon.

War Through The Camera's Eye

Prove that pictures really do speak a thousand words with this Civil War activity. Explain to your students that many of the most famous and poignant photos of the Civil War were taken by the famous photographer Mathew Brady and his team of more than 100 photographers. Collect several of Brady's Civil War photos from reference books. Have each student select one of these photos for further exploration. Then challenge each student to write a narrative that tells the story behind his photo choice.

A Nation Divided

Explore the complicated issues that led to the onset of the Civil War with this critical-thinking exercise. Divide your class into two groups—the North and the South. Then make a three-columned chart on the board as shown. In the first column of the chart, record the suggested events or issues listed below that contributed to the deterioration of relations between the northern and southern states prior to 1861. Subdivide the northern and southern groups into smaller cooperative groups of two to three students. Assign one cooperative group from each side the same topic to research from its perspective.

After the groups have researched, have them present their Confederate or Union viewpoints, in turn, to the class. As the groups present their positions, record relevant information on the board as shown. Ask students to analyze why the two sides held such different positions on the issues and how such differences could have caused the two regions to go to war against each other. (For a research contract about the Civil War, see page 251.)

Suggested Topics

- The Compromise of 1850
- The Fugitive Slave Law
- The impact of *Uncle Tom's Cabin* by Harriet Beecher Stowe
- The abolitionist movement
- Lincoln's election to the presidency
- The Kansas-Nebraska Act
- The Dred Scott decision
- The raid on Harpers Ferry
- The secession of South Carolina from the Union

Event/Issue	North	South
Fugitive Slave Law	The North was against the law because they were against returning escaped slaves to their owners. Abolitionists established the Underground Railroad to help slaves escape to freedom.	The South was for the law because it forced the return of all escaped slaves.

Branches Of Government

Introduce your students to the three branches of the U.S. government with this activity. Begin by drawing a large triangle on the board. Label each of the triangle's angles with a different branch of government as shown—*executive, legislative,* and *judicial.* Explain that our Constitution provides the framework for the federal government, as well as a system of *checks and balances* that keeps any one branch of the federal government from becoming too powerful. Point out that this triangular organization allows each branch to interact with the other two branches. Visually demonstrate this concept by having three student volunteers come to the front of the room and stand with joined hands in a triangular formation. Strengthen students' understanding of how the three branches of government are related by giving each student a copy of page 252.

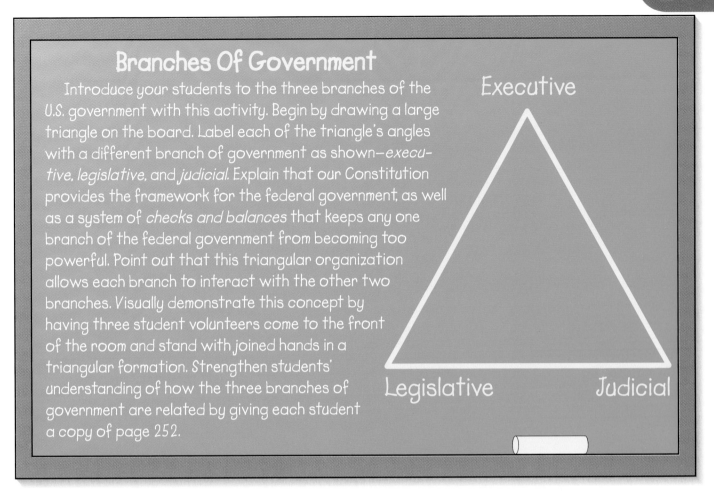

Off To Work We Go

Familiarize your students with the Industrial Revolution by introducing them to some of its key players. Explain to your students that during the Industrial Revolution, lots of new machines were invented that changed the nature of American life. Challenge your students to scour their social-studies texts and reference materials to contribute to a class list of American inventors and inventions. Compile and duplicate this list for every student. Next have each student fold a plain sheet of 8 1/2" x 11" paper lengthwise into thirds. Direct each student to label the three resulting sections "Inventor And Invention," "Life Before," and "Life After." Have each student record the inventors and their inventions from the class list in the "Inventor And Invention" column of his chart. Then instruct each student to think about what life would have been like before and after each invention and record his thoughts in the appropriate column.

Inventor And Invention	Life Before	Life After
Henry Ford automobile		
Thomas Alva Edison electric light phonograph motion picture camera and projector		
Alexander Graham Bell telephone		

current Events

The Year In Review

This easy activity is a great way to create a cumulative record of exciting news events from the current school year! Begin by labeling a large three-ring binder "The Year In Review: Top News Events Of [current year]." Use dividers to make a different section for each month of the school year. As students bring in current-events articles, mount each one on a separate sheet of 8 1/2" x 11" paper and place it in the appropriate section. Keep the notebook in your classroom library for students to read during their free time. By the end of the school year, your students will have compiled a comprehensive record of all the major news events that occurred.

A Nose For News

Keep your students in the know about current newsmakers with the following current-events exercise. Cut out several photos of newsmakers published in recent newspapers and magazines, making sure that an individual's name does not appear on his or her photo. Mount each photo on a sheet of construction paper and assign it a different number. Have each student number her paper with matching numbers; then— as you display the photos in sequential order—challenge her to identify by name each featured person next to the corresponding number on her paper. Also have her tell why that person has recently been in the news. Give one point to each student for every photograph she correctly identifies and one point for correctly naming the news event in which the individual took part. Review the answers as a group, discussing each individual and the role he or she played in that news event.

Writer's Block

Square off on current events with this hands-on activity. Direct each of your students to bring in a current news article. Tell each student to wash and dry a one-pint milk carton saved from lunch in the school cafeteria. Next have the student cut off the top of his carton, leaving only the sides and bottom portion. Provide each student with 8 1/2" x 11" construction paper for covering all sides of the carton—including the top opening—to make a cube. On each side of the cube except the base, instruct the student to write a different one of the *five Ws*—"Who?", "What?", "When?", "Where?", and "Why?" as shown. Then have each student read his newspaper article and record the answer to each question on its corresponding section of the cube. The result will be a visual aid that provides a quick overview of a current news event.

World Map

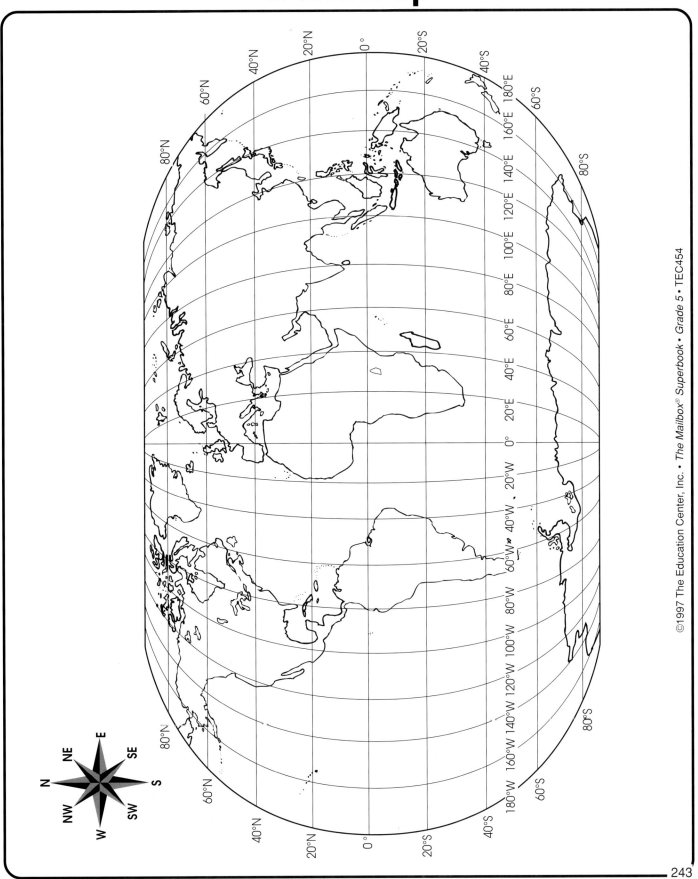

United States Map

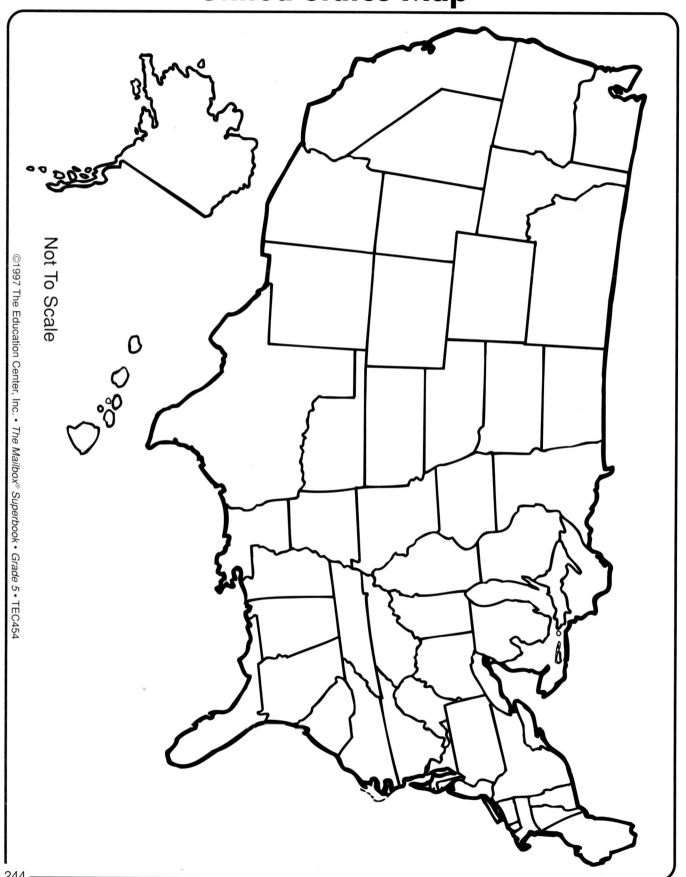

Not To Scale

©1997 The Education Center, Inc. • The Mailbox® Superbook • Grade 5 • TEC454

Portrait Of A Region

Follow the directions from your teacher to write a poem about a state from the region you are studying.

Pennsylvania

COAL

My region, the Middle Atlantic, is like a crowded mall just one week before the holidays.

My capital is Harrisburg and my nickname is the Keystone State.

My population is large and includes Italian, German, and Polish descendants.

Tourists come to visit historic Philadelphia and the Pocono Mountains.

My hills and valleys are like a colorful roller-coaster track at your favorite amusement park.

My land holds anthracite coal that is as black as the night sky.

I share this land with white-tailed deer and hemlock trees.

Some of my residents work in service industries and eat Hershey's® chocolates.

CHOCOLATE

_____
(name of state)

My region, the _____, is like _____
             (region)

_____.

My capital is _____, and my nickname is _____.
             (capital)   (nickname)

My population is _____ and includes _____ descendants.
             (adjective)   (nationality)

Tourists come to visit _____ and _____.
                (tourist attraction)   (tourist attraction)

My _____ are like _____.
     (physical features)

My land holds _____ that is _____ as _____.
             (natural resource)   (color)

I share this land with _____ and _____.
                (animal)   (plant)

Some of my residents work _____ and eat
                                         (job)

_____.
(popular food from state)

Bonus Box: On the back of this sheet, list three words that describe your region. In a paragraph, explain why you chose each word.

©1997 The Education Center, Inc. • *The Mailbox® Superbook* • Grade 5 • TEC454

Note To The Teacher: Use with "Portrait Of A Region" on page 234.

Name _____

Destination: U.S. Regions

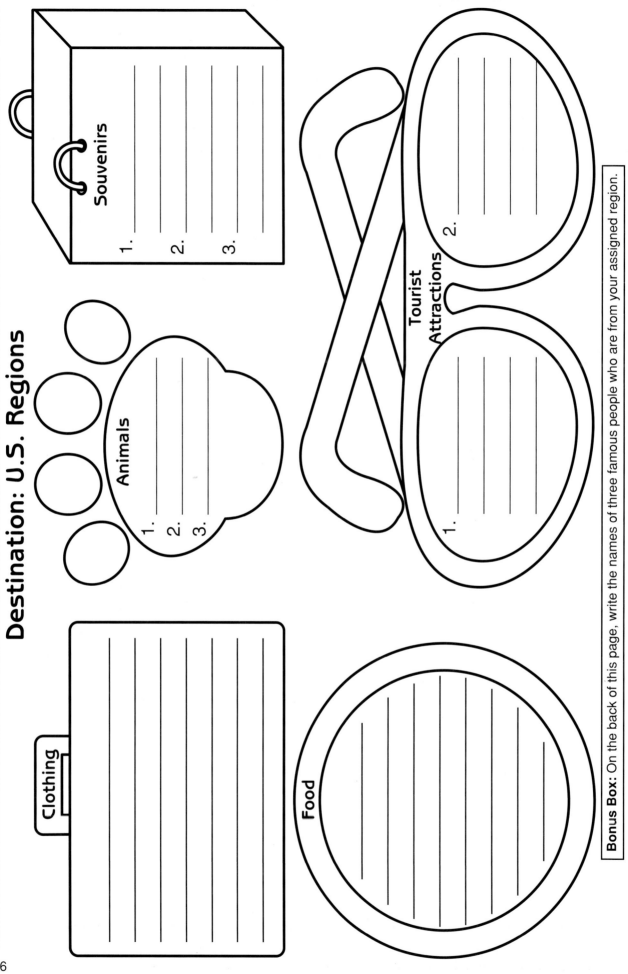

Souvenirs

1.
2.
3.

Animals

1.
2.
3.

Tourist Attractions

1.
2.

Clothing

Food

©1997 The Education Center, Inc. • The Mailbox® Superbook • Grade 5 • TEC454

Bonus Box: On the back of this page, write the names of three famous people who are from your assigned region.

Note To The Teacher: Use this page with "Destination: U.S. Regions" on page 235.

Fredericton	Halifax	Yellowknife	Whitehorse	North Saskatchewan River
St. John's	Regina	Lake Winnipeg	Bay Of Fundy	Winnipeg
Hudson Bay	St. Lawrence Seaway	Great Bear Lake	Newfoundland	Rocky Mountains
Yukon Territory	Montreal	Toronto	Edmonton	Ottawa
Ontario	Prince Edward Island	Quebec	Saskatchewan	Northwest Territories
Nova Scotia	Alberta	British Columbia	Manitoba	New Brunswick

Note To The Teacher: Use this page with "State The Location" on page 236.

Imagination "State-tion"

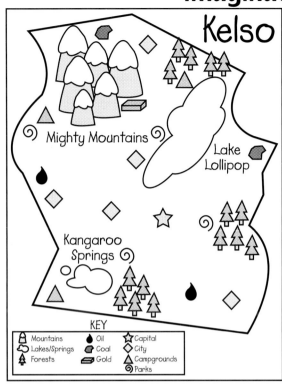

Kelso

KEY

⌂ Mountains	● Oil	☆ Capital	
⌂ Lakes/Springs	⬟ Coal	◇ City	
⬥ Forests	▱ Gold	△ Campgrounds	
		๑ Parks	

Directions: Follow the steps below to create a map of a brand-new state.

1. Draw the shape of your new state on the paper your teacher gives you.
2. Write the name of your state on the map.
3. Decide which landforms and bodies of water you want your new state to have. Give each landform or body of water a creative name—such as Echo Valley or The Flaky Desert.
4. Design at least ten different symbols to use in a key for your map. Have three of these symbols each represent a different natural resource. The other symbols could represent the capital of your state and its cities, landforms, and bodies of water.
5. Position the symbols on your map throughout the state to show their locations.
6. Make a key for your map in the lower-left or -right corner of your map.

Note To The Teacher: Use with "Imagination 'State-tion' " on page 232.

Write All About It!

Extra! Extra! Write all about it!

Directions:
1. Using research materials and your textbook, complete the steps in Part A below to create newspaper articles about your assigned region.
2. Complete the steps in Part B below to design a two-page newspaper layout that will inform others about your region.
3. Copy the articles created in Part A onto the layout created in Part B. Write the name of your newspaper in its designated place.

Part A:
1. Write a weather report that is typical for this time of year.
2. Find out what natural resources are found in your region. Write a short news article about one or more of these resources.
3. Find out what people in your assigned region do for entertainment. Write a short news article that tells about an upcoming event in your region.
4. Design an advertisement for one of the tourist attractions in your assigned region.
5. Write a short news article about an animal found in your assigned region.
6. Find out what types of jobs the people in your assigned region have. Write three classified ads that announce current job openings.

Part B:
1. Study the front page of any local newspaper to see how it is organized. Compare the layout of the front page to that of the other newspaper pages.
2. On a sheet of drawing paper, design a front-page layout. Include space for the name of your paper.
3. On another sheet of drawing paper, create a layout for a second newspaper page.

©1997 The Education Center, Inc. • *The Mailbox® Superbook* • Grade 5 • TEC454

Colonial America: map skills

Mapping Out The Thirteen Colonies

Directions: Find each item listed in the word bank and label it on the map. Then label the directions on the compass rose.

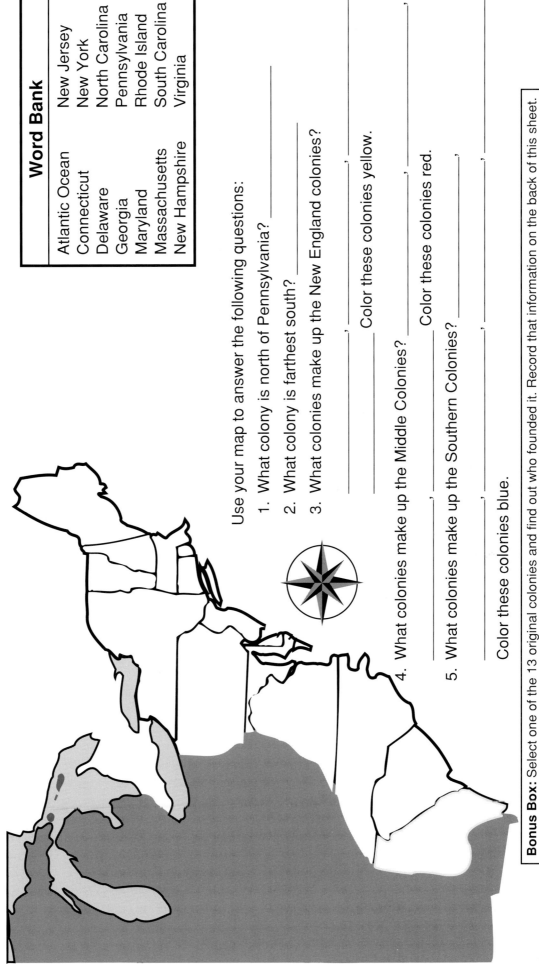

Word Bank	
Atlantic Ocean	New Jersey
Connecticut	New York
Delaware	North Carolina
Georgia	Pennsylvania
Maryland	Rhode Island
Massachusetts	South Carolina
New Hampshire	Virginia

Use your map to answer the following questions:

1. What colony is north of Pennsylvania? _____

2. What colony is farthest south? _____

3. What colonies make up the New England colonies? _____
   _____, _____, _____,
   _____. Color these colonies yellow.

4. What colonies make up the Middle Colonies? _____
   _____, _____, _____.
   Color these colonies red.

5. What colonies make up the Southern Colonies? _____
   _____, _____, _____,
   _____. Color these colonies blue.

Bonus Box: Select one of the 13 original colonies and find out who founded it. Record that information on the back of this sheet.

©1997 The Education Center, Inc. • *The Mailbox® Superbook • Grade 5 • TEC454 • Key p. 318*

Note To The Teacher: Use with "Colonial Craftsmanship" on page 238. Duplicate one copy of the reproducible for each student. Have the student complete the sheet as directed to learn more about the location of the 13 original colonies.

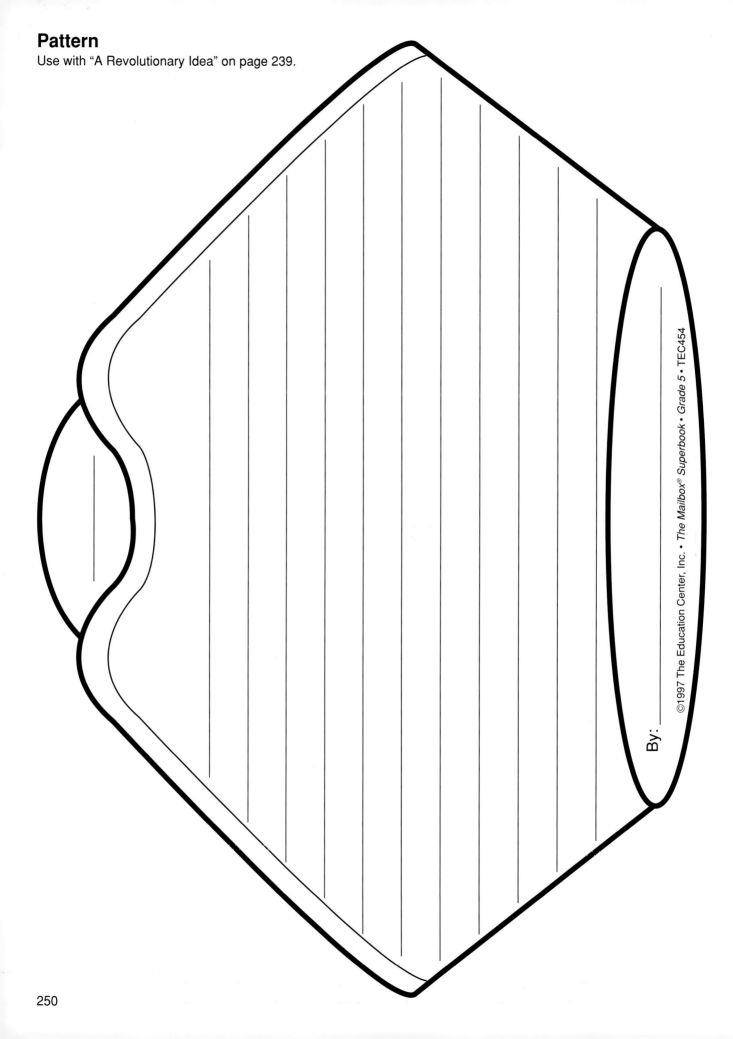

By: _____

©1997 The Education Center, Inc. • *The Mailbox® Superbook • Grade 5* • TEC454

A Nation Divided

Directions: Select _____ projects from the list below to learn more about the Civil War.

1. Many soldiers fighting in the Civil War kept journals. Pretend that you are a Union or Confederate soldier and write three journal entries about your wartime experiences.

2. During the Civil War many new songs were written. On a poster write either the words to "The Battle Hymn of the Republic," a northern tune, or "Dixie," a song of southern origin. Then illustrate your poster.

3. Harriet Beecher Stowe's famous novel, *Uncle Tom's Cabin,* is an antislavery novel that was first published in 1851. The novel increased tension between the North and the South. Find out what this controversial novel was about and why it caused tension between the two groups.

4. Mathew Brady was a famous Civil War photographer. Design a page of Civil War events that might have appeared in one of Brady's photo albums. Be sure to include a detailed caption under each photo.

5. Draw and color replicas of the Confederate and Union flags.

6. The Underground Railroad was not under the ground, and it wasn't a railroad. Research to find out exactly what the Underground Railroad was, and why it was important to so many people during the Civil War.

7. During the Civil War, the United States was a divided nation. On an outline map of the United States, color the Union states blue and the Confederate states gray.

8. During the Civil War, hot-air balloons were used by the military. Find out the purpose of these balloons. Then make a diorama with a scene that includes a hot-air balloon.

9. The battles of the Civil War took place in many different locations. On a map of the United States, label the sites of at least ten major Civil War battles.

10. The Union forces were led by General Ulysses S. Grant, and the Confederate forces were led by General Robert E. Lee. Research one of these two men and write a biography about him.

Note To The Teacher: Use with "A Nation Divided" on page 240. Before duplicating, write the number of projects you want each student to complete. Then duplicate a copy of the contract for each student.

A Balancing Act

The Constitution provides the framework for the U.S. government. It provides for three branches of government—the executive, legislative, and judicial branches. The Constitution also outlines a system of checks and balances to help ensure that no single branch of government becomes too powerful.

Directions: Research and record in the correct box below the duties of each of the three branches of the federal government. Then find out how each branch checks—or limits the power of—the other two branches. Write your findings inside the arrows on the diagram.

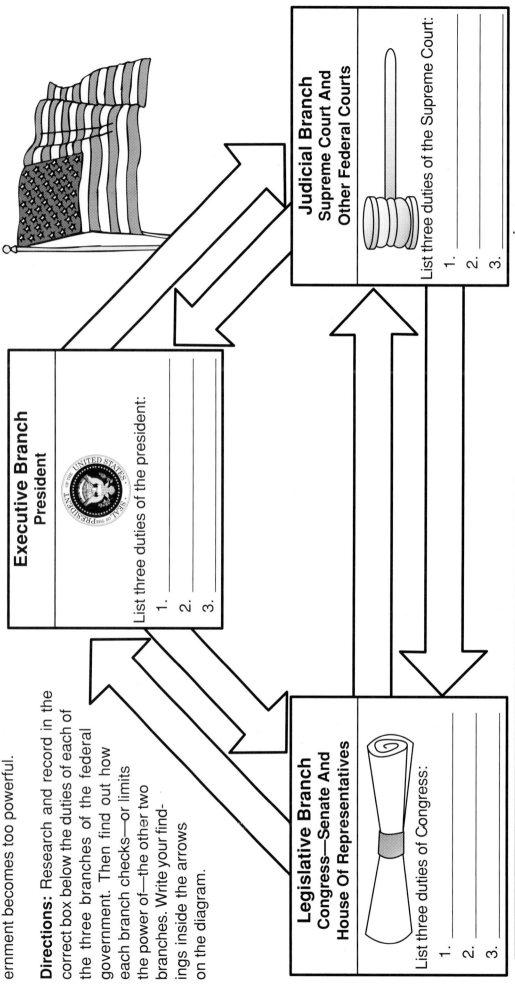

Executive Branch
President

List three duties of the president:

1. _____
2. _____
3. _____

Legislative Branch
Congress—Senate And House Of Representatives

List three duties of Congress:

1. _____
2. _____
3. _____

Judicial Branch
Supreme Court And Other Federal Courts

List three duties of the Supreme Court:

1. _____
2. _____
3. _____

Bonus Box: Using an almanac, find the names of the president's current cabinet members. List each member and his or her title on the back of this sheet.

©1997 The Education Center, Inc. • *The Mailbox® Superbook* • *Grade 5* • TEC454 • Key p. 318

Note To The Teacher: Use with "Branches Of Government" on page 241. Duplicate one copy of this reproducible for each student.

SCIENCE & HEALTH

THE SCIENTIFIC METHOD

Familiarize your students with the scientific method by having them work in groups to conduct the following simple experiments. For each experiment give each student one copy of the form on page 268 to guide him or her through the proper procedures.

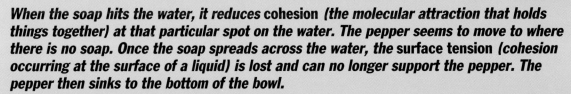

EXPERIMENT 1: Does Soap Affect Cohesion?

Materials: bowl of water, pepper, liquid soap

Procedure:
1. Sprinkle some pepper on the surface of the water in the bowl.
2. Hypothesize about what will happen when you place a drop of liquid soap on the water near the edge of the bowl.
3. Place one drop of liquid soap on the water near the bowl's edge.

When the soap hits the water, it reduces cohesion (the molecular attraction that holds things together) at that particular spot on the water. The pepper seems to move to where there is no soap. Once the soap spreads across the water, the surface tension (cohesion occurring at the surface of a liquid) is lost and can no longer support the pepper. The pepper then sinks to the bottom of the bowl.

EXPERIMENT 2: Can Rocks Absorb Water?

Materials: scale, four plastic cups 3/4 full of water, one sample of each type of rock: granite, marble, limestone, and sandstone

Procedure:
1. Weigh each rock in turn on a scale and record the results.
2. Place each rock in a different cup of water. Allow the rocks to soak overnight.
3. Hypothesize about whether or not the weight of each rock has changed after it has soaked overnight.
4. One at a time, remove each rock from its cup and weigh it.
5. Compare the two weights of each rock.

Some rocks are permeable, *or able to soak up fluids. Sedimentary rocks are the only types of rock capable of absorbing some water from a cup. Because sandstone and limestone are sedimentary rocks, they will weigh more after soaking overnight in water. The granite and marble will not weigh more.*

EXPERIMENT 3: How Do Acids Affect Tooth Enamel?

Materials: three raw eggs, vinegar, three plastic cups, cola, water, masking tape, permanent marker

Procedure:
1. Label and fill one cup with vinegar, one cup with water, and one cup with cola.
2. Carefully place an egg in each cup so that the egg is completely covered with liquid.
3. Hypothesize about what you think will happen to the egg in each cup.
4. Let the eggs stand overnight and then make your observations.
5. Think of the outer shell of the egg as the enamel on your teeth. What can this mean?

The vinegar eats away the outer shell of the egg, the egg in the water remains unchanged, and the cola stains the outer shell of the egg. Generally acids can be harmful to teeth. Just as vinegar and cola can affect the outer shell of the egg, acids in the mouth can affect the enamel on teeth.

Geology

JUST A BAG O' ROCKS?

All rocks are not created the same, and this classifying activity will prove it! Gather a variety of rocks—sedimentary, igneous, and metamorphic—in a Ziploc® bag for each group of students. Give one bag of rocks to each group and one magnifying glass to each student. Have each group classify its rocks using any criteria it desires and share its method of classifying with the class. Challenge each group to tell whether any rock could fit into more than one of its groups. Next refer students to a textbook illustration of the rock cycle. Introduce the three types of rocks, and explain how each type is formed. Again have each group attempt to classify its bag of rocks, this time according to the known types of rocks.

If desired, extend this activity by having students complete the reproducible on page 269 as directed. Afterward instruct each group to compare the results of the experiment with the classification method it used in the activity above.

EARTHQUAKE!

Right in your classroom, model the action of the earth's plates just before an earthquake! Measure and cut two strips of cloth three inches longer than a cake pan. Place the strips in the bottom of the pan adjacent to each other, allowing the excess cloth to extend over either side of the pan. Cover the strips with damp soil; then pack it down firmly. Place model houses, cars, and trees on top of the soil to represent a neighborhood, being sure to place some models over the area where the two pieces of cloth meet. Gather students around the model. Grasp the edges of both pieces of excess cloth; then simultaneously pull them away from the pan. Have your students observe the effect that the shifting cloth has on the soil and the objects on top of the soil. Challenge your students to compare the results of this experiment to what might really happen during an earthquake.

COMICAL ROCKS

Assess your students' knowledge of the rock cycle with this fun, creative activity. Give each student a sheet of drawing paper, scissors, and colored pencils or crayons. Have her fold and cut the paper in half lengthwise, making two strips. Direct her to use the first strip to make a rough draft and the second strip for the final copy of a comic strip that explains the rock cycle. Suggest that the student make up names—such as Molly Magma, Inga Igneous, Sally Sedimentary, and Metamorphic Matt—for her rock during its different stages. Make sure that each section of the comic strip includes a picture and caption. Collect the comic strips and display them on a bulletin board titled "Comical Rocks."

I'm Molly Magma. I used to live deep inside the earth.

Then I was pushed out through a volcano. Now my friends call me Lava.

That cold surface air made me harden.

Now I'm a whole new rock with a brand new name—Inga Igneous!

Uncovering The Bare Facts About Seeds

Introduce your students to the wonderful world of seed plants with this activity in observation. Gather a handful of corn and bean seeds for each group of students. Set aside a few of the seeds; then soak the remaining seeds overnight in a cup of water. The next day drain the water from the cups; then divide your class into small groups.

Display the seeds that were not soaked in water; then give each group one of the cups of soaked seeds, a magnifying glass (optional), and a few toothpicks. Guide the group to conclude that the soaked seeds expanded. Next instruct each group to follow the steps below.

BEAN SEED   CORN SEED

Embryo
Seed Coat
Food Supply
Cotyledons
(seed leaves)

Embryo
Seed Coat
Food Supply

1. Carefully remove the seed coating from a few of the corn and bean seeds.

2. Locate and separate the main parts of a seed—the *covering,* the *embryo* (baby plant), and the *food supply.*

3. Notice any differences between the corn and the bean seeds.

Point out that the corn seed has only one food-supply part (called a *seed leaf*) and that the bean seed has two seed leaves. Tell students that botanists separate seed plants into two different classes—*monocotyledons* (monocots), flowering plants with one seed leaf; and *dicotyledons* (dicots), flowering plants with two seed leaves. Explain that corn is a monocot and beans are dicots.

To extend the activity, give each group two plastic cups containing soil. Have each group plant a soaked corn seed in one cup and a soaked bean seed in the other. Allow time for the seeds to germinate; then follow up by having students discuss the characteristics of and differences between a monocot and a dicot.

FAR-TRAVELING SEEDS

Have your students spread the word about seed dispersal with this research activity! Explain to students that seeds are *dispersed,* or scattered, from the parent plant to increase their chances of landing in a place suitable for successful growth. Without going into detail, tell students that different seeds travel from the parent plant in various ways. Divide your class into small groups. Assign each group one of the plants listed below; then provide the group with a variety of reference materials. Instruct each group to research how the seeds from its parent plant are dispersed. Direct each group's members to pretend that they are seeds from their assigned plant. Have them tell the class what kind of seeds they are, and use pictures or diagrams to show how they traveled from their mother plant to the place where they began to grow.

After each group has shared, classify each seed by the way it travels—*wind, water, animals, expulsion,* or *other.* If desired, follow up by reading aloud *How Seeds Travel* by Cynthia Overbeck (Lerner Natural Science Books, 1982).

LIST OF PLANTS
- milkweed
- **witch hazel**
- maple
- **dandelion**
- coconut
- **burdock**
- cocklebur
- **mistletoe**
- impatiens (touch-me-not)
- **willow**
- cottonwood
- **oak**

Physically Fit Plants

So why do plants bend like that? Introduce your students to *tropism*, the bending movement in living things caused by an outside factor. Explain that there are four types of tropisms: *thigmotropism*, *hydrotropism*, *geotropism*, and *phototropism*. Thigmotropism is the bending of a plant in response to touch. For example, when the leaves of the Mimosa pudica plant are touched, they fold up and the branches fall against the stem. Hydrotropism is the tendency of a plant's roots to grow toward water. Have your students think of plants and trees living along the edges of ponds and lakes with roots that grow toward the water. To illustrate phototropism—a plant bending in response to light, or geotropism—a plant bending in response to gravity—conduct one or both of the experiments below.

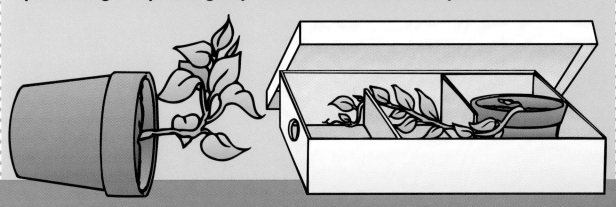

Geotropism

- Position a small potted plant on its side. After a few days (or sooner), observe the stem and leaves bending away from gravity—a display of negative geotropism.
- Soak two bean seeds in water overnight. Roll up six moistened paper towels and place them in a glass jar. Insert the two bean seeds between the jar and the paper towels; then put the jar in a sunny area. After a few days, watch the roots begin to grow downward, displaying positive geotropism. When the roots are about one inch long, place the lid on the jar and turn the jar upside down. After a few days, observe the roots turn and grow downward (again displaying positive geotropism) while the stem grows upward (displaying negative geotropism).

Phototropism

- Place a bean plant in a shoebox that has dividers similar to those shown. Cut a two-inch hole in the end of the box opposite the plant. Keep the lid on the box for about a week, removing the lid only to water the plant. Watch as the plant grows rapidly around the box's dividers toward the light.
- Remove one side from a large box; then position the box upside down so that the open side faces a window. Slide a potted plant into the box. Observe the plant's leaves and stems begin to bend toward the light source.

PICTURING PHOTOSYNTHESIS

Challenge your students to exercise their higher-level thinking skills for this group assignment. After teaching about photosynthesis, divide your class into small groups. Give each group a sheet of chart paper and colored pencils or markers. Tell the groups that the class plant is in trouble! Explain that it is unable to carry out photosynthesis. Instruct each group to create an artificial system to keep the plant alive. Explain that the created system must carry out every function that photosynthesis would normally do for the plant. Have each group describe its new system, its parts, and its functions on chart paper using pictures and words. After each group shares its new system, display it on the classroom wall for others to enjoy.

BY THE LIGHT OF THE MOON

Demonstrate what makes the moon shine with this easy activity. Show the class a bicycle reflector. Point out that the reflector does not have a light source. Ask your students what makes a reflector visible in the dark. Turn out the lights and shine a flashlight on the reflector. Explain that the reflector reflects the light of the flashlight. Apply this concept to the sun and moon. Help your students conclude that the moon reflects the light of the sun, and without the sun there would be no moonlight.

Sky Patterns

What do Leo, Pisces, and Orion have in common? They're constellations, of course! Name several constellations and see if your students can identify them as a group of stars. Then explain that a *constellation* is a group of stars that can be seen within a particular area of the night sky. Tell your students that ancient Romans, Greeks, and other cultures identified and named groups of stars in the Northern Hemisphere after animals and mythological characters. For example, Leo was named for a lion. Further explain that mapmakers and explorers named the star groups in the Southern Hemisphere after scientific instruments, animals, and many other things. For example, the constellation Telescopium was named after the telescope. Share the story of one of the well-known constellations, such as Orion or Pegasus.

Next pair your students; then assign each pair a different constellation (see the list). Instruct partners to use reference materials to find out what their assigned constellation looks like, the story behind its name, and an interesting fact about it. When the research has been completed, guide each pair through the steps at the right for creating a star can. After the constellation cans have been constructed, darken the room. Have each pair in turn share information about its constellation while displaying it.

Extend this activity by distributing one copy of "Cool Constellations" at the top of page 270 and the materials listed on that page to each student. Instruct each student to complete the page as directed.

Materials: empty tin can, pencil, drawing paper, hammer, two or three different-sized nails, flashlight

Steps:
1. Trace one end of the can onto the drawing paper.
2. Draw your assigned constellation within the circle on your paper. Mark the location of the stars heavily so that you can see them from the back of the paper.
3. Turn the paper upside down and place it over the bottom of the can.
4. Use the hammer and nails to punch holes in the bottom of the can to represent each star. Use different-size nails to show the varying brightness of the stars.
5. Remove the paper and place the flashlight inside the can. Darken the room; then point the flashlight toward the ceiling to project your constellation.

Constellations:

Andromeda	Hercules
Aquarius	Leo
Aries	Libra
Auriga	Pegasus
Boötes	Pisces
Cancer	Sagittarius
Canes venatici	Scorpius
Capricornus	Taurus
Cassiopeia	Ursa major
Cygnus	Ursa minor
Gemini	Virgo

Sun, Moon, Earth— How Big?

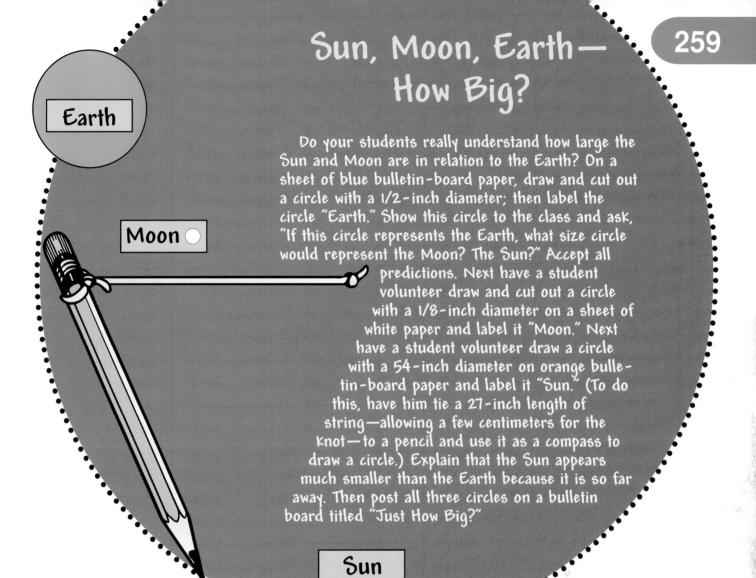

Do your students really understand how large the Sun and Moon are in relation to the Earth? On a sheet of blue bulletin-board paper, draw and cut out a circle with a 1/2-inch diameter; then label the circle "Earth." Show this circle to the class and ask, "If this circle represents the Earth, what size circle would represent the Moon? The Sun?" Accept all predictions. Next have a student volunteer draw and cut out a circle with a 1/8-inch diameter on a sheet of white paper and label it "Moon." Next have a student volunteer draw a circle with a 54-inch diameter on orange bulletin-board paper and label it "Sun." (To do this, have him tie a 27-inch length of string—allowing a few centimeters for the knot—to a pencil and use it as a compass to draw a circle.) Explain that the Sun appears much smaller than the Earth because it is so far away. Then post all three circles on a bulletin board titled "Just How Big?"

CREATE AN ALIEN

Are there other life forms in outer space? There will be after your students complete this research project! Show your class a picture of a giraffe or other animal. Ask your students which features or characteristics help that animal survive in its habitat. For example, the color of a giraffe's coat allows it to blend with trees, and its nostrils can close completely to keep out dust and sand.

Next assign each student a different planet, excluding Earth. Give each student a copy of page 271 and a variety of reference materials. Instruct him to follow the directions on the reproducible to describe the characteristics of his assigned planet and to create an alien that could inhabit that planet. Have each student share with the class his findings about his planet and the picture of the alien he created. Then direct each student to cut out his alien picture from the bottom half of the reproducible for display on a bulletin board titled "Life On Other Planets."

JOURNEY TO THE CENTER OF THE UNIVERSE

After teaching your students the different parts of the solar system, challenge them with this problem-solving mission. Give each student a sheet of drawing paper and colored pencils or crayons. Instruct each student to design a transportation device that will take him to the center of the universe. Explain that his device must be able to survive changes in air pressure and temperature, and withstand encounters from foreign objects—such as meteor showers—along the way. Tell each student to describe in paragraph form how his device will work and attach it to his drawing. Display your students' creations on a bulletin board titled "Ready For A Challenging Journey?"

ENERGY

SAVE THE CUBE!

Introduce how energy is conducted with this hands-on project. Tell students that when they arrive at school the next morning, each group of students will be given an ice cube in a tin can. Explain that the challenge will be to design a container to keep the ice cube from melting for as long as possible. Instruct each student to bring any materials he will need for his container to school the next day. Establish the following three rules for the project: (1) students will **not** be allowed to use ice buckets, coolers, or bags of ice for their containers; (2) a tin can must be used in some way; and (3) the ice cube must be accessible for periodic checks.

On the next school day, divide your class into small groups. Give each group time to design its container. Provide additional materials—such as plastic bags, tape, small pieces of packaging material, empty cartons or boxes, tin foil, and pieces of wood or plastic—for each group to use. Once each container has been built, give each group an ice cube to place in its container. Put all the containers in the same area of the classroom. Plan for each group to check its cube once every hour, checking more frequently as the cubes become smaller. Declare the team whose cube lasts the longest—and reduces conduction the most—as the winner. What a great springboard for a discussion on conductors and insulators!

Consider The Source!

Familiarize your students with the different sources of energy with this group project. Explain that there are many sources of energy (see the list below). Next divide your students into small groups; then assign each group one of the energy sources from the list. Provide each group with reference materials, one sheet of poster board, and markers. On the left half of the poster board, instruct each group to diagram how its assigned energy source is used to produce electricity. On the right half of the poster board, have each group show a chart that lists the pros and cons of its energy source. Then schedule a time for each group to present its information to the class.

Energy Sources: oil, gas, coal, uranium (nuclear), water, sun, biomass, geothermal, wind

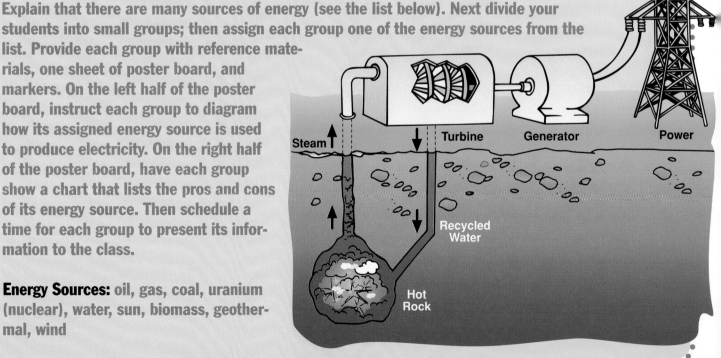

Electricity On The Way

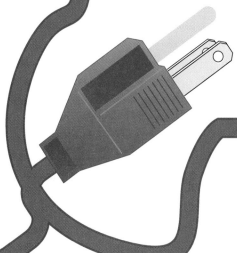

Help your students understand how electricity gets from the power plant to their homes with this creative project. Distribute one copy of page 273 to each student. Have the student follow the diagram on the sheet as you explain the transmission and distribution of electricity. Next divide your class into groups. Give each group a sheet of poster board, markers, glue, tape, scissors, and a variety of scrap materials—such as empty milk cartons, small boxes, construction paper, and yarn. Challenge each group to create a model that shows what is explained on the reproducible. Have the group use the poster board as a base for its model. Require that each model include the following labeled items: a house with a meter, a power plant, two transformers (one outside the power plant and one near the house), transmission lines, a substation, distribution lines, and service lines. Assess by having each group refer only to its model to explain the transmission and distribution of energy to the class.

TO CONSERVE OR NOT TO CONSERVE

This tasty activity will really get your students thinking about energy conservation! Give each student one pretzel log and a napkin. On your signal instruct each student to begin eating his pretzel. Tell the student to raise his hand and keep it raised when he is finished eating. Every 15 seconds, count and record on the chalkboard the number of students who have finished eating their pretzels. Continue in this manner until all students have finished eating. Then give each student another pretzel and instruct him to take a bite on your signal. This time instruct him to stand when he is finished eating. Call out "Take a bite" every 15 seconds until all students have finished their pretzels. Each time you signal, count and record on the chalkboard the number of students who are finished.

Next allow students to study the recorded information; then explain that the first set of information represents *unlimited consumption* and the second represents *conservation*. Discuss both of these concepts by asking the following questions:

- How long did it take before all the resources (pretzels) were depleted in the first activity? In the second activity?
- Were there more resources in the second activity?
- How was the rate of consumption regulated in the second activity?
- Based on the information you gathered, how can the consumption of oil, natural gas, coal, and electricity be regulated?
- What effect does conservation have on our resources?

Follow up this activity with a research activity. Divide your class into groups; then assign each group a different resource to research from the list below. Duplicate one copy of the earth pattern on page 272 for each group. Instruct the group to find out uses for its resource, the outlook for that resource (how long before this resource is depleted), what is being done to conserve that resource, and what can be done to help conserve that resource. Then have the group record its information on the pattern and cut it out. Display the completed patterns on a bulletin board titled "A Look At Conservation."

Research Topics: natural gas, oil, coal, water, uranium, rain forests, various minerals

MATTER

Modeling The States Of Matter

Familiarize your students with the states of matter with an activity that gets them up and moving! Take your class outside to a basketball court or another sectioned

area of the playground. Instruct your students to stand on the basketball court together. Explain that each student represents an atom and the basketball court represents a cooking pot. Then direct each student to act out or move in the way that you explain as you read the descriptions below:

- You are a liquid. You are moving slowly inside the pot. (Have students slowly walk around the court.)
- It's starting to get cold. (Have students walk slower and slower.)
- Now you are frozen. (Have students stand very close together at one end of the court—representing the bottom of the pot.)
- It's starting to warm up. (Have students slowly walk around.)
- It's getting hot. (Have students walk very fast around the court.)

- You're boiling! (Have students begin to leave the court, one at a time.)
- You're now a gas!

Bring students back together and discuss the different states of matter that were demonstrated. If desired, repeat the activity!

SOLID OR LIQUID?

Investigate solids and liquids with this perplexing experiment. Hold up a cup of water and ask students to identify it as a solid or liquid. Question students as to which characteristics make water a liquid. *(A liquid has a definite volume but no definite shape, is easily visible, and has molecules that are not tightly packed.)* Next show students a mound of cornstarch on a plate. Ask students which characteristics make cornstarch a solid. *(A solid has a definite volume and shape, is easily visible, and has molecules that are tightly packed and cannot move easily.)*

Next divide your class into groups of four or five students. Give each group 200 mL of water in a mixing bowl, 350 mL of cornstarch, a craft stick, and the directions below.

1. Use the craft stick to stir the cornstarch into the water, a little at a time. (You may not need all the cornstarch.)
2. Stop stirring the mixture when it becomes difficult to do.
3. Explore the mixture by hand.
4. Determine whether the mixture is a solid or a liquid. Explain your answer.

Then tell students that the mixture has properties of both a solid and a liquid. *(When the mixture is squeezed, it feels like a solid. When the mixture is not being squeezed, it returns to a liquid.)* Explain that the molecules in this mixture don't flow easily under pressure (squeezing). During cleanup put the mixture in the trash to avoid clogging a drain.

Demonstrate the presence of an invisible gas with this quick experiment. Place a small votive candle inside a beaker or glass jar. Pour a small amount of baking soda mixed with water into the beaker. Light the candle. Tell students that you are going to add a liquid to the beaker. Instruct the class to observe the candle as you add the liquid. Without telling students what the liquid is and being careful not to pour any vinegar directly on the candle, add a small amount of vinegar to the beaker *(the flame will go out)*. Ask students what made the flame go out. After a few student responses, allow a student to try to identify the mystery liquid by smell *(vinegar)*. Explain that when vinegar is poured into the dissolved baking soda, carbon dioxide is released. Explain further that carbon dioxide fills the beaker, pushing out the oxygen; without any oxygen, the flame cannot burn. Help your students conclude that even though gas cannot be seen, it is still present.

Ready...Set...GO!

Test the *viscosity* of various liquids by having your students stage a marble race! Explain that viscosity is a liquid's resistance to flow, and since liquids have no definite shape, they can flow. Fill five jars, each with a different liquid—such as water, cooking oil, shampoo, syrup, clear liquid soap, or vinegar. Also have a stopwatch and five marbles on hand. Make sure that the level of liquid in each jar is equal; then instruct a student to hold a marble just above the surface of the liquid. On your signal, have her drop the marble into the jar. Use a stopwatch to time how long it takes for the marble to reach the bottom of the jar. Record the time on the chalkboard; then repeat the process using a different marble for each jar of liquid. Compare the recorded times. Point out that the slower the marble falls, the higher the viscosity of the liquid. Next follow the steps below to have the class predict whether or not the viscosity of a liquid changes when it is heated.

1. Gather a bottle of syrup and two marbles.
2. Have your students think about the viscosity of both cold and hot syrup and make predictions about dropping marbles into these liquids.
3. Use the stopwatch to time a marble being dropped into the cold syrup; then record the time on the board.
4. Heat the syrup and return it to the jar.
5. Time a marble being dropped into the heated syrup, again recording the time.
6. Have students compare the two times to determine which syrup allowed the marble to fall faster *(the hot syrup)*.

Explain that molecules move faster when heated, reducing the attraction between them. Then help your students conclude that raising the temperature of a liquid decreases its viscosity.

OCEANS

The Octopus
The octopus is a mollusk with a soft and boneless body. It uses its eight arms to help it move and to catch food. Many octopuses live only one year.

OCEAN COLLAGE

This sea-life research project will make a great classroom display! Assign each student a different sea animal. Instruct the student to research basic information about his assigned animal and write it on an index card. Then have each student draw and cut out an outline shape of his animal from construction paper. Next provide each student with old nature magazines to scour for ocean-related pictures. Have him create a collage by covering his animal shape with cut-out pictures from the magazines. Finally post each completed animal collage along with its matching index card on a bulletin board titled "In The Deep-Blue Sea." Follow up this activity by giving each student a copy of page 274 to complete as directed.

NATURE'S MEDICINE CHEST

Your class will discover a wealth of new sea plants and animals with this activity. Share that many medicines come from ocean plants or animals. Tell students that plantlike organisms called *red algae* give us anticoagulants—drugs that prevent blood from clotting. Also share that we get a substance that relaxes muscles from a species of marine snail. Explain how there may be countless cures for cancer and other illnesses in the ocean just waiting to be discovered! Next use blank file-folder labels to cover the old labels of clean, empty medicine bottles. Then give one bottle and a sheet of drawing paper to each student along with the directions below.

1. Imagine that you have just discovered a new sea animal or plant that was previously unknown.
2. Draw a picture of this life form and write a sentence telling how this plant or animal will help relieve or cure an illness.
3. Write your name and the name of the medicine which comes from your plant or animal on the outside of the bottle.
4. Roll up your sheet of drawing paper and place it inside the medicine bottle.

Collect the bottles and display them on a bulletin board titled "Fishing For Cures."

Joe Lorenzetti
COLD AWAY
Rx

WHALE SONGS

Your students will be ready to dive into your oceans unit after this introductory activity! Obtain a tape recording of humpback-whale songs and a copy of *Winter Whale* by Joanne Ryder (Morrow Junior Books, 1994) from your local library. Play the whale songs as you ask your students to close their eyes and imagine what undersea life is like. Have your students discuss how the music makes them feel. Afterward stop the tape and read aloud *Winter Whale*—a book about a child who is transformed into a humpback whale so that he can experience life in the ocean among other whales. Finally start the tape again and have your students write words to a humpback whale verse that might express what a whale is communicating. Then allow each student to share his verse as the whale music plays in the background.

Ecology Corner

Heighten your students' awareness of ecological issues with this weekly activity. Reserve a small bulletin board or corner of a chalkboard to post an "Ecology Question Of The Week." Next check out from your school or local library *50 Simple Things Kids Can Do To Save The Earth* (Greenleaf Publishers, 1990), a book that lists 50 ecology-related questions and answers. Once a week write a different ecology-related question on the board (see the illustration). Instruct each student to write his name and an answer to the question on a slip of paper and place it in an envelope positioned by the posted question. At the end of each week, place all the slips of paper that contain a correct answer in an envelope and draw one name. Reward that student with a homework pass or other small incentive. Then use the posted question as a springboard for a related discussion.

How many milk cartons can you fill with the water from a five-minute shower?

Extend this activity by having your students conduct surveys among their families, friends, and neighbors about environmentally friendly practices. Give each student a copy of the reproducible at the bottom of page 270. Afterward direct the class to total their findings and create bar graphs that represent the answers to each survey question.

EARTH BUDDIES

These little recycled buddies will help teach responsibility to their fifth-grade buddies! Guide each student through the steps at the right to create an Earth Buddy. Then encourage each student to care for her buddy by watering it and trimming its hair.

Materials for each student: 1 leg from an old pair of panty hose, 2 cups of sawdust (from a local lumberyard), 1 tablespoon of grass seed, 1 large plastic cup, one 12-inch length of fishing line, plastic eyes, scrap materials for facial features, scissors, and glue

Steps:

1. Cut off all but about six inches of the toe end of the panty hose.
2. Place the toe end of the panty hose inside the plastic cup as if you were placing a trash bag in a garbage can.
3. Place one tablespoon of grass seed inside the toe of the panty hose.
4. Fill the panty hose with sawdust until it is the size of a solid round baseball.
5. Tie the open end with fishing line; then decorate the Earth Buddy as desired.
6. After the glue has dried, hold the Earth Buddy underwater for about two minutes.
7. Place the Earth Buddy on a dish containing water in a sunny location and wait for its hair to sprout!

BODY SYSTEMS

Food On The Move

Introduce the concept of peristalsis with this small-group activity. Explain to your students that peristalsis is the process by which food is pushed through the esophagus and intestinal tubes. In advance cut pairs of old stockings into long tubes. Divide your class into small groups; then give each group one tube. Next provide each group with a tennis ball. Explain that the ball represents the bolus, the ball of food formed in the mouth by chewing and saliva. To demonstrate peristalsis, instruct one student from each group to place the ball inside the stocking and hold it as shown. Then have the student squeeze the stocking behind the ball so that it moves through the stocking. Direct the students in each group to take turns, allowing each group member to try his hand at this experiment.

IT'S DIGESTION TIME!

So where does food go after you eat it? Copy the chart below onto the chalkboard. Use a diagram of the digestive system and the information in the chart to explain each step of the digestive process to your students. Then distribute one copy of page 275, scissors, colored pencils or crayons, and a glue stick to each student. Instruct the student to complete the page as directed to make his own diagram of the digestive system.

DIGESTIVE TIMETABLE

Number Of Hours	Action
0	You start eating.
1/2	Your stomach is full.
2	Partly digested food called **chyme** enters the duodenum.
6	Your stomach is almost empty.
12	Your small intestine absorbs nutrients.
18	Wastes begin to form in the large intestine.
24	Solid wastes called **feces** are ready to leave the body.

SIZING UP THE INTESTINES

Just how long are the small and large intestines? This partner activity will let your students discover the answer for themselves. Pair your students; then give each pair a 28-foot length of twine or string. Instruct each partner to hold one end of the string, extending it as far as possible. Explain that the length of the twine represents the approximate length of an adult's intestines. Next challenge each pair to neatly fold the twine so that it fits on a sheet of notebook paper. Explain that this represents how the intestines fit inside the body. Finally display a diagram of the digestive system, pointing out both the large and small intestines. Your students will be amazed at the way their bodies utilize space!

REACTION-TIME CHECKUP

Use this fast-paced game to introduce the nervous system. Divide your class into groups of six to eight students each.

TO PLAY:

1. Give one student from each group a stopwatch and a calculator, designating him as the timekeeper.

2. Instruct the remaining group members to join hands and form a circle around its timekeeper.

3. Select one member from each group as the starter.

4. Explain that on your signal, the starter should squeeze the hand of the person to his right, who should then squeeze the hand of the person to his right, and so on around the circle.

5. When the starter feels his left hand being squeezed, have him call out, "Stop!"

6. Instruct the timekeeper to record the time and divide it by the number of people in his group.

7. Have the class compare the times recorded by each group.

8. Declare the team with the shortest time the winner.

Discuss the sequence of events that enabled the message to be passed along. *(The nerves in your hand feel the squeeze. The message travels along the nerves in your arm and spinal cord to your brain. The sensory part of your brain processes the message and sends a signal to the cerebellum with specific instructions for the muscles. These signals then travel down your spinal cord and arm to the muscles in your hand. The muscles in your hand contract.)* Play additional rounds to see if each group can shorten its reaction time. Then have each group send the signal around the circle twice before stopping or by passing the signal to the left instead of the right. Extend your study of the nervous system with the reproducible on page 276.

How deep can you go into a forest?

Halfway. If you go deeper, you start to come out again!

Brainy Bulletin Board

Stimulate your students' brains with this interactive bulletin board. Cut out several brain shapes from different colors of construction paper. For each cutout, write a different brain-teaser question on the front and its answer on the back. Use pushpins to arrange each cutout on a bulletin board titled "Have You Used Your Cerebral Cortex Today?" Introduce the display by explaining that the largest part of your cerebral cortex is responsible for processing information. Then invite each student to visit the board during free time to put his brain to the test.

TEST YOUR MEMORY

Test your students' memories for faces with this learning-center activity. Collect 20 different pictures of faces that are relatively the same size. Be sure to choose pictures that are all color or all black-and-white. Paste each picture to a different 5" x 8" white index card. Place 15 of the mounted pictures in an envelope labeled "Envelope One" and the remaining 5 pictures in an envelope labeled "Envelope Two." Position both envelopes at a learning center with an index card displaying the directions below. Then invite pairs of students to the learning center to test their memories.

How To Test Your Memory
1. Study the 15 pictures in Envelope One for one minute only.
2. Look away while your partner mixes in five new pictures from Envelope Two.
3. Study all 20 pictures. Can you identify the five new pictures that your partner added?

Date_____

Science Lab Report

Group Members: _____   _____

_____   _____

Assignment/Purpose: _____

Question: _____

Hypothesis: _____

_____

Materials: _____

_____

Procedure: _____

_____

_____

_____

_____

_____

_____

Observations: _____

_____

_____

_____

_____

Conclusions: _____

_____

_____

_____

_____

Note To The Teacher: Use this form with the experiments on page 254 or whenever a student conducts an experiment. Duplicate one copy for each student.

Fizzes And Bubbles

Do you think you can make a rock fizz or bubble? If it's the right type of rock, you can! Many sedimentary rocks and some metamorphic rocks have calcium deposits within them. If calcium deposits are in a rock, it will fizz and bubble when vinegar is poured on the rock. Follow the steps below to test your bag of rocks for calcium deposits.

Materials: bag of various rocks, plastic cup filled with vinegar, eyedropper, paper towels, magnifying glass, several sheets of old newspaper, marker

Procedure:
1. Spread out the newspaper on your work surface. Arrange your rocks on the paper; then label each rock by writing "A," "B," "C," and so on in the space below each rock.
2. Use the eyedropper to place a few drops of vinegar on rock "A." Does it fizz? Are there any bubbles? Use your magnifying glass if necessary. Record your observations in the chart below by writing *yes* or *no* in the appropriate column.
3. Repeat Step 2 on another area of the same rock. Record your observations; then decide whether or not the rock contains calcium deposits by writing *yes* or *no* in the last column of the chart.
4. Complete Steps 2 and 3 for each different rock.

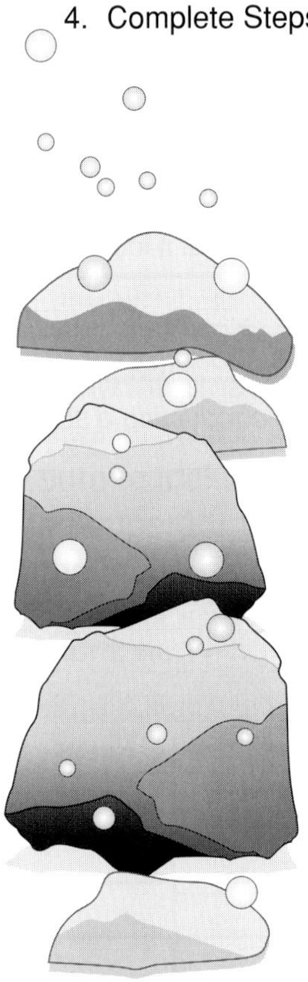

Rock	Test One		Test Two		Calcium Deposits?
	Fizz?	Bubble?	Fizz?	Bubble?	
A					

Conclusions: _____
_____
_____
_____
_____

Bonus Box: Trade rocks with another group; then repeat the procedure with the new set of rocks. Record your observations on the back of this sheet.

Note To The Teacher: Use with "Just A Bag O' Rocks?" on page 255. Provide each group of students with the materials listed above and one copy of this sheet.

Pattern

Use with "To Conserve Or Not To Conserve" on page 261.

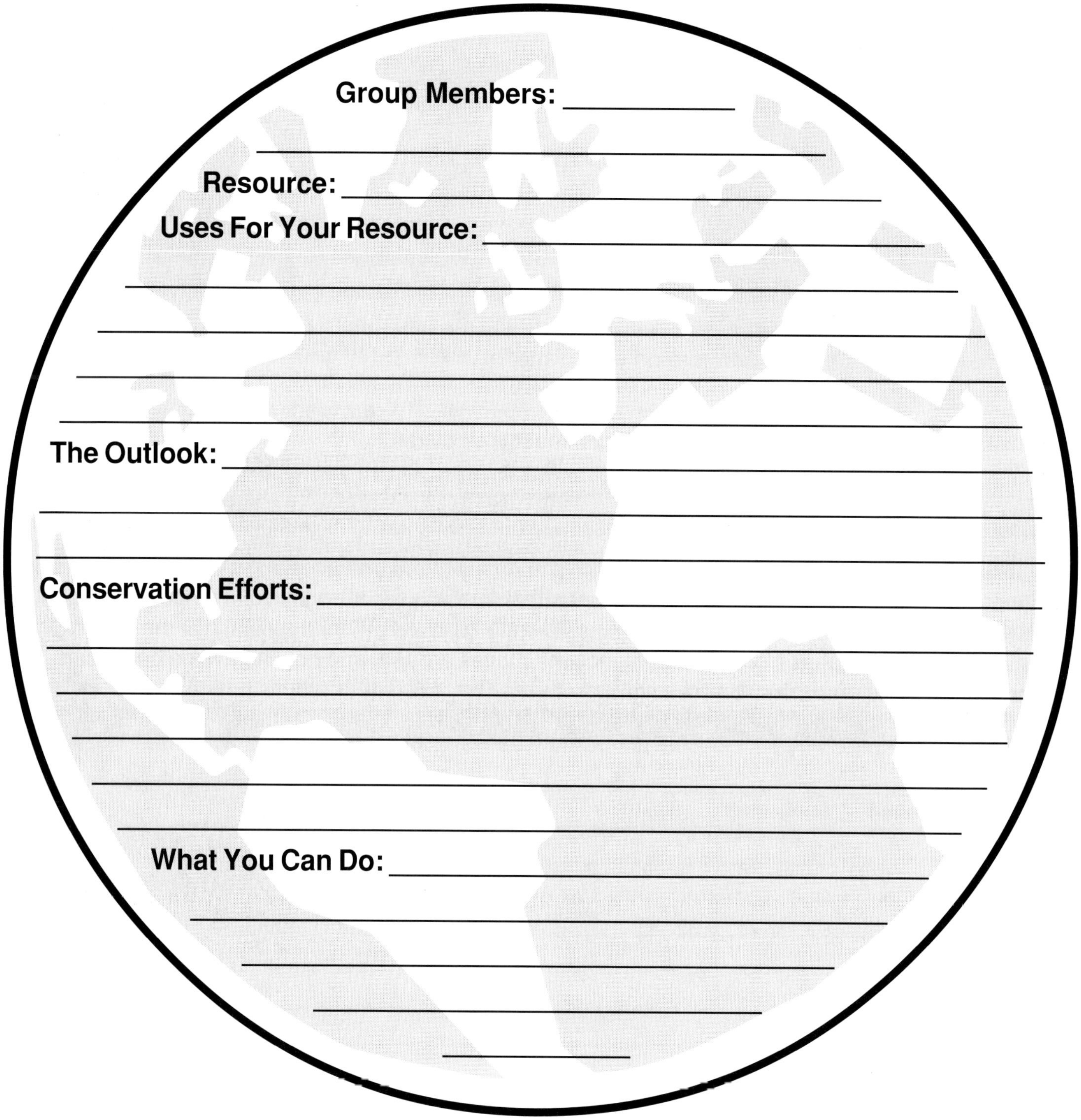

Group Members: ____________
Resource: ____________
Uses For Your Resource: ____________
The Outlook: ____________
Conservation Efforts: ____________
What You Can Do: ____________

Bringing Electricity To Your House

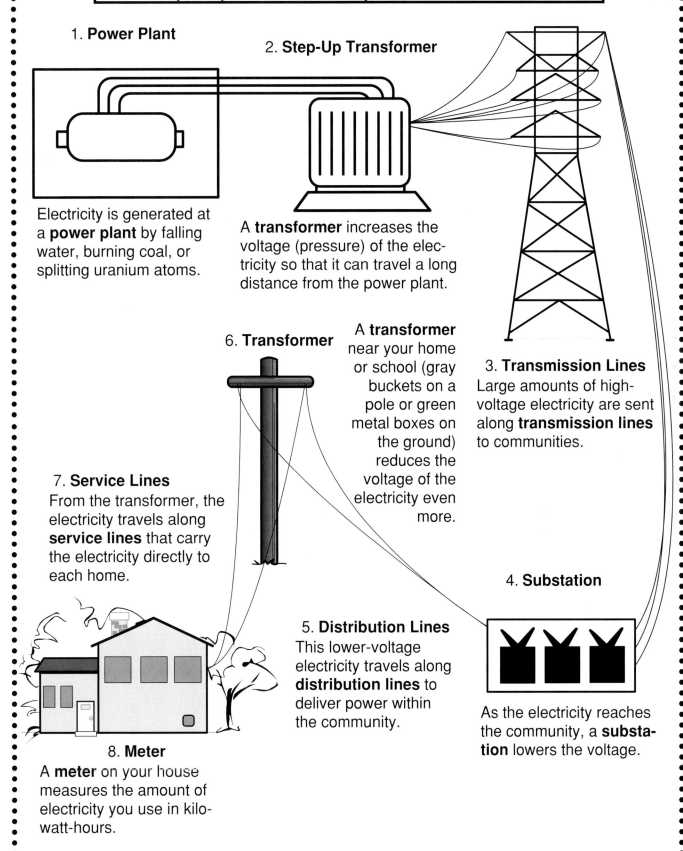

1. **Power Plant**

Electricity is generated at a **power plant** by falling water, burning coal, or splitting uranium atoms.

2. **Step-Up Transformer**

A **transformer** increases the voltage (pressure) of the electricity so that it can travel a long distance from the power plant.

6. **Transformer**

A **transformer** near your home or school (gray buckets on a pole or green metal boxes on the ground) reduces the voltage of the electricity even more.

3. **Transmission Lines**
Large amounts of high-voltage electricity are sent along **transmission lines** to communities.

7. **Service Lines**
From the transformer, the electricity travels along **service lines** that carry the electricity directly to each home.

5. **Distribution Lines**
This lower-voltage electricity travels along **distribution lines** to deliver power within the community.

4. **Substation**

As the electricity reaches the community, a **substation** lowers the voltage.

8. **Meter**
A **meter** on your house measures the amount of electricity you use in kilowatt-hours.

©1997 The Education Center, Inc. • *The Mailbox® Superbook* • Grade 5 • TEC454

Note To The Teacher: Use with "Electricity On The Way" on page 261.

In The Deep-Blue Sea

In 1979, Dr. Sylvia Earle spent 2 1/2 hours 1,250 feet below the ocean's surface exploring a coral reef off the coast of Hawaii. Dr. Earle was able to withstand the tremendous water pressure this deep in the ocean because she wore a special diving suit called a *Jim*. The *Jim* is named in honor of a diver, Jim Jarrett, who was the first to test the suit. The suit looks similar to a space suit, but weighs 1,000 pounds!

Solve each fraction puzzle below to discover some of the sea life that Dr. Earle saw during her amazing dive. The first one is done for you.

1. Add the first 3/6 of "corner" to the first 2/8 of "aluminum."

   bamboo <u>c</u> <u>o</u> <u>r</u> <u>a</u> <u>l</u>

2. Add the first 1/7 of "reading" to the last 2/5 of "today."

   deep-sea ___ ___ ___

3. Add the first 3/5 of "shrug" to the first 3/7 of "improve."

   red ___ ___ ___ ___ ___ ___

4. Add the first 3/4 of "pint" to the last 1/5 of "truck."

   ___ ___ ___ ___ coral

5. Add the first 1/3 of "fiddle" to the middle 1/3 of "wished."

   lantern ___ ___ ___ ___

6. Add the first 5/8 of "hatching" to the last 2/5 of "basket."

   ___ ___ ___ ___ ___ ___ ___ fish

7. Add the last 3/7 of "cleared" to the first 2/6 of "crunch" and the first 1/2 of "able."

   ___ ___ ___ ___ ___

8. Add the first 1/4 of "earn" to the first 2/8 of "elephant."

   gray ___ ___ ___

9. Add the first 2/3 of "letter" to the last 1/3 of "introduce."

   sea ___ ___ ___ ___ ___ ___

10. Add the last 3/4 of "knee" to the last 1/2 of "middle."

    ___ ___ ___ ___ ___ ___ fish

Bonus Box: Imagine that you are exploring a coral reef and discover a new type of sea life. On the back of this sheet, draw what it looks like; then name your new sea creature.

Tracking Digestion

Your body doesn't stop working after you finish eating. It has to prepare what you ate for use by your body. All the body parts that help in digesting food are part of the *digestive system.*

Make your own model of the digestive system by first coloring each part below a different color. Next cut out each colored part along the bold line. Afterward glue each digestive-system part in the correct place on the body outline. Then draw a line pointing to each part, labeling it correctly with a word from the Word Bank. *Hint: Each digestive-system part is like a piece of a puzzle.*

Word Bank: esophagus, stomach, liver, small intestine, large intestine

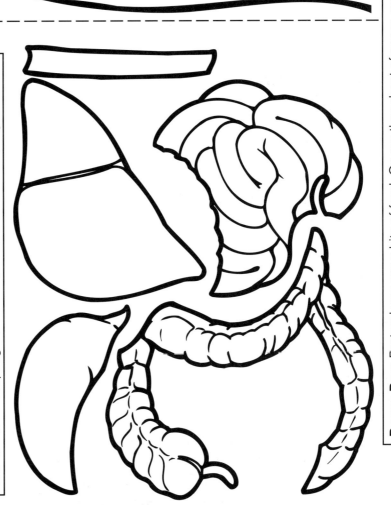

Bonus Box: Pretend you are a bite of food. On another sheet of paper, write a story telling about your journey through the digestive system.

Note To The Teacher: Use with "It's Digestion Time!" on page 266.

On Your Nerves: **A Play**

If you thought about all of your body's functions—including the blinking of your eyes or breathing—it would be overwhelming. Many nerves control themselves without any direction from you at all. This network of nerves is called the *autonomic nervous system.* It includes the *parasympathetic nervous system,* which takes care of normal functions such as digestion, and the *sympathetic nervous system,* which takes care of emergency situations.

Practice and perform this play with your group to learn more about how the *sympathetic nervous system* works to help protect you.

[**Setting:** A big dog is charging at you, barking ferociously.]

Eyes: My, what large teeth you have, Spike! Optic Nerve, send this picture to Brain.

Optic Nerve: Well, okay, if you insist. Brain, look at this!

[Meanwhile] **Ears:** My, what a loud bark you have, Spike! Auditory Nerve, send this sound to Brain.

Auditory Nerves: Do I have to? Okay, Brain, listen to this!

Brain: I don't like this! I'm scared! Spinal Cord, tell the Body to run!

Spinal Cord: Sympathetic Nerves, do your stuff!

Sympathetic Nerves: Spinal Cord, tell the Heart to beat faster, the Air Passages in the lungs to get wider, and the Stomach and Intestines to slow down their work!

Spinal Cord: Heart, beat faster! Air Passages, get wider! Hey, Stomach and Intestines, slow down and give your blood to the Heart and other muscles!

Heart, Air Passages, Stomach, and Intestines: [whining] But why?

Spinal Cord: Do you want to be a dog's dinner?

Sympathetic Nerves: Adrenal Glands, pump that adrenaline fast!

Adrenal Glands: Coming up!

All: Run!

Bonus Box: On the back of this sheet, describe two other situations when your sympathetic nervous system might be at work.

Note To The Teacher: Use after "Reaction-Time Checkup" on page 267. Duplicate one copy for each student. Divide your class into groups; then have each group practice and perform the play, using props if desired.

TECHNOLOGY

Computer-Management Tips

WHEN SOFTWARE WISHES COME TRUE

Get ready for the day when your software wishes come true by keeping data on your favorite software now. Each time you come across a great piece of software, record information about that program in a notebook or on a computer database. Be sure to include any information that will be helpful in finding the software when funds do become available.

Software Wish List

Software Title: *Math-a-rama*

Publisher: *Computer Inc.*

Grade Level(s): *4-5*

Curriculum Area(s): *Math*

Type Of Software: *Game*

Floppy Disk or CD: *CD*

Cost: *$39.95*

Ordering Information: *page 26*

Rating/Comments: *Great math-facts practice*

MANAGING STUDENT COMPUTER TIME

Use the "Equal Time" reproducible on page 284 to help ensure equity in students' use of computer(s). Post one copy of the reproducible next to each computer in the classroom. Instruct each student to complete the chart every time she uses the computer. You'll be able to tell at a glance who is using the computers and what software is being used.

Computer Whiz Kids

Keep track of each student's computer-training progress with the "Computer Training Checklist" on page 285. Duplicate one copy of the checklist for each student. Each time a student masters a specific task on the list, have her check it off. When the student has checked off each item on the list, award her with a "Computer Operator's Permit" (see page 285).

Use "Computer Whiz Kids" on page 286 to help track student progress with mastering specific pieces of software. Each time a student masters a particular application, place a sticker in the appropriate column by her name. This simple strategy will motivate your students to explore new programs. Award students who have mastered all the programs listed with a special treat or certificate.

Computer Tutors

Looking for an efficient way to train your students on how to use the software applications you have in the classroom? Round up some parent as well as student volunteers and train them on the proper usage of each application. Then schedule times for the computer tutors to come into the classroom and train individual students or small groups of students. This will allow you time to continue teaching while your students receive the much-needed software training.

MOBILE COMPUTER CARTS

If you have a limited number of computers in your school, you'll love this great management tip! Ask your school to purchase an A/V cart with a built-in electrical outlet and wheels. Place your computer and printer on the cart, then plug both pieces of equipment into the cart. Now it can be wheeled around your room or from room to room easily. Simply plug the cart into a wall outlet, and you're ready to go! This ease of access will encourage even the shiest "techy-wanna-be" to borrow and use the computer.

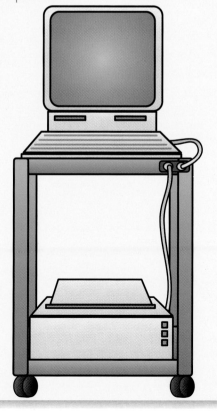

DISK MANAGEMENT

It's important for every student to have her own disk, but storage can sometimes be a problem. Assign each student a different number; then give each student a plastic Ziploc® sandwich bag. Instruct the student to label her disk with her assigned number, then place it in the bag. Pin each student's bag to a bulletin board in numerical order. Students will be able to easily find their disks as well as have a designated place to return their disks. If bulletin-board space is not available, purchase a computer-disk storage box. Have each student write her assigned number on the end of her disk as well as on the disk's label so the number can easily be seen when stored in the box.

Classroom Library Database

Take advantage of a database program to create a computerized classroom library card catalog. For each book create various categories such as *genre, author, title, copyright date,* and s*tudent/teacher comments.* Have student or parent volunteers help you enter the data for each book into the computer. This will help you keep an inventory of your collection as well as help students quickly see if a particular book is housed in the classroom library before heading to the school's main library.

My Side Of The Mountain

Genre: Adventure
Author: Jean George
Copyright: 1959
Comments: Great adventure story. Very descriptive and lots of good facts and information.

Computer Activities

FROM THE EDITOR'S DESK

Here's a great way for your students to improve their proofreading skills while learning how to edit on the computer. Have each student design/create his own worksheet using a word-processing program. Instruct each student to use the program to write ten sentences that contain spelling and/or grammatical errors. Instead of printing out the worksheet, have each student save his worksheet on the computer's hard drive. Next have student pairs visit the computer to edit each other's sentences using the *cut* and *paste* options as well as a *spell-checker*, then print out a copy of the corrected versions. Remind each student pair not to save their corrections to the hard drive. (Saving changes will alter the original student's worksheet template.) Be sure to direct each student designer to then check the printout to see if the proofreader was able to find all the mistakes.

Can You Find All The Mistakes?

1. The Boy run all the way to store the.
2. A wild gaot chased Liz threw the garten.
3. Stephanie meet Debra at the moovies.
4. Irv one the race!
5. Chris eight too much candi and became eel.
6. Cindy wus krowned queen of the ball.
7. The dog barked at Sharon as buy she walked.
8. The gurl found the lost purs.
9. Hour teem one the game!
10. Wee ordered tin pizzas.

Computerized Spelling Tests

This activity is great for students who have missed a spelling test or for students who have individualized spelling lists. Pair the student needing to take a spelling test with another student who will be the *tester*. Send both students to a computer. Instruct the tester to call out each spelling word and have the other student enter each word on the computer using a word-processing application. After completing the test, instruct the pair to print out a hard copy of the student's word list. Then have the pair run a spell-check on the list, directing the tester to use the spell-checker to correct any misspelled words on the hard copy. This process gives the student immediate feedback, and the teacher can easily record the grade.

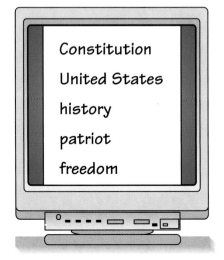

Constitution

United States

history

patriot

freedom

WEEKLY REPORTERS

Assign student pairs to be Weekly Reporters. Instruct each pair of reporters to document important classroom and school activities or events that occur during their assigned week. At the end of the week, have each pair write a news article about that week's events using a word-processing application such as the Student Writing Center™. Encourage each pair to include appropriate clip art or original computer-generated art with their article. At the end of each month, combine each pair's article into a monthly newsletter. Distribute one copy to each student and keep a class copy in a three-ring binder.

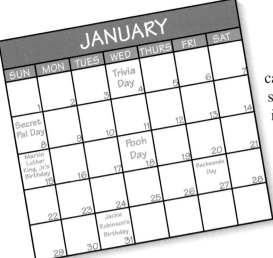

JANUARY

SUN	MON	TUES	WED	THURS	FRI	SAT
			Trivia Day 3	4	5	6	7
Secret Pal Day 1	2	3	Pooh Day	11	12	13	14
Martin Luther King, Jr.'s Birthday 15	16	17	18	19	Backwards Day 20	21
22	23	Jackie Robinson's Birthday 24	25	26	27	28
29	30	31				

Create A Calendar

Most graphics programs and desktop-publishing programs are capable of creating calendars. Each month assign a new team of students to create a class calendar. Instruct the team to research important dates, historical events, holidays and celebrations, as well as school functions that occur during its assigned month. Teachers who have access to the Internet might want to check out the Media Designs Education Calendar site on the World Wide Web at the address below.

http://home.earthlink.net/~mediadesigns/Calendar.html

Student Software Reviews

Get feedback from your students on the software used in the classroom with this great idea. On your classroom computer, set up a separate document/file for each piece of software used in your classroom. Schedule a time for each student to visit the computer and write a brief critique of each software application. Be sure to remind each student to save his work after writing the critique. *(The next student will write his critique beneath the previous student's critique.)* Tell students to respond to the following questions in their critiques:

► 1. Was this program one of your favorites? Why or why not?

► 2. What skills did this software teach you?

► 3. Did you use this software often?

► 4. Would you recommend this software to another student?

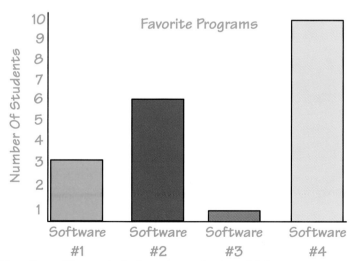

Use the critiques to help you evaluate which programs were the most effective. If a spreadsheet application is accessible, compile the results into a bar graph that shows students the most and least favorite programs as well as the programs most and least used.

BIRTHDAY BANNERS

Each month assign a new group of students to be on the celebrations committee. It will be this group's responsibility to generate birthday banners, cards, and signs for each student who has a birthday during that group's assigned month. Students will enjoy and look forward to this responsibility as well as learn how to use the various aspects of your desktop-publishing software.

Computer Projects/Research

Exploring The Web

Need a method to monitor whether students are making efficient use of their time on the World Wide Web? Have each student use a copy of the reproducible on page 287 to record and define his search topic and what he hopes to accomplish during his on-line search session. Also instruct the student to use the reproducible to record the address for each site that he visits during his research. At the bottom of the reproducible, ask each student to record what he learned from the session. Did he learn any good shortcuts for accessing information or find any good sites with helpful information?

CHECK IT OUT

Ever find a great web site, then forget to jot down the address? Problem solved! Use the reproducible on page 288 as a log to record useful web sites you encounter. On the lines provided, record the name and address of each site as well as a brief summary of the information available at that site. Separate each entry by cutting along the dotted lines; then paste each entry in alphabetical order or by topic in a three-ring binder for quick and easy referencing.

Topic: General References
Site: The Internet Public Library
URL Address: http://www.ipl.org/newspaper,
This site contains...References materials, special exhibits, on-line texts

KEYING IN ON KEYWORDS

Doing research on the World Wide Web or even on a multimedia encyclopedia CD-ROM can be very time-consuming. For example, typing in the word *music* may give a student over 500 articles to preview. However, using a keyword or phrase such as "Beethoven" or "classical music" greatly narrows the search, providing more specific and useful information. Have your students practice generating keywords and phrases by writing broad topics on the board such as *sports, art,* and *medicine.* Direct students to brainstorm a list of keywords for each topic; then write your students' responses on the board underneath the corresponding topic. Together discuss which keywords listed are best and why. To make searching more efficient for students, have each student make a list of two or three keywords (approved by you) for his topic before allowing him to use the computer.

SPORTS

Football
NFL
Troy Aikman
Super Bowl

Travel Brochures

This geography-centered project will help your students learn about the many possible uses of the computer. Pair your students; then assign each pair a different country, state, or city to research. Have the pair find information such as the location, climate, landforms, economy, and points of interest of its assigned topic. Encourage students to use the Internet as well as multimedia encyclopedias on CD-ROM to find the information they need. After the facts have been collected, have each pair design and create a brochure about its assigned location using a desk-top-publishing program. Suggest that students use appropriate clip art or original computer art to decorate their brochures. If possible print the brochures on a color printer. Pin the bro-chures to a bulletin board for everyone to enjoy.

Menu Makers

Display several menus gathered from restaurants in your community. Point out the catchy names, the descrip-tive phrases, and any slogans used to tell about the food items and prices that help capture the consumer's attention. Have each student create his own menu using a computer, a desktop-publishing program, and appropriate clip art. Instruct each student to include in his menu a restaurant name and slogan, several entrees with tantalizing descriptions, and, of course, prices. Use these student-made menus in learning centers or with your math groups for a variety of critical-thinking activities.

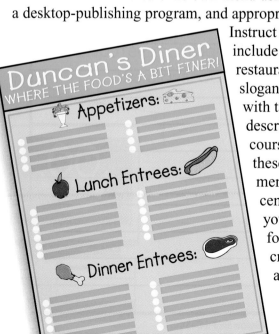

ON-LINE DEBATE

Looking for an easy way to get your students involved in an on-line project? Find another teacher on the same grade level in your school system, city, or state who has access to the Internet and E-mail. (Do not tell your students where the class is located. Keeping this a mystery will add to the fun.) Together decide on a curriculum-related issue that will lend itself easily to a good debate; then follow the steps below to get the ball rolling.

1. Assign one class the role of opposer and the other the role of supporter.

2. Have the opposing class research five to ten reasons for opposing the selected issue or topic.

3. Direct the supporting team to re-search five to ten reasons for sup-porting that issue or topic.

4. Instruct each class to send the other class an E-mail message containing its opposing or supporting reasons.

5. Have each class read the other class's reasons and write a rebuttal for each one.

6. Direct each class to E-mail its list of rebuttals back to the other class.

7. After both classes have read the other class's rebuttals, discuss the process and what they learned during it.

8. Reveal the location of the other class.

Computer Whiz Kids

Student's Name	Software Title #1	Software Title #2	Software Title #3	Software Title #4	Software Title #5

Note To The Teacher: Use with "Computer Whiz Kids" on page 278.

Name _____

Exploring The Web

Use this form to help organize information you find on the World Wide Web.

1. What is your search topic? _____

2. What information do you hope to find on the web?

   _____

   _____

3. Use the space below to record important information about each site you visit. If more space is needed, use the back of this sheet to record additional site names and addresses.

Site #1	Site #2
Name: _____	**Name:** _____
URL Address:	**URL Address:**
_____	_____
Important Information: _____	**Important Information:** _____
_____	_____
_____	_____
_____	_____

Site #3	Site #4
Name: _____	**Name:** _____
URL Address:	**URL Address:**
_____	_____
Important Information: _____	**Important Information:** _____
_____	_____
_____	_____
_____	_____

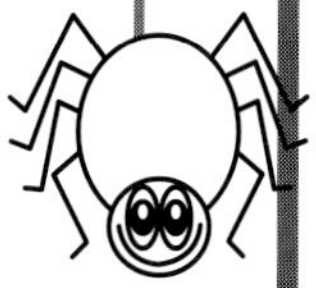

4. What did you accomplish during your search session? What did you learn?

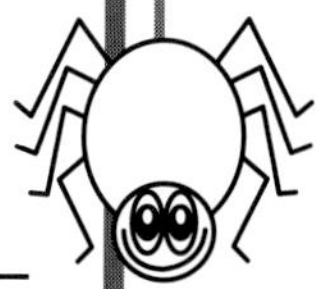

   _____

   _____

   _____

   _____

   _____

Topic: _____   **This site contains...** _____

Site: _____   _____

URL Address: _____

Topic: _____   **This site contains...** _____

Site: _____   _____

URL Address: _____

Topic: _____   **This site contains...** _____

Site: _____   _____

URL Address: _____

Topic: _____   **This site contains...** _____

Site: _____   _____

URL Address: _____

Topic: _____   **This site contains...** _____

Site: _____   _____

URL Address: _____

Topic: _____   **This site contains...** _____

Site: _____   _____

URL Address: _____

Topic: _____   **This site contains...** _____

Site: _____   _____

URL Address: _____

Topic: _____   **This site contains...** _____

Site: _____   _____

URL Address: _____

©1997 The Education Center, Inc. • *The Mailbox® Superbook* • Grade 5 • TEC454

288 **Note To The Teacher:** Use with "Check It Out" on page 282.

HOLIDAY & SEASONAL

Holiday & Seasonal

GREAT PUMPKINS!

Most pumpkins weigh between 15 and 30 pounds, but some can weigh up to 800 pounds! Use this interesting bit of trivia to "scare up" some interest in a challenging math lesson on pumpkins. First enlist the aid of parent volunteers in supplying pumpkins for—and assisting groups of four students with—completing the activity. Make a class chart like the one shown on a large sheet of bulletin-board paper. Divide students into groups; then give each group a pumpkin, a tape measure, a scale, and paper and pencil. Supply the parent assisting each group with newspaper and a knife for carving the pumpkin. Have each group record estimates about its pumpkin: its weight, height, circumference, and the approximate number of seeds it contains. Then direct each group to use its measuring tape and scale to make actual measurements. Have the parent volunteer cut open the pumpkin so the group can count the seeds. Finally instruct each group to record its estimated and actual measurements on the chart. Display the chart, having each group share its data; then top off the activity by toasting the seeds for a great snack!

Estimated/Actual Measurements

	Weight	Height	Circumference	# Of Seeds
Group 1	10 lb./	8 in./	22 in./	200/
Group 2				
Group 3				
Group 4				
Group 5				

Dress To Impress

Involve your students in celebrating the season by having a custom-made costume contest. Direct each student to choose a character who's real or imaginary and school- or study-related, such as a teacher, an administrator, a book character, a scientist, or an explorer. Require costumes to be made from materials found at home or school. (Supply materials to any student needing them.) Also supply each student with a 4" x 6" index card, directing him to write a speech from his character's point of view that explains whom he is and why he should win the contest. Enlist staff members to judge the costumes and speeches. After the judging, give each student a small treat and announce the top three "most impressive characters."

Some Big Thank-Yous!

What are your students most thankful for? Find out by creating a gigantic thank-you card for your school. Fold a six-foot sheet of white bulletin-board paper in half, greeting card–style. Open the paper, and then write the title "Thank You, [your school's name]!" across the top. Place the card on a classroom table along with a supply of colorful markers and crayons. Have each student write a brief message for the card to someone in the school she wishes to thank for a kind deed. Suggest that each student draw a decorative illustration next to her message. After each student has added her thanks, display the card on a wall at the front of the school. If desired, invite other faculty members and students to add to this gigantic Thanksgiving Day thank-you.

Holiday Economi$ts

Give your students a little insight into the cost of holiday gift giving with this real-life activity. First have each child write a list of ten gifts he'd like to receive on a sheet of loose-leaf paper along with an estimated cost of each item. Then divide students into groups of four, and provide each group with several store catalogs or newspaper sale pages. Instruct each student to search the catalogs for each item on his list and record its actual price on his sheet. Finally have the student calculate an estimated and an actual total for his ten items. As a class, discuss the differences between the totals. Extend the activity by posing problems such as those in the illustrations, having each student calculate an answer for each one. You'll soon see your students develop an understanding of holiday economics and an appreciation for gift giving.

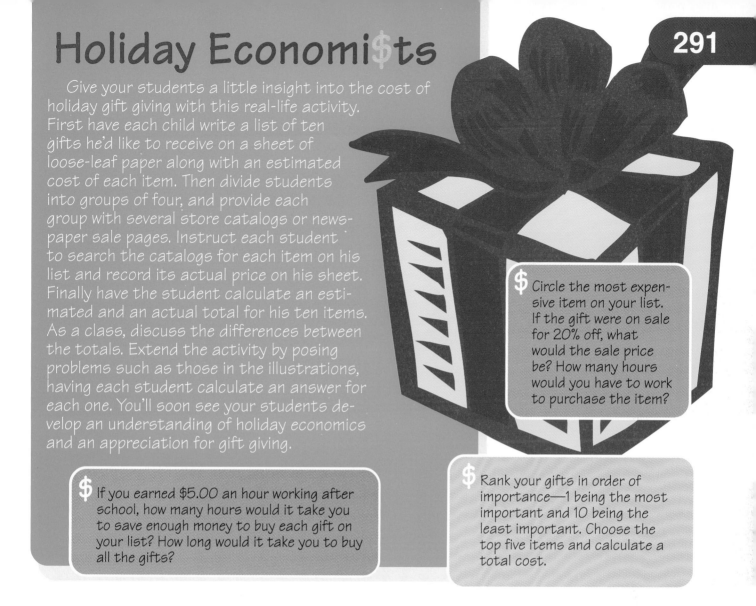

$ Circle the most expensive item on your list. If the gift were on sale for 20% off, what would the sale price be? How many hours would you have to work to purchase the item?

$ If you earned $5.00 an hour working after school, how many hours would it take you to save enough money to buy each gift on your list? How long would it take you to buy all the gifts?

$ Rank your gifts in order of importance—1 being the most important and 10 being the least important. Choose the top five items and calculate a total cost.

In Pursuit Of Holiday Trivia

Who doesn't love a good trivia game? Gather resources on the season's various holidays, such as Christmas, Kwanzaa, and Hanukkah. Then divide students into groups of four or five. Direct each group to research the holidays for 15–20 interesting facts. Next give each group a sheet of poster board, about twenty-five 4" x 6" index cards, markers, and scissors. Instruct the group to design a trivia game that includes a gameboard, game cards, game markers, an answer key, and a rules sheet. Afterward place each completed game in a different area of the room; then assign each group to a game other than the one it designed. Direct each group to appoint one member as moderator, then follow the rules for playing the game. After about 15 minutes, have each group rotate to the next game. Continue in this manner until each group has played every game except its own. Students will enjoy this novel approach to learning about the season's holidays.

Name That Resolution!

The New Year just wouldn't be the same without making a few resolutions. Have each student brainstorm a list of resolutions for the upcoming year. Ask several volunteers to share their resolutions; then lead a discussion about how many resolutions aren't accomplished because they are unrealistic and too difficult to achieve. Direct each student to scan her list and cross out any resolutions that aren't realistic. Next provide each student with a 12" x 18" sheet of light-colored construction paper and colorful markers or crayons. Instruct the student to write her name vertically in large, decorative letters down the 18-inch side of her paper. Challenge the student to write a different, realistic resolution that begins with each letter in her name. Have each student share her goals; then display them on a wall or bulletin board titled "Name That Resolution."

Poetry Readers' Theater

Lead your students in a celebration of Afro-American History Month with a series of dramatized poetry readings. Write on the chalkboard the list of famous African-American poets shown below. Pair students; then direct each pair to find a poem of interest written by one of the poets on the list. Give students time to gather props or musical selections to dramatize the poem and rehearse reciting it. On the day of the presentations, hang a decorative sheet or a large sheet of bulletin-board paper from the ceiling to the floor as a backdrop. Invite parents, staff members, or another class to the presentation—or videotape it for a later viewing. Students will delight in adding their own creative touches and interpretations to their poetry presentations.

- **Maya Angelou**
- **Arna Bontemps**
- **Gwendolyn Brooks**
- **Paul Laurence Dunbar**
- **Langston Hughes**
- **Naomi Long**
- **Frank Marshall**
- **Claude McKay**
- **Lucy Terry**

Electronic Valentines

Harness your students' love of computers to create thoughtful Valentine's Day greetings for others. Enlist the aid of your media specialist in searching the Internet for names of schools and specific classrooms in other cities, states, or countries. Pair students; then assign each pair an E-mail address. Direct the pair to send a special Valentine's Day message via E-mail to its assigned class or school. Students will eagerly await receiving their replies, and who knows? It could be the beginning of some interesting friendships!

Why is St. Patrick honored by the Irish?

He performed many brave and kind deeds for the people.

St. Patrick's Day Puzzle

Help your "little leprechauns" recognize facts about St. Patrick's Day with the following activity. Obtain an old puzzle that has about 10–15 different interlocking pairs. On each pair write one question and its answer from the list below, with the question on one piece and the answer on the matching piece. Separate and mix up the pieces; then place them in a bag. Have each student draw a puzzle piece from the bag and find the classmate with the matching question or answer. Instruct student pairs to double-check that the question and answer match by interlocking the pieces. After all matches have been found, have each pair share its question and answer for a fun-filled trivia session about St. Patrick's Day!

- Who was St. Patrick? He was a priest who brought Christianity to Ireland.
- Why is St. Patrick honored by the Irish? He performed many brave and kind deeds for the people.
- In Irish lore, what happens if you catch a leprechaun? He is supposed to lead you to a pot of gold.
- What is special about a four-leaf clover? It is supposed to bring good luck to its finder.
- By the end of the 1850s, how was St. Patrick's Day often celebrated? With parades being held each year in cities across the country.
- What does the Irish flag look like? It is divided into three equal sections of orange, white, and green.
- What is Ireland often called? The Emerald Isle.
- What are some of the many symbols associated with St. Patrick's Day? Shamrocks, leprechauns, harps, gold coins, and the color green.
- What does one legend about St. Patrick state? He drove out all the snakes in Ireland.
- What is a shamrock? A *trifolium,* or clover.

EASTER-EGG SURPRISE

Spring is viewed as a time of new beginnings. Invite your students to contemplate the season's meaning with this thought-provoking activity. Discuss the season with your students, and have them give examples of events and activities that they associate with this time of year. Examples may include the birth of animals, the growing of plants, the blooming of flowers, and the onset of warm weather. Record their responses on the chalkboard. Next provide each student with a plastic egg (found in most discount stores) and a strip of light-colored construction paper. Direct each student to write a sentence on his strip that describes a favorite seasonal event, using nouns, verbs, and descriptive adjectives. Have the student place the strip in his egg. Afterward collect all the eggs and place them in a decorative basket. Pass around the basket and have each student choose one egg, open it, and read the description inside. If desired, replace the eggs in the basket and share the surprise messages with other classes.

The sun's warm rays reflect off the dewy green grass in the first light of dawn.

Earth Day Envelopes

Help your students understand and appreciate the importance of protecting the earth and its quickly dwindling resources. On strips of paper, write different problems facing the earth today, such as the need for recycling; the overflowing of landfills; acid rain; the depletion of the ozone; and air, water, and land pollution. Make a strip for each group of four students. Place each strip in a different envelope. Then, after discussing the meaning behind Earth Day, divide students into groups of four and give each group an envelope. Direct each group to research the causes and effects of the problem contained in its envelope and devise a plan for solving that problem. Afterward instruct the group to write a letter to a local government official or an environmental agency explaining its findings and plan. Finally have each group share its letter with the class; then, if desired, mail each letter to the official or agency indicated.

The average American produces about three pounds of trash each day. Where does all the trash go? Most of it just keeps piling up in already overflowing landfills.

See You At The Beach!

By the time the end of the year rolls around, everyone is yearning for sunshine and sandy beaches. Bring a warm day at the beach to your students with this fun-filled idea. Enlist the participation of other teachers at your grade level by asking each teacher to plan a beach-related lesson for one activity period. Suggest that lessons and activities include sand painting, learning to identify seashells, and studying interesting ocean creatures. Then devise a schedule that rotates each class to a different classroom and lesson for each planned period. If desired have students dress in touristy attire, and culminate the day with an outside beach party that includes beach towels, beach balls, good food, and popular music.

A Day At The Beach!

9:00–10:00

Room 202: Sand Painting—Mrs. Ferrell's Class
Room 203: Shell Study—Mr. Davis's Class
Room 204: Ocean Animals—Miss McDole's Class

10:00–11:00

Room 202: Sand Painting—Miss McDole's Class
Room 203: Shell Study—Mrs. Ferrell's Class
Room 204: Ocean Animals—Mr. Davis's Class

11:00–12:00

Room 202: Sand Painting—Mr. Davis's Class
Room 203: Shell Study—Miss McDole's Class
Room 204: Ocean Animals—Mrs. Ferrell's Class

ALWAYS sharpen more than one pencil.
Bob

Keep a NEAT & ORDERLY desk area.
Cynthia

You'll love the great books Mrs. Cox will share!
Sue

Welcoming Advice For The New Crew

Get your students involved *this* year in welcoming and helping *next* year's students! Cover a classroom bulletin board with white paper. Add the title "How To Survive 5th Grade!" near the top of the display. Provide a supply of colorful markers and crayons nearby. Direct each student to use the markers to write a brief, positive message like those in the illustration; then watch as this display fills up quickly with lots of great messages! Invite each student to share her words of wisdom; then save the dynamic display for the upcoming school year.

A Roomful Of Learning

The end of school is a perfect time to do a little reflecting upon the year's successes. Give your students the chance to see just how much they've learned with this simple activity. Post several large sheets of paper—one for each subject your students have studied—around your classroom. Label each sheet with a different subject. Place containers of colorful markers in several areas for easy student access. Then, during free time throughout the day, invite each student to write an interesting fact she's learned about the subject listed on each sheet. Suggest that she also add a colorful illustration. Keep the sheets posted until every student has had a chance to add to them. Then review the sheets together, inviting each student to share the facts she contributed. You and your students will be amazed at such a roomful of learning!

See you next year, Sam!

Juan

Thanks for being such a good friend.

Jasmine

SAM SMITH

I'm glad you were in my class this year!

Katie

We had lots of fun on our field trip to the Marine Science Museum!

Marty

"TEE-RIFIC" T-SHIRTS

Cap off the end of the school year with this "tee-rific" idea! Have each student bring in a plain, white T-shirt from home. (Supply a T-shirt for any student who needs one.) Place a supply of colorful laundry markers or fabric paints in an area of the classroom for easy student access. Direct each student to use the markers or paints to write his name and draw a decorative summer design (such as a favorite summer activity) on the front of his shirt. Afterward direct students to sign one another's T-shirts, adding a brief, positive message about the school year or the upcoming summer vacation. Then, on the last day of school, instruct each student to wear his T-shirt—proudly displaying the positive, personalized messages!

We had lots of fun this year! Have a great summer
Jason

I hope we're in the same class again next year, Sam!

Molly

Naming Special Memories

End the school year by having students share feelings of friendship and good wishes with one another. Arrange students in a circle; then give each student a 9" x 12" sheet of light-colored construction paper. Direct the student to write her first and last names in decorative block letters in the center of the paper. After each student has written her name, have her pass her sheet to the classmate sitting to her right. Direct each student receiving a paper to use a colorful marker to write a positive comment about the person whose name is on the paper. Suggest that students write positive comments related to that person's skills, talents, or friendliness, or simply have them write good wishes for a great vacation. Instruct the student to sign her comment, then pass it on to the next student. After all students have signed one another's papers, give each paper back to its owner. If desired, laminate each student's page to create a long-lasting memory of a special year.

Name_____

FALL FAIR FUN

The weather is crisp, the leaves are turning different colors, and you and your friends are headed to a fall fair! Read each statement below. Use your mental-math skills to estimate how much money each friend will spend, and how much he or she will have left. Then use paper and pencil or a calculator to find the exact amounts. Record your answers in the table below.

Ticket Information
All Tickets $.25 Each
Gonzo's Guess Your Weight .... 2 Tickets
Fanny's Fabulous Face Painting .... 4 Tickets
Zigfield's Zany Zoo .... 3 Tickets
Babette's Balloons .... 2 Tickets
The Twister .... 5 Tickets
Harry's Hair-Raising Haunted House .. 5 Tickets
Madame Zelda's Fortune-Telling .... 3 Tickets
Ferris Funkweller's Ferris Wheel .... 4 Tickets
Go-For-It Game Room; Each game .... 2 Tickets

Concession Stand
Super-size any item for just $.25 more!
Hamburger $1.65
Hot Dog $1.30
Corn Dog $1.50
Popcorn $1.25
Cotton Candy $0.75
Caramel Apple $0.55
Soft Drink $0.95

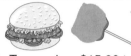

	Estimated Amount		Exact Amount	
	Cost	Change	Cost	Change
1. Tommy has $15.00 to spend on tickets. He wants to buy enough tickets to try all nine games at the carnival one time.				
2. Debbie's friends sent her to the concession stand with $15.00. They told her to buy three hot dogs, two hamburgers, two caramel apples, and three drinks.				
3. Marcos had $7.00. He bought 16 tickets, then headed for the concession stand.				
4. Josh and Janet were given $10.00 to spend at the fair. Josh bought tickets for the haunted house and the Twister, then six more tickets for the game room. Janet bought tickets to have her face painted and to visit the zoo.				
5. Missy wants to spend her $5.00 on tickets for the Ferris wheel and the fortune-teller. She also wants to get some cotton candy and popcorn.				
6. Albert had $20.00 in his pocket. He bought tickets to ride the Twister three times, then lost five dollars.				
7. Paco has $3.00 and Maria has $1.75. Each plans to purchase six tickets.				
8. Marvin is really hungry. With his $6.50 he purchased two corn dogs, popcorn, cotton candy, and a soda.				
9. Zelda's throat is parched after telling so many fortunes. With the $18.75 she earned, she bought super-sized soft drinks for herself, Ferris, and Harry.				
10. Trina loves balloons! She gave $4.75 to Babette for nine balloons.				

Weighty Words

Would you describe a vampire as friendly—or a werewolf as joyous? Probably not! Each boldfaced word below can be associated with Halloween, but one of the descriptive words that follows the Halloween word does not fit with the others. Circle the word that does not belong; then tell why it does not go with the others on the line provided. Use a dictionary or a thesaurus for help.

1. **pumpkin:** orbicular compacted ambitious textured

_____

2. **Frankenstein:** altitudinous frolicsome brawny repugnant

_____

3. **bat:** swift felicitous fanged sensatory

_____

4. **candy:** delectable unsavory callous pliant

_____

5. **trick:** homely shocking mischiefful ingenious

_____

6. **graveyard:** eerie uninhabited somber finicky

_____

7. **ghost:** corporeal ominous translucent quadrate

_____

8. **haunted house:** lonesome dilapidated splendiferous austere

_____

9. **skeleton:** gaunt clattery modish frail

_____

10. **mummy:** malodorous aged cadaverous fragrant

_____

11. **night wind:** empathetic clamorous frigid frenzied

_____

12. **costume:** defiant dappled inventive ghastly

_____

13. **black cat:** titanic svelte ebony agile

_____

14. **witch:** cackling surly formidable comely

_____

Bonus Box: Choose one of the boldfaced Halloween words listed above. Find three more words to describe it; then draw a picture of it based on the word descriptions.

Not Just Talkin' Turkey

Combining two or more shorter sentences into a longer, more detailed sentence helps make your writing smoother and livelier. Use the following examples to help you combine each set of sentences below. Write your combined sentences on the back of this sheet. Then, in the turkey before each number, write the number of the example that you used for help.

How to combine two or more shorter sentences:

1. **Use an adjective.**
   My mom made a fabulous pie. It was coconut cream.
   My mom made a fabulous coconut-cream pie.

2. **Use an adverb.**
   We are going to roast the turkey. We will roast it tomorrow.
   We are going to roast the turkey tomorrow.

3. **Use a series of words.**
   The turkey weighs 20 pounds. The turkey is golden brown. The turkey smells delicious.
   The turkey weighs 20 pounds, is golden brown, and smells delicious.

4. **Use an appositive phrase.**
   Mrs. Reichart makes the best apple strudel. Mrs. Reichart is our German neighbor.
   Mrs. Reichart, our German neighbor, makes the best apple strudel.

5. **Use a compound subject or predicate.**
   Joe watched the football game on TV. Jim watched the game, too.
   Joe and Jim watched the football game on TV.

6. **Use *and, but,* or *or*.**
   I love to go outside after eating Thanksgiving dinner. I won't go outside if it's raining.
   I love to go outside after eating Thanksgiving dinner, but I won't go outside if it's raining.

---

 1. Aunt Myra ate too much food. The food was rich.

 2. Our next-door neighbor is coming over for dinner. Dinner is at noon.

 3. Thanksgiving Day is a time for family. It is a time for food and fun.

 4. Ruff is my dog. Ruff likes sweet potatoes.

 5. My brother Waldo started a food fight. My sister Wilma started one, too.

 6. My dad heaped my plate full of stuffing. My dad heaped my plate full of mashed potatoes. My dad also heaped my plate full of cranberry sauce.

 7. My five-year-old cousin got the wishbone. He gets the wishbone every year.

 8. Thanksgiving is my favorite holiday. Christmas is my favorite holiday, too.

 9. Bob is my friend. Bob can crack walnuts with his teeth.

 10. My Uncle Al loves fresh corn. He doesn't like corn-on-the-cob.

 11. Our cat curls up on top of the table. Our cat goes to sleep right in the middle of dinner.

 12. We have a turkey named Terrell. He is a pet.

Bonus Box: On another sheet of paper, write a story about Terrell the turkey. Be sure to combine your sentences to make your writing better. Underline the sentences that you combined.

It's A Turkey's Life

Have you ever wondered what a turkey would say if it could talk and tell you a little bit about itself? Imagine that the turkey below had human qualities. Fill in each blank with information about the turkey. Then dress the turkey according to his or her character, adding creative details. For example, if your turkey likes sports, you may show him or her holding a basketball and wearing sneakers.

Name: _____

Nickname: _____

Address: _____

Place of birth: _____

Family members: _____

Job description: _____

Pets: _____

Favorite TV show: _____

Favorite hobby/sport: _____

Favorite snack food: _____

Favorite song: _____

Favorite book: _____

Favorite holiday: _____

Bonus Box: On another sheet of paper, write a story about the turkey you've described above.

Note To The Teacher: Supply each student with a pencil, markers or colored pencils, scissors, glue, and a sheet of 9" x 12" construction paper. After each student completes the activity, have him cut out his turkey and description paper. Then direct each student to glue his cutouts to the sheet of construction paper. Post each student's work on a wall or bulletin board titled "It's A Turkey's Life."

Embarrassed Elory

Santa's head elf, Elory, has to keep his elves working hard because Christmas is right around the corner! About this time each year, he writes a special letter to his elves. But poor Elory just doesn't know how to use the "right words." Help Elory by reading his letter. Circle the words that he used incorrectly; then spell correctly the words he should have used on the blanks below. Use a dictionary if you need help. Elory will be forever grateful for your efforts!

Dear Fellow Elves,

As ewe know, Christmas is fast approaching so we must keep ourselves busy! Eye no that buy this time we all our very tired, but we must bare the burden and keep our spirits hi! Four months now (since last December 25), we have each made thousands of toys. (Accept for Ernie's Ant Betty, who in August tripped over a train car and acquired a nasty brake in her arm.) Still we have many more toys to make, so please do not dessert our cause. The children of the world depend on us! Ellen has suggested that we all be aloud to take an extra day off this year—I think that is a capitol idea! I shall talk to Santa before the holiday arrives.

I'll clothes my letter by saying that the cent of Christmas is in the heir, and snow is on the bow. So dew not despair, my friends. You will soon bee rewarded with the laughter of happy children everywhere!

Sincerely,
Elory Edwards
Head Elf

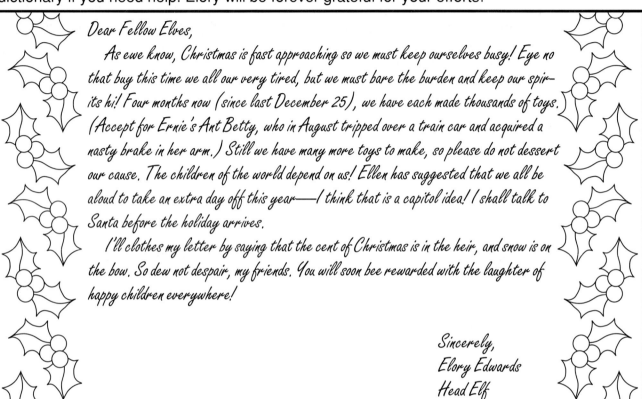

1. _____
2. _____
3. _____
4. _____
5. _____
6. _____
7. _____
8. _____
9. _____
10. _____

11. _____
12. _____
13. _____
14. _____
15. _____
16. _____
17. _____
18. _____
19. _____
20. _____

Bonus Box: Write a list of other word pairs that are often misused; then use those words incorrectly in a letter of your own. Afterward have a classmate identify the words you used incorrectly.

Just In Time For Christmas!

Ron, the reindeer coach, has to get Santa's reindeer into shape in time for their big day—Christmas Eve, of course! He keeps a record of each day's training and gives it to Santa. Help Ron prepare his report by finding out how much time each reindeer spent on the activity described. Work each problem on the back of this sheet; then record your answer on the line next to the problem.

_____ 1. Comet started his weight training at 12:35 P.M. and ended at 2:50 P.M.

_____ 2. Dasher attended nutrition classes from 10:10 A.M. to 1:37 P.M.

_____ 3. Blitzen got on the treadmill 2 hours and 10 minutes before 3:00 P.M., then stopped at 1:16 P.M.

_____ 4. Dancer started breakfast 25 minutes before 7:45 A.M., then left for the gym at 7:50 A.M.

_____ 5. Prancer sure put in a long day. After starting practice at 8:22 A.M., he didn't quit until 5 hours and 13 minutes before midnight.

_____ 6. Donner read about the benefits of aerobic training from 11:56 P.M. to 2:24 A.M.

_____ 7. Rudolph started landing practice 7 minutes before 11:09 A.M. and finished 48 minutes after noon.

_____ 8. Vixen took an early-morning walk from 5:18 A.M. to 11:05 A.M.

_____ 9. Cupid did 20 laps in the heated pool 17 minutes before 2:10 P.M. and finished at 2:44 P.M.

_____ 10. Dancer took a much-needed break at 11:56 A.M. and finished at 12:29 P.M.

_____ 11. Donner was in the gym for 8 hours and 27 minutes except for his lunch break that lasted one hour and 14 minutes.

_____ 12. Cupid spent one hour and 32 minutes in a step-aerobics class, and two hours and 33 minutes in the weight room.

_____ 13. Rudolph stepped into the sauna at 5:20 P.M. and left at 5:47 P.M.

_____ 14. Beauregard, Santa's newest recruit, ended his in-class training at one o'clock in the afternoon. He then studied until 3:37 P.M.

_____ 15. At a quarter to four in the afternoon, the whole herd—except for Prancer and Donner—got together for a fun game of Dodge Ball. They played until twenty minutes after five in the evening.

Bonus Box: Make up a schedule that describes each reindeer's day for Christmas Day. Write the schedules on the back of this sheet.

The Great Gift Exchange

The elves in the Elfonso family exchange gifts with one another every year. This year, though, the name tags fell off the gifts! To help the Elfonsos know how to distribute the gifts, write a √ in the grid to show the gift that each elf should receive. (Hint: Write an *X* in the grid to show the gifts that each elf should not receive.)

Gifts:

Elves:	fruitcake	toy-making tools	hot-chocolate maker	bunny slippers	art book	antique ornament
Egbert						
Englebert						
Erwin						
Ethel						
Edna						
Elvira						

Clues:

1. Erwin's gift is edible.
2. Ethel is not artistic.
3. Elvira receives neither the hot-chocolate maker nor the art book that her sisters receive.
4. Egbert knows his sister's favorite animal is a bunny.
5. Englebert's twin brother collects antiques.

Bonus Box: On the back of this sheet, write a story about the Elfonso family's holiday. Include a description of each gift and explain the gift exchange.

The Magic Of Eight

Hanukkah is a Jewish holiday celebrated in December. Each evening of this eight-day celebration, a candle is lighted on a special eight-branched candelabra called a *menorah*.

Directions: For each clue, write a word that rhymes with the word *eight*. Write one letter in each blank. Use a dictionary for help. The first one is done for you.

1. You don't have to ask a sleepy bear to do this during the winter. <u>h</u> <u>i</u> <u>b</u> <u>e</u> <u>r</u> <u>n</u> a t e

2. Do this if you want to stretch a story to make it funny. __ __ __ __ __ __ __ a t e

3. This is quite the opposite of crooked. __ __ __ a i __ __ __

4. This object is definitely not a Frisbee®. __ __ a t e

5. These wheels will get you where you want to go. __ __ __ __ __ __ __ __ a t e __

6. Beat the clock or you'll be this. __ a t e

7. An artist does this every day. __ __ __ __ __ __ __ a t e __

8. Blood, air, and memos may do this. __ __ __ __ __ __ a t e

9. A fisherman would say you can't fish without this. __ a i t

10. To give a little dough away. __ __ __ a t e

11. To put off doing something until another day. __ __ __ __ __ __ __ __ __ __ a t e

12. Mimes will do this to you every time. __ __ __ __ a t e

13. If you want to get going, do this. __ __ __ __ __ __ a t e

14. To vanish into thin air. __ __ __ __ __ __ a t e

15. If you do this, you'll brighten up the place. __ __ __ __ __ __ __ a t e

16. It's all part of a detective's job. __ __ __ __ __ __ __ __ a t e

17. Every sentence must have its mark. __ __ __ __ __ __ a t e

18. If you do this, you may be seeing double. __ __ __ __ __ __ a t e

19. To cut something short. __ __ __ __ __ __ __ a t e

20. A ship's captain must know how to do this. __ __ __ __ __ a t e

Bonus Box: Work with a partner to create more clues for words that rhyme with *eight*. Exchange your clues with another pair of students.

Nguzo Saba (en-GOO-zoh SAH-bah)

The Seven Principles Of Kwanzaa

Each year from December 26 until January 1, African-Americans celebrate the season of *Kwanzaa*. Kwanzaa, meaning "fruits of the harvest," is a time for showing pride in one's heritage, building strong family relations, and sharing ideas. Each day during the holiday, a candle is lit on a *kinara* (kee-NAH-rah) to celebrate one of the seven different principles shown below.

Directions: Read each of the 12 statements. In the flame next to each statement, write the number of the principle or principles that action matches. Explain each of your answers on the back of this sheet.

3. UJIMA
(oo-JEE-mah)
COLLECTIVE WORK
AND RESPONSIBILITY
We work together to
make life better.

4. UJAMAA
(oo-JAH-ma)
COOPERATIVE ECONOMICS
We build and support our own
businesses.

5. NIA
(NEE-ah)
PURPOSE
We have a reason
for living.

2. KUJICHAGULIA
(koo-jee-cha-goo-LEE-ah)
SELF-DETERMINATION
We decide things
for ourselves.

6. KUUMBA
(koo-OOM-bah)
CREATIVITY
We use our minds and
hands to make things.

1. UMOJA
(oo-MOH-jah)
UNITY
We help each other.

7. IMANI
(ee-MAH-nee)
FAITH
We believe in ourselves, our
ancestors, and our future.

_____ 1. Katrina decided to spread the word about the holiday by creating posters and displaying them throughout her neighborhood.

_____ 2. Randy made a Kwanzaa greeting card for his parents.

_____ 3. Shenika decided that she wants to go to college and become a doctor.

_____ 4. Alex studied his family's history and labeled a genealogy chart with the information he found.

_____ 5. Nicole, along with her brother Tomario and sister Shonda, prepared a traditional meal of catfish, collard greens, and sweet-potato pie for themselves and their family.

_____ 6. The members of the Saunders family created special gifts for one another.

_____ 7. Kimberly interviewed several African-American businesspersons and prepared a report for her social-studies class.

_____ 8. A *bendera*—a flag with black, red, and green stripes—was displayed at the local Kwanzaa festival.

_____ 9. Tomeka shared an African folktale with a kindergarten class at her school.

_____ 10. Marcus created a poem about his life and his plans for the future.

_____ 11. Kinara's mother made long, colorful dresses called *bubas* for her and her sisters.

_____ 12. Marian and her brother kept a scrapbook of special family events.

Bonus Box: On another sheet of paper, create a poster that tells others about Kwanzaa and its seven principles.

The Season Is The Reason

The winter season is often a difficult time for many animals. There is little to eat, and it is hard for them to keep warm. In order to survive the cold winter months, animals must adapt to their environments. Match each adaptation with an animal from below. After you make each match, cut out each animal's picture and paste it in the box next to its description.

1. Its body temperature drops, its blood circulation slows, and it falls into a deep sleep.

2. It spends the northern summer in the Arctic, then migrates 12,500 miles to the Antarctic during the southern summer.

3. It spends its summer thousands of feet above sea level. When winter weather arrives, this animal walks down into a valley.

4. It migrates 2,100 miles south from the northeastern United States to Mexico.

5. It spends the southern summer in the Antarctic, then travels 5,000 miles toward the equator to its breeding ground.

6. Its brown coat turns white in winter, then turns brown again for summer.

7. It has feathers that cover its toes to protect it against extreme cold.

8. It eats as many wooded plants as it can in the summer, storing this food as fat on its humped body for the harsh months ahead.

9. It has a thick fur coat that's orange on its throat and chest to keep it warm.

10. It has a thick oily coat and a lodge to keep it warm.

11. During severe storms, it scoops out a hollow shelter in the snow and sleeps until the storm is over.

12. It often stores large supplies of seeds and nuts in the ground, under fallen leaves, or in stockpiles near its nest.

| pine marten | beaver | squirrel | brown bear | humpback whale | polar bear |
| mountain quail | arctic tern | monarch butterfly | snowshoe hare | moose | snowy owl |

Bonus Box: Choose one of the animals above. Find five facts about the animal—such as its physical traits, habitat, food sources, predators, special abilities, or other interesting facts. Illustrate these facts on the back of this sheet.

Note To The Teacher: Each student will need scissors, glue, and appropriate reference materials.

The Resolution Solution

Many people make New Year's resolutions, but don't follow through with them. Why not? Maybe one reason is that they don't make a plan. A well-thought-out plan is a key to sure success! Complete the plan below to help you achieve a goal that you've set for the new year. Then go for it!

My Resolution Solution

1. Define your goal—*What is it that I want to accomplish?*
   _____
   _____
   _____

2. List all possible options—*What can I do to help me reach my goal?*
   _____
   _____
   _____

3. Study your options—*What are the pros and cons of each plan?*
   _____
   _____
   _____

4. Test each option—*Which plans will help me reach my goal?*
   _____
   _____
   _____

5. Choose the best option—*Which plan will work best for me?*
   _____
   _____
   _____

6. Evaluate your success—*Is my plan working? Should I pick another plan?*
   _____
   _____
   _____

I'm going to increase my batting average!

I'm going to read a new book every day!

Note To The Teacher: After each student completes his plan, have him cut out the paper, roll it up, and tie it with ribbon or yarn. Then display your students' plans on a bulletin board titled "Our Resolution Solutions!"

"King–ly" Words

Dr. Martin Luther King, Jr., was a man dedicated to a dream of equality for all people. Read each definition below. Fill in the blanks beside the definition with a word that has the letters *k-i-n-g* in it. Write one letter in each blank. Use a dictionary for help.

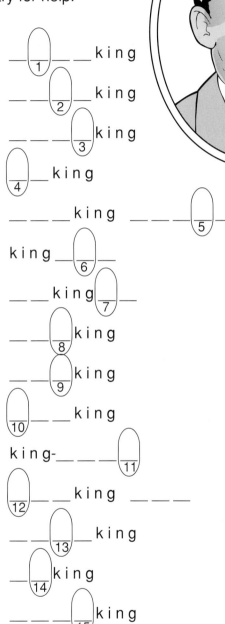

1. rapping ___ ①___ ___ k i n g

2. sock ___ ___ ②___ k i n g

3. pondering ___ ___ ___ ③k i n g

4. an early pirate from Scandinavia ④___ k i n g

5. a moving chair ___ ___ ___ k i n g ___ ___ ___ ⑤

6. land ruled by a king or queen k i n g ___ ⑥___

7. in a kidding manner ___ ___ k i n g⑦___

8. searching ___ ___ ⑧k i n g

9. going under the water ___ ___ ⑨k i n g

10. preparing food ⑩___ ___ k i n g

11. unusually large k i n g-___ ___ ___ ⑪

12. a place for cars ⑫___ ___ k i n g ___ ___ ___

13. collapsing ___ ___ ⑬k i n g

14. coming out of sleep ___ ⑭k i n g

15. piling ___ ___ ___ ⑮k i n g

16. pulling sharply ___ ⑯___ k i n g

Write the circled letter from each number above in the blanks below.
The words will spell two ideas in which Dr. King strongly believed.

___ ___ ___ ___ ___ ___ ___ ___ ___ ___ ___ and ___ ___ ___ ___ ___
1 2 3 4 5 6 7 8 9 10 11   12 13 14 15 16

Bonus Box: Use a dictionary to find five other *king* words. Then, on the back of this sheet, write a clue for each word like those shown above. Give your puzzle to a friend to solve.

Plotting Their Achievements

African-Americans have made many significant contributions to our nation's history—both past and present. Find out more about these famous Americans by completing the activity below. Match the first name of each African-American with his or her last name and achievement. In the blanks that follow each name, write the **letter** of the **column** and the **number** of the **row** in which the matching answer is found. The first one is done for you.

1. Patricia **E**, **3**
2. Harriet ____, ____
3. Thurgood ____, ____
4. Jackie ____, ____
5. Rosa ____, ____

6. Mary McLeod ____, ____
7. Jesse ____, ____
8. George Washington ____, ____
9. Sidney ____, ____
10. Alex ____, ____

11. Wilma ____, ____
12. Shirley ____, ____
13. Henry ____, ____
14. Martin Luther ____, ____
15. Crispus ____, ____

	A	B	C	D	E
1	**Tubman** slave who helped others escape to freedom	**Carver** scientist known for agricultural research with peanuts	**Bethune** educator who tried to improve educational opportunities for African-Americans	**Poitier** first African-American actor to win an Academy Award®	**Marshall** first African-American associate justice of the U.S. Supreme Court
2	**Chisholm** first African-American woman to serve in Congress	**Owens** winner of Olympic® gold medal in men's track	**Robinson** first African-American player in major-league baseball	**Haley** author of *Roots*	**Parks** arrested for refusing to give up her bus seat to a white man
3	**Aaron** major-league baseball player who hit the highest number of home runs	**Rudolph** first American woman to win three gold medals in track and field	**King, Jr.** a leader of the Civil Rights movement	**Attucks** first American killed in the fight for independence at the Boston Massacre	**Harris** first African-American woman to hold a U.S. cabinet post

Bonus Box: Choose a famous African-American listed above. Find three more facts about this person's life and achievements. Write your information on the back of this sheet.

Note To The Teacher: Provide each student with appropriate reference materials.

PARTY PACKAGES

I. M. Even is planning a party for Valentine's Day. He is purchasing party supplies for 30 guests. Help I. M. by filling in the chart below with the number of packages he needs to purchase so that there are no leftover items. The first one has been done for you.

Item	Number Of Items Per Package	Number Of Items Each Guest Will Receive	Number Of Packages I. M. Should Buy
1. balloons	10	2	6
2. marshmallow hearts	5	2	
3. Valentine's Day cards	10	1	
4. lollipops	12	2	
5. sugar cookies	6	3	
6. chewing gum	8	4	
7. party hats	5	1	
8. conversation hearts	50	20	
9. cinnamon sticks	9	3	
10. stickers	15	8	
11. pretzels	20	10	
12. party favors	5	3	
13. paper cups	15	1	
14. noisemakers	3	2	

Bonus Box: If candy bars are sold in packages of 8, how many packages does I. M. need to purchase for his guests so there will be fewer than four bars leftover after each guest has one?

SWEETHEART ACRONYMS

An acronym is a kind of abbreviation. It is a word made out of the first letters of a title or group of words. An acronym doesn't have periods, and it is usually written in capital letters. For example, *SCUBA* stands for **S**elf-**C**ontained **U**nderwater **B**reathing **A**pparatus.

Directions: For each valentine word below, think of a title or group of words that the acronym could represent. (Your answer does not have to relate to Valentine's Day.) The first one has been done for you.

1. HEARTS  Henry's Edible And Really Tasty Sweets

2. LOVE _____

3. CUPID _____

4. ROSES _____

5. PARTY _____

6. CARDS _____

7. CANDY _____

8. SWEETS _____

9. FLOWER _____

10. FRIEND _____

11. SECRET _____

12. COOKIES _____

Bonus Box: Write a secret message in the form of an acronym to a special valentine. Examples: WYBAF—Will you be a friend? YAASP—You are a special person!

©1997 The Education Center, Inc. • *The Mailbox® Superbook* • *Grade 5* • TEC454

Shamrock Shake-Up

Imagine that on Saint Patrick's Day a leprechaun appears at your house and fills your backyard with lucky shamrocks and pots of gold. The leprechaun then gives you three long poles and presents the following challenge: Use the poles to divide your yard into six parts. Each part must contain three shamrocks and one pot of gold. If you complete the challenge, you can keep the shamrocks and gold.

Directions: Move three long pencils, straws, or sticks around on the diagram below until you find the solution to the leprechaun's challenge. Then draw three lines on the diagram to show your final answer.

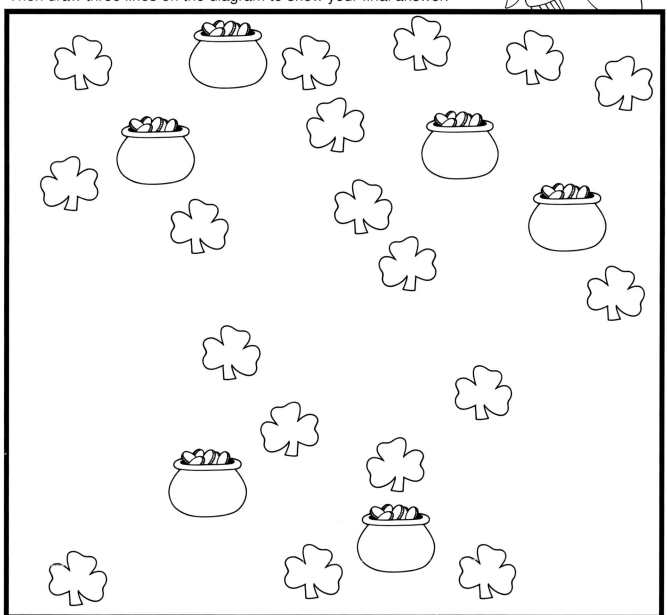

Bonus Box: Saint Patrick, for whom this day is celebrated, lived in Ireland during the fifth century. Ireland, once one country, is now divided into two parts. On the back of this sheet, write the names of the two countries and their capital cities.

Note To The Teacher: Provide each student with three long pencils, straws, or sticks.

Spring-Cleaning

The members of the Tidy family are at it again—they are busy with their annual spring-cleaning. Since the Tidys do everything in an orderly manner, they have decided to arrange all the items into eight different groups. Below is a list of the items they have cleaned and sorted to sell at a garage sale. But one of the items in each group doesn't belong. Help the Tidy family by writing a category title on the sign above each group. Then cross out the item that does not belong in that group.

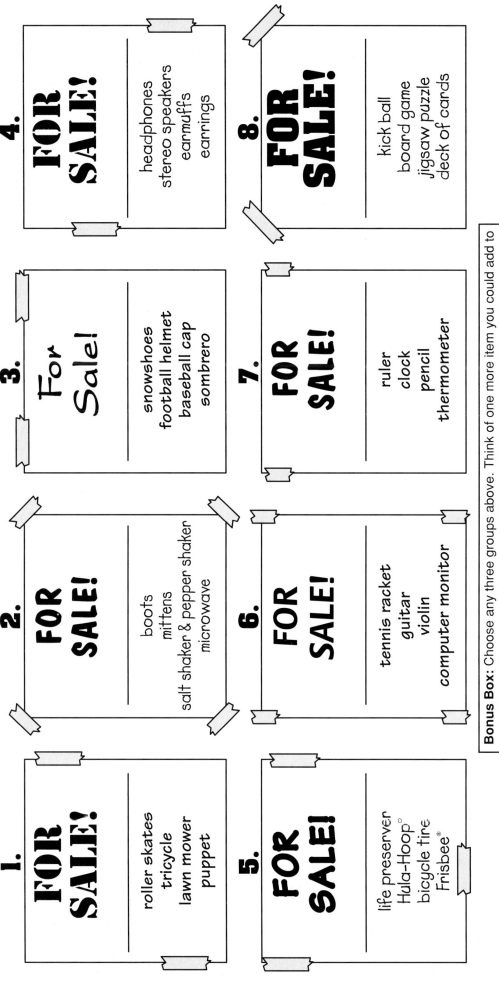

1.

FOR SALE!

_____

roller skates
tricycle
lawn mower
puppet

2.

FOR SALE!

_____

boots
mittens
salt shaker & pepper shaker
microwave

3.

For Sale!

_____

snowshoes
football helmet
baseball cap
sombrero

4.

FOR SALE!

_____

headphones
stereo speakers
earmuffs
earrings

5.

FOR SALE!

_____

life preserver
Hula-Hoop°
bicycle tire
Frisbee®

6.

FOR SALE!

_____

tennis racket
guitar
violin
computer monitor

7.

FOR SALE!

_____

ruler
clock
pencil
thermometer

8.

FOR SALE!

_____

kick ball
board game
jigsaw puzzle
deck of cards

Bonus Box: Choose any three groups above. Think of one more item you could add to each list that fits that group's category. Then add the name of that item to its sign.

Hot On The Trail Of An Easter Egg!

Barbara Bunny is going on a hunt, an Easter-egg hunt to be exact! She's just been given directions that will lead her to a huge chocolate egg! Follow the directions below to see if you can find the egg, too. Use a ruler and a colored pencil to lightly trace your path on the diagram below. Then mark the spot where you find the egg with a decorative Easter egg.

1. Walk west 20 steps.
2. Wander north 20 steps.
3. Amble east 15 steps.
4. Gallivant north 10 steps.
5. Travel west 35 steps.
6. Go south 10 steps.
7. Take 10 steps east.
8. Journey north 15 steps.
9. Saunter east 30 steps.
10. Proceed south 20 steps.
11. Push west 15 steps.
12. Trek south 10 steps.
13. Traipse east 30 steps.
14. Wend north 25 steps.
15. Meander southwest 55 steps.
16. Mark this spot with a colored egg.

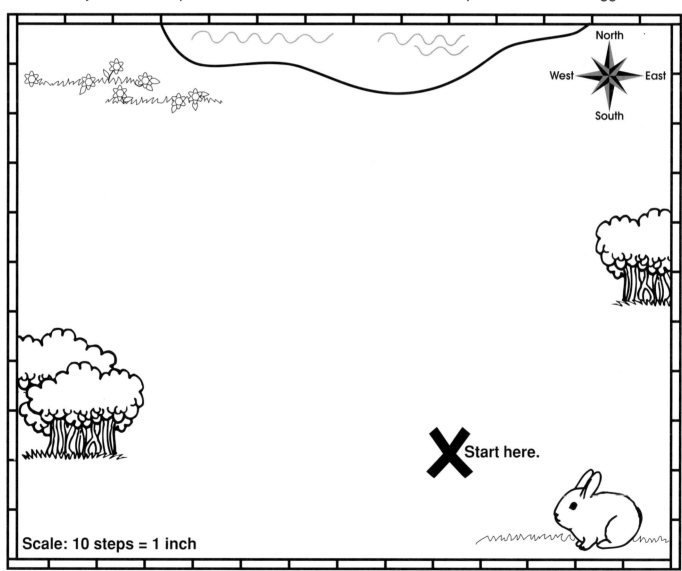

Bonus Box: On another sheet of paper, draw a map and write a set of directions for another Easter-egg hunt. Trade papers with a classmate to see if he or she can find the egg at the end of the trail.

©1997 The Education Center, Inc. • *The Mailbox® Superbook* • *Grade 5* • TEC454 • Key p. 320

Note To The Teacher: Supply each student with a ruler and colored pencils or crayons.

A Perfect Pair

Why are the words *heart* and *earth* such a perfect pair? These two words are *anagrams*—a word pair formed by rearranging the same letters. On the blanks provided, write an anagram for each five-letter word below.

1. taste _____

2. petal _____

3. crate _____

4. ocean _____

5. groan _____

6. early _____

7. melon _____

8. horse _____

9. scent _____

10. bread _____

11. teach _____

12. teams _____

13. steam _____

14. pages _____

15. plane _____

16. reams _____

17. spear _____

18. pools _____

19. angle _____

20. stale _____

We make the perfect pair!

Bonus Box: On the back of this sheet, write five different anagram word pairs.

Year-End Calculations

Wow! Another school year has come and gone. Do you know how much time you've spent in school this past year? To find out, complete each activity below. Write your equations and answers on the blanks that follow each activity. Use a calculator for help.

HOW MUCH TIME HAVE YOU SPENT IN SCHOOL?

1. Write the number of days you're in school during a year. (Most schools attend about 180 days.)

   _____

2. Subtract the number of days you missed due to illness, doctors' appointments, vacations, etc., from the number of days spent in school.

   _____ – _____ = _____

3. Write the starting and ending times of your school day. Then calculate how many hours and minutes you spend in school each day. Use this to determine the number of minutes you spend in school each day.

   starting time _____ ending time _____

   hours _____ minutes _____

   minutes you spend in school each day _____

4. Calculate the number of minutes you spend at lunch, recess, and other breaks each day. Subtract this number from the minutes you spend in school each day (see Number 3) to see how much time you spend working in school each day.

   minutes spent during break times _____

   _____ – _____ = _____

5. Multiply the number of days you spend in school (see Number 2) by the number of minutes you spend working in school each day (see Number 4). This gives you the total number of minutes you've spent working in school this year.

   _____ x _____ = _____

6. Divide the number of minutes spent in school working (see Number 5) by 60 to find the total number of hours you've spent in school working this year.

   _____ ÷ _____ = _____

7. Divide the number of hours spent in school working this year (see Number 6) by 24 to find the total number of 24-hour days you've spent in school working this year.

   _____ ÷ _____ = _____

8. Divide the number of days spent in school (see Number 2) by 7 to find the total number of weeks you've spent in school this year.

   _____ ÷ _____ = _____

Bonus Box: Calculate the approximate number of hours you've spent watching TV for each day, week, and month of the school year. Write your calculations and answers on the back of this sheet.

Note To The Teacher: Provide each student with a calculator.

THE END IS NEAR!

Yes, the end of the school year is near, and summer is right around the corner! But before you head off for your summer vacation, put your brain to work one last time with this positively perplexing set of puzzles!

List as many words of four or more letters as possible using only the letters in the title of this sheet. There are at least 28 words. Write any extra words you find on the back of this sheet.

1. _____
2. _____
3. _____
4. _____
5. _____
6. _____
7. _____
8. _____
9. _____
10. _____
11. _____
12. _____
13. _____
14. _____
15. _____
16. _____
17. _____
18. _____
19. _____
20. _____
21. _____
22. _____
23. _____
24. _____
25. _____
26. _____
27. _____
28. _____

See how many words from your list can be found in this word search. Circle each word that you find. There are 28 words.

H	N	R	H	H	E	D	I	N	D
T	I	E	E	T	A	N	E	A	I
A	E	N	A	R	S	E	E	A	A
E	R	N	D	A	T	R	A	H	R
D	E	I	E	E	E	T	T	E	I
E	E	D	E	E	R	E	N	A	S
E	N	H	R	A	N	I	I	R	E
N	S	E	E	I	D	R	A	I	N
I	H	H	N	R	E	T	S	E	R

Write the words from your list that you did not find in the word-search puzzle.

Homophones, or *homonyms,* are words that are pronounced alike, but are spelled differently and have different meanings. The words *blue* and *blew* are homophones. Write the homophones that are in your list of words.

Bonus Box: Find another way to group the words from your list. For example, the words can be grouped by parts of speech or the sounds with which they begin. Write your grouping on the back of this sheet.

©1997 The Education Center, Inc. • *The Mailbox® Superbook* • *Grade 5* • TEC454 • Key p. 320

Answer Keys

Page 14
Polishing Up The Pledge
I pledge **allegiance** to the **flag** of the United **States** of America and to the **Republic** for which it stands, one **nation**, under God, **indivisible**, with liberty and justice for **all**.

Basic Facts Tune-Up
3 x 5 = **15**
2 x 9 = **18**
6 x 8 = **48**
9 x 5 = **45**
7 x 6 = **42**
4 x 9 = **36**
27 ÷ 3 = **9**
40 ÷ 8 = **5**
12 ÷ 1 = **12**
49 ÷ 7 = **7**
54 ÷ 6 = **9**
35 ÷ 7 = **5**

Page 149
Nouns
mouse
staircase
librarian
bus driver

Verbs
sang
purrs
fell
ate

Adjectives
beautiful
lazy
easy
short

Adverbs
swiftly
loudly
quietly
quickly

Pronouns
they
We
she
you

Page 152
1. H
2. C
3. I
4. D
5. F
6. J
7. B
8. G
9. A
10. E

Possible cause-and-effect sentences:
1. Paulette, Pamela, Parker, and Patrick didn't attend the party because their invitations got lost in the mail.
2. Penelope's mom said that there were hardly any decorations left at the Party Palace, so none of the decorations matched.
3. Penelope's Doberman pinscher got loose and jumped on the table that held the cake. As a result, chocolate cake flew from one corner of the room to the other!
4. Prudence, Penelope's best friend, said her stomach felt queasy; therefore she had to leave the party early.
5. Peter put a fake snake in a gift box and gave it to Penelope. Consequently, Penelope screamed and knocked the punch bowl on the floor.
6. Paul and Perry insisted that they saw a UFO flying over the backyard, so everyone left in the middle of Penelope's game and ran outside to look at the sky.
7. A freak thunderstorm caused the electricity to go out. For this reason, Penelope's guests couldn't listen to the music recordings they brought.
8. Penelope's baby brother, Preston, took the tags off two identically wrapped gifts, so Penelope didn't know which gift was from whom.
9. The pizza delivery person was late because of a flat tire. For this reason, everyone was starving by the time the pepperoni pizza arrived.
10. Because Penelope tripped over her new pair of Rollerblades®, she crashed to the floor and bruised her patella.

Page 153
1. Clues: holidays, heart-shaped, red paper, Abraham Lincoln, George Washington, African-Americans
   Answer: February
2. Clues: adventure, goggles, fins, crystal-clear water
   Answer: scuba diving or snorkeling
3. Clues: heart thumping, podium, note cards, audience
   Answer: give a speech
4. Clues: quiet room, opening and closing of books, shuffling of papers, occasional cough, rows of shelves filled with assortment of books, magazines, and reference materials
   Answer: a library
5. Clues: mother's present, floral fragrance, crushed, water, wilt
   Answer: a bouquet of flowers
6. Clues: parents, job, feeding, changing diapers, reading bedtime story
   Answer: baby-sit
7. Clues: lab coat, lens, microscope, specimens, slide, assistant
   Answer: a scientist, researcher, or doctor
8. Clues: cushioned seat, offered a drink and a snack, abrupt jerking movement, flashing message, seat belt
   Answer: on an airplane

Page 154
1. C
2. B
3. E
4. A
5. D

Page 220
1. $39.99
2. $24.99
3. $8.99
4. $37.99
5. $12.99
6. $9.99
7. $29.99
8. $19.50
9. $34.99

Page 222
1. 5 miles
2. 5 4/5 miles
3. 4/5 mile farther
4. 13 miles
5. 8 11/20 miles
6. 4 3/10 miles
7. Camper group B hiked the farthest.
8. 11 1/20 miles
9. 8 11/20 miles
10. Answers will vary.

Page 223
1. Possible answers:
   750.4   5407.
   754.0   5470.
   4057.   5704.
   4075.   5740.
   4507.   7045.
   4570.   7054.
   4705.   7405.
   4750.   7450.
   5047.   7504.
   5074.   7540.
2. 540.7 or 547.0
3. Possible answers:
   0.457   04.75
   0.475   4.057
   0.547   4.075
   0.574   4.507
   0.745   4.570
   0.754   4.705
   04.57   4.750
4. 70.45
5. 0.457 or 0.475
6. 5.047 or 5.074
7. Possible answers:
   4.507   5.047
   4.570   5.074
   4.705   5.407
   4.750   5.470
8. 40.57
9. 0.457
10. .0457

Page 224
1. $6.09
2. $2.99
3. $6.98
4. $5.01
5. $14.49
6. $5.05
7. $14.15
8. $6.75
9. $61.51
10. Ireland $3.38; Denmark $5.67

317

Answer Keys

Page 225
1. 12 sq. cm
   4 sq. cm
   16 sq. cm
2. 2 sq. cm
   22 sq. cm
   24 sq. cm
3. 1 sq. ft.
   6 sq. ft.
   7 sq. ft.
4. 8 sq. yd.
   2.5 sq. yd.
   10.5 sq. yd.
5. 600 sq. mm
   375 sq. mm
   975 sq. mm
6. 7.5 sq. cm
   1.5 sq. cm
   9 sq. cm
7. 4 sq. cm
   5 sq. cm
   9 sq. cm
8. 11.5 sq. ft.

Bonus Box answer:
1. $4.00
2. $6.00
3. $1.75
4. $2.63
5. $243.75
6. $2.25
7. $2.25
8. $2.88

Page 226
Possible design:

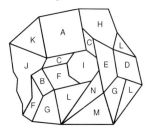

Page 228
1. 2 hours
2. 3 hours and 10 minutes
3. 3 hours and 20 minutes
4. 1 hour and 15 minutes
5. 5 hours and 38 minutes
6. 2 hours and 15 minutes
7. 55 minutes
8. 1 hour and 40 minutes
9. 5:30 P.M.
10. 7:00 A.M.
11. 11:25 P.M.
12. 12:40 P.M.
13. 10:40 P.M.

Page 229
"Organization, Please!"
1. Margo can use 10 different combinations of coins.

Quarters	Dimes	Nickels
2	0	0
1	2	1
1	1	3
1	0	5
0	5	0
0	4	2
0	3	4
0	2	6
0	1	8
0	0	10

2. Answers will vary.
3. Possible scores: 25, 23, 21, 19, 17, and 15.

Bonus Box answer: Possible scores: 50, 48, 46, 44, 42, 40, 38, 36, 34, 32, and 30.

Page 229
"Check This Out!"
1. Vince won 2 marbles the first day, 5 marbles the second day, 8 marbles the third day, 11 marbles the fourth day, and 14 marbles the fifth day.
2. The numbers are 21 and 35.
3. 652 x 8

Bonus Box answer: 568 x 2

Page 230
"Picture This!"
1. The first jar contains 45 gumballs.
2. Jerry is the oldest.
3. Courtney got on the elevator at the 10th floor.

Bonus Box answer: Answers will vary.

Page 230
"Reverse Your Thinking"
1. Jenna originally had $108.75 in her piggy bank.
2. There were 129 students enrolled in Joshua's school during the first year.
3. Cory must get started at 6:35 P.M.

Bonus Box answer: Cory will arrive home at 10:05 P.M.

Page 249
1. New York
2. Georgia
3. New Hampshire, Massachusetts, Connecticut, Rhode Island
4. Pennsylvania, New York, New Jersey, Delaware
5. Maryland, Virginia, North Carolina, South Carolina, Georgia

Page 252

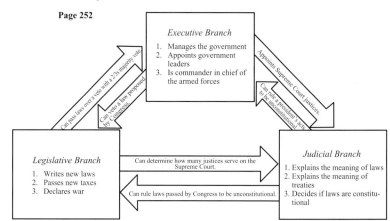

Page 274
1. bamboo coral
2. deep-sea ray
3. red shrimp
4. pink coral
5. lanternfish
6. hatchetfish
7. red crab
8. gray eel
9. sea lettuce
10. needlefish

Page 275

esophagus
liver
stomach
small intestine
large intestine

Answer Keys

Page 296

Answers may vary. Accept reasonable estimates.

	Estimated Amount		Exact Amount	
	Cost	Change	Cost	Change
1.	$7.00	$8.00	$7.50	$7.50
2.	$11.00	$4.00	$11.15	$3.85
3.	$4.00	$3.00	$4.00	$3.00
4.	$7.00	$3.00	$5.75	$4.25
5.	$4.00	$1.00	$3.75	$1.25
6.	$9.00	$11.00	$8.75	$11.25
7.	$3.00	$2.00	$3.00	$1.75
8.	$6.00	$0.50	$5.95	$0.55
9.	$4.00	$15.00	$3.60	$15.15
10.	$5.00	$0.00	$4.50	$0.25

Page 297

1. ambitious
2. frolicsome
3. felicitous
4. unsavory
5. homely
6. finicky
7. quadrate
8. splendiferous
9. modish
10. fragrant
11. empathetic
12. defiant
13. titanic
14. comely

Page 298

1. Aunt Myra ate too much rich food. (1)
2. Our next-door neighbor is coming over for dinner at noon. (2)
3. Thanksgiving Day is a time for family, food, and fun. (3)
4. Ruff, my dog, likes sweet potatoes. (4)
5. My brother Waldo and my sister Wilma started a food fight. (5)
6. My dad heaped my plate full of stuffing, mashed potatoes, and cranberry sauce. (3)
7. My five-year-old cousin gets the wishbone every year. (2)
8. Thanksgiving and Christmas are my favorite holidays. (5)
9. Bob, my friend, can crack walnuts with his teeth. (4)
10. My Uncle Al loves fresh corn, but he doesn't like corn-on-the-cob. (6)
11. Our cat curls up on top of the table and goes to sleep right in the middle of dinner. (5)
12. We have a pet turkey named Terrell. (1)

Page 300

These words are written in the order in which they appear in the letter.

1. you
2. I
3. know
4. by
5. are
6. bear
7. high
8. For
9. Except
10. Aunt
11. break
12. desert
13. allowed
14. capital
15. close
16. scent
17. air
18. bough
19. do
20. be

Page 301

1. 2 hours and 15 minutes
2. 3 hours and 27 minutes
3. 26 minutes
4. 30 minutes
5. 10 hours and 25 minutes
6. 2 hours and 28 minutes
7. 1 hour and 46 minutes
8. 5 hours and 47 minutes
9. 51 minutes
10. 33 minutes
11. 7 hours and 13 minutes
12. 4 hours and 5 minutes
13. 27 minutes
14. 2 hours and 37 minutes
15. 1 hour and 35 minutes

Page 302

Egbert's gift is the antique ornament.
Englebert's gift is the toy-making tools.
Erwin's gift is the fruitcake.
Ethel's gift is the hot-chocolate maker.
Edna's gift is the art book.
Elvira's gift is the bunny slippers.

Elves:	fruitcake	toy-making tools	hot-chocolate maker	bunny slippers	art book	antique ornament
Egbert	✗	✗	✗	✗	✗	✔
Englebert	✗	✔	✗	✗	✗	✗
Erwin	✔	✗	✗	✗	✗	✗
Ethel	✗	✗	✔	✗	✗	✗
Edna	✗	✗	✗	✗	✔	✗
Elvira	✗	✗	✗	✔	✗	✗

Page 303

1. hibernate
2. exaggerate
3. straight
4. plate
5. roller skates
6. late
7. illustrates
8. circulate
9. bait
10. donate
11. procrastinate
12. imitate
13. accelerate
14. evaporate
15. illuminate
16. interrogate *or* investigate
17. punctuate
18. duplicate
19. abbreviate
20. navigate

Page 304

Answers may vary. Accept all reasonable responses.

1. Principles 6, 7—She is using her creativity to share knowledge of a holiday that celebrates her heritage.
2. Principles 6, 7—He is using his creativity to share and celebrate his heritage.
3. Principles 2, 5—She is deciding for herself what career path she will follow.
4. Principle 7—His research shows his belief in his ancestors and heritage.
5. Principles 1, 3, 6, 7—They work together to share a traditional meal of Kwanzaa.
6. Principles 1, 6—The family is showing its unity through creative gift giving.
7. Principle 4—She is showing support for African-American businesses.
8. Principle 7—It is a display of cultural pride.
9. Principles 1, 7—She is helping the children understand the holiday by way of a traditional tale.
10. Principles 2, 5, 6, 7—He shows purpose and self-determination through a creative poem.
11. Principles 1, 6, 7—She uses her creativity to share her cultural heritage with her family.
12. Principles 3, 6, 7—They work together to create a history of their family.

Page 305

1. brown bear
2. arctic tern
3. mountain quail
4. monarch butterfly
5. humpback whale
6. snowshoe hare
7. snowy owl
8. moose
9. pine marten
10. beaver
11. polar bear
12. squirrel

Answer Keys

chair
6. kingdom
7. jokingly
8. seeking
9. sinking
10. cooking
11. king-size
12. parking lot
13. breaking
14. waking
15. stacking
16. jerking

nonviolence and *peace*

Page 308
1. E, 3
2. A, 1
3. E, 1
4. C, 2
5. E, 2
6. C, 1
7. B, 2
8. B, 1
9. D, 1
10. D, 2
11. B, 3
12. A, 2
13. A, 3
14. C, 3
15. D, 3

Page 309
1. 6
2. 12
3. 3
4. 5
5. 15
6. 15
7. 6
8. 12
9. 10
10. 16
11. 15
12. 18
13. 2
14. 20

Bonus Box answer: 4

Page 311

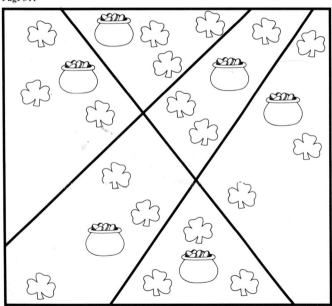

Bonus Box answer: Belfast, Northern Ireland; Dublin, Ireland

Page 312
Answers may vary.
1. Things with wheels, puppet; Toys, lawn mower
2. Things that come in pairs, microwave
3. Things worn on the head, snowshoes; Sports equipment, sombrero
4. Things worn on the ears, stereo speakers
5. Things with holes in their centers, Frisbee®
6. Things with strings, computer monitor
7. Things used to measure something, pencil
8. Playthings with more than one piece *or* playthings that require the use of the hands, kick ball

Page 313
Student's drawings for the southwest path may vary.

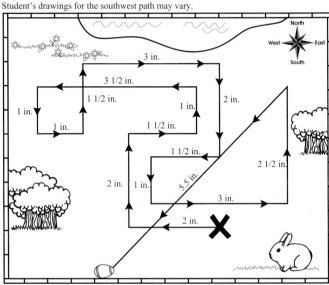

Page 314
Answers may vary.
1. state
2. plate
3. trace
4. canoe
5. organ
6. relay
7. lemon
8. shore
9. cents
10. beard
11. cheat
12. mates, tames, steam, meats
13. meats, teams, mates, tames
14. gapes
15. panel
16. mares
17. pares, pears, spare
18. spool, loops
19. glean, angel
20. least, steal, tales, slate

Page 316
The following is a possible list of words, each of which is found in the word-search puzzle. Accept other reasonable answers.
1. arise
2. dinner
3. hear
4. nine
5. rest
6. teen
7. dear
8. earth
9. heart
10. raid
11. saint
12. trend
13. death
14. eastern
15. here
16. rain
17. sheet
18. reed
19. deer
20. hart
21. hinder
22. read
23. sneer
24. diner
25. head
26. need
27. rein
28. stern

The words from each student's list that are not found in the word-search puzzle will vary. Accept all reasonable answers.

Homophones: heart/hart, dear/deer, hear/here, rain/rein, read/reed